MÀSTERY OF THE
SAUCES

THE CULINARY LIBRARY
VOLUME 3
D. & P. GRAMP

3

Fig: 1

ISBN: 149360788X
ISBN 13: 978-1493607884

ABOUT THE AUTHORS

Between them the authors have trained in the Culinary Arts at Elizabeth Russell's School of French Cookery & The Cordon Bleu Cookery School, London, worked as a professional chef in Mayfair and as a food lecturer. With post graduate degrees in the Visual Arts and Psychology and a Medical Degree underway, they have also launched a successful Artisan Tea business, studied food photography and cheese making and are both published authors. They co-founded TheCulinaryLibrary.com food blog in 2011.

Many thanks to our editor James Treloar.

Cover image, *Cactus*, used under license from Kew Gardens, England. See cactus sauce recipes, pages, 109, 113, 124 and 146.

Dedication

For Charlotte

CONTENTS

———◆◆◆———

Duck—Fish—Hoi Sin—Honey-Ginger—Japanese Mayonnaise or Kewpie—Lemon—Lime Caramel—Mango—Massumam—Master Sauce or Stock—Miso—Oyster—Nam Jim—Pad Thai—Plum—Ponzu—Satay—Sesame—Soy—Sriracha—Sweet & Sour—Tamarind—Teriyaki—Thai Curry—Tom Yum—Tonkatsu—Tosa—Vinaigrette Asian Style—Wasabi—XO—Yakisoba—Yakitori.

Major Grey's Chutney—Mango Chutney—Mint Chutney—Mustard Pickle Relish—Piccalilli Cauliflower Relish—Pineapple Chutney—Red Onion Chutney—Sweet Corn Relish—Tomatillo Chutney—Tomato & Apple Chutney.

Champagne—Chantilly—Choron—Citron—Divinity—Maltese—Mousseline—Noisette.

Mother Tomato: Creole—Françoise—Hussarde—Marinara—Matriciana—Napoletana—Primavera—Parmigiana—Provençale—Siciliana.
Bread—Gravy—Piquant—White Italienne.

Definition—Dumplings & Quenelles—Eggs—Fish—Frogs Legs—Fruit—Game, Feathered—Game, Furred—Gratins—Meat—Offal—Pasta—Pastries, Savory—Pastries, Sweet—Potatoes—Poultry—Rice—Shellfish, Crustaceans & Mollusks—Snails—Soups—Vegetables.

Aioli—Alicante—Andalouse—Avocado—Barbeque—Basil—Cambridge—Caesar Salad—Chantilly—Chimichurri—Chipotle—Cumberland—Dijonnaise—Green—Gremolata—Gribiche—Horseradish—Horseradish & Sour Cream—Horseradish & Apple—Hummus—Minted Spicy Yoghurt—Mayonnaise—Mint, English—Oxford—Pesto—Piri Piri—Ranch—Ravigote—Rémoulade—Romesco—Rouille—Russian—Seafood—Suedoise—Tapenade—Tartare—Thousand Island—Verde, Salsa—Vinaigrette—Walnut.

Apple—Apple Brandy—Brandy Custard—Butterscotch—Caramel—Cherry—Chocolate—Chocolate (hard shell)—Choc Mint—Chocolate Toblerone—Coconut—Coconut Creams—Coffee—Coulis—Cream Cheese—Crème Anglaise—Crème Pâtissière—Crêpe Suzette

Orange—Custard—Fruit—Fudge, hot—Gooseberry—Hard—Lemon—
Lemon Curd—Maple Cream—Marshmallow—Mocha—Orange—
Orange Custard Cream—Peanut Brittle Sauce—Praline—Rhubarb—
Sabayon—Toffee—Turkish Delight Sauce—Yoghurt Honey—
Zabaglione.

INTRODUCTION

"A great meal without a sauce is like a beautiful woman without clothes."
—BRILLAT-SAVARIN

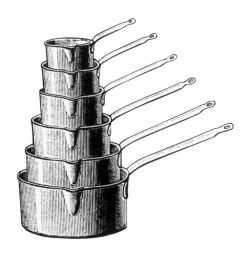

"The difference between good and bad cookery can scarcely be more strikingly shown than in the manner in which sauces are prepared and served. If well made, they prove that both skill and taste have been exerted in its arrangements. When coarsely or carelessly prepare, they greatly discredit the cook."
—ELIZA ACTON, *Modern Cookery for Private Families*, 1845

THE CULINARY LIBRARY ....

Mastery of the Sauces is a definitive recipe and reference book for all cooks wanting to understand and master the world of Sauce making. Covering hundreds of descriptions and recipes, its range spans from the classic mother sauces and their derivatives through to modern sauces including foams, gelées, jus and pan reductions. Like other volumes of *The Culinary Library*, *Mastery of the Sauces* is a compact practical tool designed to work hard and earn its place on your kitchen shelf, to be used frequently and lead beginners and experienced cooks to Mastery.

SAUCE MAKING IS EASY ....

No one book can cover every sauce ever invented, but detailed instructions on making the five classic French mother sauces and the formula for their derivatives will alone provide the foundation for beginner cooks to successfully build over 100 sauces. Many sauces are simple and quick to make, using few techniques to produce a wide range of flavors, but it is the continual tasting and adjusting of flavors required of the sauce maker that provides an excellent opportunity to train the cook's palate. No matter what you have read or been told, balancing sweet, sour, salty, bitter and umami (savory) flavors in a sauce is not a difficult culinary skill to acquire, it just requires practice and the knowledge of what end result is sought. Sauce making is easy; it begins with mastering the techniques of the sauté, sieving, blending and using thickeners, mixed with patience, an occasional strong wrist and always a good recipe.

INTRODUCTION

Professional and celebrity chefs sometimes tell us they 'own' a particular recipe or 'their' sauce can only be paired with a certain food. This is elitist nonsense; it excludes and erodes the confidence of beginner cooks and misses the whole point of cooking. Like any relationship, certain food flavors and textures complement each other better than others, but food pairings and preferences – like recipe ingredients and techniques – are not and never can be owned by any one chef.

Recipes come to us via a rich history of shared ideas. Even Molecular Cookery is not unique, but built on the foundations of colloidal chemistry and the work of a French physical chemist called Hervé This. So when working out which sauce to serve with which food, follow the Classic French tradition, or take the lead from modern chefs: investigate, experiment, invent and work out taste profiles and pairings for yourself. For beginners we suggest trying known pairings first as a base-line experience, and then go from there. Make the sauce, taste it, balance it and then *you* decide what foods *you* think will work with it. To aid in this process, we explain flavors and their balancing tips and tricks in the Terminology chapter, and if you are seeking guidance on the flavor pairings of other cooks and chefs, which sauces they *prefer* to serve with which foods, then our chapter on Classic Sauce & Food Pairings provides a comprehensive list.

To paraphrase Fernand Point, one of the fathers of Modern French cuisine: in a professional kitchen if the staff are the orchestra and the head chef the conductor then the sauce chef is the soloist, his music creates the sweetest perfection of all.

Another master, Picasso, once said that he grew younger as he got older because he learned more about what he didn't know. The same we think, is true for cooks, chefs and anyone with a passion for food. As we mature we realize that although our love of food, kitchens and cooking paraphernalia keeps us young at heart, we can never learn even a fraction of all there is to know or discover. And so it is with the topic of Sauces.

There is depth in mastering the sauces, more than enough to swim or drown in, depending on whether you decide to learn a few basics or aim for a greater level of knowledge and skill.

A good recipe + repetition + tasting + adjusting = Mastery

So what do we mean by a Sauce? Many of us know sauces as something we buy in bottles from the grocery store or enjoy when we eat out. We know they are primarily liquids of varying viscosity that are made to accompany our food, but how many of us would know that purées, salsas, vinaigrettes and foams are also classified as sauces? And what about chutneys, broths, gels and essences? If we take the view that a 'sauce' is any mixture of moist food designed and used primarily to complement another food then we have our first definition.

If made and served separately, we call them accompanying sauces. If they are an essential foundation of a dish, we call them cooking or cook-in sauces, and if they are an added component of a dish, we call them a dressing or coating sauce.

Too narrow a definition and we restrict ourselves to the classics of the past, too broad a definition and we open the door to allow in the soup family, the pretentious pre-packaged powders and commercial synthetic glues that masquerade as sauces; even that sticky set, the fruit jams and the whole nutty-butter family would be vying for inclusion.

In this book we haven't quite been so inclusive, we've tried to restrict our guest list, aiming for something wide ranging but manageable, sauces we can make ourselves from real food rather than just pluck off the shelf in downtown, anywhere shops. That's not to say commercial condiment sauces don't have their place, they certainly do. Their wide popularity is not only evidence that we love sauces in all their forms, but also 'condiments' are the largest and fastest growing section of the global retail food economy.

Sauces have not only survived but have increased in number for hundreds of years, and their form and texture have changed dramatically. Part of the original role of sauces was to make pre-refrigeration decaying food more palatable, so they tended to be heavy or spicy 'smotherers'. Then came the classic period of French cooking, where new sauces were extravagant flights of fancy reserved for those with fully developed palates, kitchens and wallets. It has been during some of the most difficult of economic times, like recessions, poverty and war rationing, that sauces were appreciated the most. They provided bulk and flavor using very few but widely available and inexpensive ingredients. Tomato Sauce is a peasant food, as is Asian Soy, both daily staples. And who can forget the days when Tuna Mornay was small flakes of canned fish swimming in a sea of white sauce, or when Macaroni and Cheese sauce was every child's favorite, or when thin slices of meat or chicken were submerged under a plate full of gravy in times when a roast had to serve not only as the family Sunday lunch, but was expected to provide leftovers for tea and then stretch to mid-week sandwiches.

We have made and still make sauces for many reasons. For bulk, for texture, for visual appeal, for variety, but most of all because, quite simply, they taste wonderful and they make other foods taste better. It's that old alchemical formula where 1 + 1 = 3.

A sauce elevates simple food to something magical, and there is always the feeling when you eat a good sauce that the meal has been made by someone with a passion not only for food, but for pleasure.

SIMPLIFYING COMPLEXITY ....

In this volume of *The Culinary Library* we don't cover every sauce ever invented because there are simply too many of them. Escoffier, in his *Guide to Modern Cookery*, first published in 1907, listed over 150 sauces, but by the time he wrote *Ma Cuisine* towards the end of his career he included more than 200, and after his death the *Larousse Gastronomique* increased this number to 260! And these are just the classics. We have also had to make choices about which chapter to place a sauce in; as some could go into several chapters, to avoid repetition we have selected the best fit.

INCLUSIONS & OMISSIONS ....

The sauces you will find in *Mastery of the Sauces* will all be worthy of escorting your culinary creations; they may be from one of the classic colored families – the Browns, Blondes, Whites, Reds and Yellows – and you will definitely find the five French matriarch or 'mother' sauces from which most other classic sauces are derived. We have also included their most popular children, the secondary and compound or 'little sauces'. We invited some family cousins to appear; especially the ones that have made the long journey from the Orient and Far East, and the luscious Indian chutneys and Mexican salsas make an appearance as well as some old sauces that have become new again. Most families have some strange characters, and sauces are no different, so for your amusement and entertainment we have included a chapter, with recipes, of some quirky characters. Make some Wow-Wow, XO or Worcestershire for your friends and they will declare you a culinary genius.

As with any guest list, we can't include everyone, so if you have a favorite that we have not included then we apologize in advance.

Once we decided what to include, we had to decide how best to introduce them. How to simplify the complexity of the past into the simplicity of the present? How to make the sauces quick and affordable, rather than endlessly tedious or outrageously expensive? How to reach a skill level of mastery before confidence or patience fails?

—We have chosen therefore to describe some sauces by every-day cooking terms like cold or hot, thick, thin or semi-solid, what flavors they have, what color they are and what they are used for.

—We have also simplified or abbreviated the ingredients lists and added short descriptions that we think are useful to an understanding of each sauce.

—Rather than write pepper and salt in every savory recipe, we assume cooks know savory recipes and sauces have to be seasoned with salt and pepper.

—We have included separate chapters on Sauce Terminology and Sauce Thickeners.

—Some sauces invented either to mask the flavor or change the outward appearance of unpalatable food we have chosen to exclude. An example of this would be the 'chaud-froids', cold-hearted slippery characters if ever we've seen them, made by mixing cream sauces or mayonnaise with gelatin until they slip-set enough for a perfect cover-up. Thankfully this practice is no longer needed nor accepted and the pretentious 'chaud-froids' of the culinary world have vanished from favor.

-We have placed the 'odd' sauces in a separate chapter called Quirky Characters, so you know they are to be made on a boring rainy day rather than everyday.

THE ROLE OF THE SAUCE ....

So why bother making a sauce? Aren't they a redundant food component in today's too-busy, time-poor world? We would argue no, just the opposite in fact; that many foods served without a sauce are boring and fail to reach their full potential, and that the emotional returns far outweigh the time and cost investment. The main purpose of a sauce, simple as it may seem, is to make food tastes better. Sauces also add moisture, texture and a rich balance or contrast of flavor to everyday foods; they add interest and lusciousness, like icing on a cake. Having said this, there are exceptions. Sauces are not meant to be deceivers, nor are they the main star of the dish, which is usually meat, fish, shellfish, vegetable, fruit, pasta or pastries. We see sauces as enhancers or enablers.

Sauces partner other foods, for one night only, as an escort, sometimes incorporating the juices their partners have been prepared in, and sometimes not; some require more care to prepare than their dishy-dates, either prepared beforehand to provide a bed for them to lay in, or afterwards as a simple splash and flash in the pan their partner was cooked in.

But whether they are fast to make or slow, simple or complex, your sauces must provide that final embellishment; they must enhance and they must flatter. Above all, they must reveal a real passion and chemistry for their partner that stirs a lingering sense of romance, magic and delight in the diners' senses, one that would absolutely be missing without them. They must be wonderful, saucy and delicious and they must always behave – even the most alcoholic ones – with utmost respect to their partner.

How lamentable, how utterly disappointing it is to encounter a wonderfully prepared, presented and luscious meal, only to find the star smothered and debased under an unworthy partner; far better to serve good food naked than to cloak it in a half-hearted gelatinous ruin, in an act of passion going terribly wrong.

HISTORY OF SAUCES

———◆◆◆———

"Despite what they claim, no one cook or chef 'owns' a recipe or a food pairing as there is always historical precedent. And there are no strict rules, only opinions. Even the Ancient Roman Emperor, Domitian (81-96 AD), had to interrupt a political debate in the senate to ask what sauce the other senators thought he should serve with his turbot that evening."
—THE CULINARY LIBRARY

Some cooks, including us, are interested in the evolution of foods; if you're not one of them you can skip this chapter. For those of you who like more detail than we cover, there are several excellent books with lengthy and more comprehensive chapters on the history of individual sauces. We have tried to kept our History of Sauces brief and concise, summarizing only the most important milestones crucial to the evolution of Sauces.

ANCIENT CHINA ....
Ancient Chinese authors thousands of years ago wrote about the importance of flavor harmonies, the craft of merging together sweet, sour, bitter and salty ingredients specifically to complement other foods. We still use these terms to describe food today, and balancing these base flavors is one of the main focuses in both

Asian and Western sauce making. There has been a resurgence of this in Western cooking recently where every TV cooking competition seems to be stressing the balancing of flavors. A fifth base flavor has now been added to sweet/sour/bitter/salty and is known as *savory* or *umami*. The Japanese Dashi sauce, with its mix of bonito (dried fish flakes) and Kombu (seaweed), is a good example of the umami taste.

ANCIENT ROME

Apicius is an Ancient Roman cookbook, written possibly by a foodie called Calius. From this amazing first cookbook we find nearly 500 ancient recipes, and most interesting of all we find that over a quarter of them are actually sauces! Herbs, spices, vinegar, honey and fermented fish provided the common ingredients, with Roman sauces being thickened with nuts, rice, liver, sea urchin, bread, pastry, eggs and wheat flour. The kitchen tool used to prepare these sauces was the Mortar & Pestle. One of the most popular Ancient Roman sauces was called 'garum', a salty, sour fermented fish sauce that Pliny the historian tells us was as popular and as prized as perfume. We have relegated the recipe for Garum to the Quirky Characters chapter, because although it was used on a daily basis, it is essentially the strained, dark brown liquid, extracted from salted mackerel or other oily fish innards, left to ferment and putrefy in the sun for a few months. From the 16th Century onwards, anchovy and anchovy sauce replaced garum in the Mediterranean diet.

THE MIDDLE AGES

The next big historical leap in sauce cookery takes us to the beginning of the Middle Ages where we find to introduction of vinegar and verjus (the sour juice of un-ripened grapes) becoming popular ingredients. Trade route spices from the exotic East had by now been established through a reliable supply chain, and almonds, along with bread, became the main sauce thickeners. The first culinary tool, the Mortar & Pestle was joined on the kitchen shelf by an array of both fine and course strainers and sieves, introducing a new textural element, smoothness, to sauce making. The words jus, coulis, gravy and salsa were all invented in the Middle Ages to describe sauces. By the 1700s, vinegar and verjus had just about had their day and were giving way to the newly arrived and exotic lemon juice, and almonds as thickeners are replace by eggs and flour. Butter also is making a first appearance as a sauce additive but it's expensive, a luxury item still and not yet widely available. It will take the next 150 years until 1869, with delays due to political upheaval and economic turmoil, before butter will manage to fully establish itself in French kitchens. We have Napoleon Bonaparte to thank for that.

FRANCE ....
Is it any wonder that the Golden Age of the culinary arts belongs to France? Why not the Italians? They were just as passionate about their food! So, not surprisingly, it was an Italian living in France who got the ball rolling.

In 1553, the 14-year-old Italian, Catherine de Medici, newly arrived at the court of Françoise I, provided the earliest foundation for French classic cookery and sauce making. Aside from being betrothed to Henry II, Catherine had a retinue of the best cooks in Europe. Another foundation came with the pre-classicists: in 1651, François Pierre de la Varenne, Henry IV's cook, published his book *Le Cuisinier François*; in the 1660s, Pierre de Lune published

Le Nouveau et Parfait Cuisinier; Massaliot in 1691 published *Le Cuisinier Roïal et Bourgeois* which discussed early roux, base and secondary sauces; and in 1733, *Le Cuisinier Moderne* by Vincent La Chapelle was published.

Laguipiere came next when he taught what he knew to a young chef called Carême. Royalty, and their desire for ostentation and excess, demanded palaces and great houses with massive kitchens. The Grande Cuisine required kitchen staff and chefs in their hundreds, with huge kitchen budgets that drained the royal coffers but in the process gave us the mother sauces and their derivatives, including rich emulsified egg sauces like hollandaise, mayonnaise and béchamel.

When the masses were liberated from the excesses of the few via the French Revolution, the growing, preparing and consuming of food became a national pastime that was elevated to patriotic status. Chefs became celebrities because revolution made access to food possible and chefs taught the masses how to cook. Following the fall of the Bastille came the rise of the cooks and their cookbooks. We would argue that the newfound liberation (unemployment) of hundreds of chefs and their staff from the royal and privileged households is just as responsible for forging France's national identity as the guillotine. The time of elite indulgence slowly eroded until by 1789 it was over. Concentrated wealth and privilege, as well as chefs, were displaced from their patrons' wealthy estates. The chefs had to survive, and so they cooked for the masses. In 1794 Carême was working in a chop house, four years later he was apprenticed to pâtissier, and later he became the first celebrity chef. A new occupational class was created; they vied for trade and became known as restaurateurs and food retailers.

Their skill with the 'soul of sauces,' those essences of meat flavors, of extracting and concentrating them, now becomes a competitive national pastime in France. Public competitions are held, kilos and kilos of the flesh and bones of beef, veal, partridge, fowl, crustaceans and game are baked, browned, deglazed and pot simmered with aromatics until reduced to 'golden cordials of flavor!' Winners are elevated to celebrity chef status.

By the early 1800s the public has begun to acknowledge the superiority of French cooking, and it was Carême who championed this. He first classified and systematized cooking and sauce making. Espagnole, béchamel, velouté and allemande he labeled the four mother sauces and identified and documented their derivative small sauces. Before the 1780s, flour as a thickener was sprinkled into sauces raw. It was Carême who first used and championed the cooked roux. He defended it against the harsh criticism of other chefs, calling them ignorant, dull, babbling, vile mountebanks! What would Carême think now of the new anti-roux faction of modern chefs? The same, probably. His contribution to the world of sauce making is unsurpassed.

Jean Anthelme Brillat-Savarin, the grand-father of French food writing, wrote a book called *The Physiology of Taste* in 1825, and told us that there is nothing more difficult than the making of a sauce and that there is not enough time to reduce the technique of sauce making to a formula. The Chef Saucier or Sauce Chef of that time was ranked second in line to the kitchen throne, almost as esteemed as the head chef.

By the time of Carême's successor, Escoffier, writing his *Culinary Guide* in 1902, there are over 200 sauces in the French chef's repertoire.

ENGLAND ....

Even before the rise of the French master chefs, the East India Company in the 1600s was importing and trading Asian soy (kecap) and fish sauces. It appears that Worcestershire, chutney and ketchup are the earliest English sauces, replicas of recipes brought back from colonial India. Hanna Glasse, an Englishwoman writing in the 1700s, had the most to say about English sauces at that time, and it is from her that we learn the English were then already making gravy, anchovy, caper, parsley, mint, egg, oyster and butter sauces. Since the days of the Classics, French chefs have thought of English chefs as inferior, but today English chefs have garnered their fair share of France's top culinary accolade, the Michelin star.

MODERN CHEFS ....

In the 1960s the French Haute (High/Fine) Cuisine and Classic (Escoffier/Carême) Cuisine movements were replaced by Nouvelle (New/Novel) Cuisine. The new chefs, Henri Gault, Paul Bocuse, the Troisgros brothers and Michel Guérard did their best in the 1970s, '80s and '90s to break up the Classic French chefs' strangle-hold on the world of food and sauces and introduced lighter, more delicate sauce making and plating. Cream and butter sauces replaced reduced meat stocks and rich sauces; broths, deglazed pans, simple vinaigrettes and sweet and savory purées became popular. Sauces became under-and-around *embracers* of their partners rather than over-the-top *smotherers*, as they evolved into artistic smears across Michelin-starred plates.

With the merging of Eastern and Western cuisines in Fusion cooking from the 1970s onwards some foods submerged themselves totally in their sauces or thin aromatic broths, or just dipped their feet in with the widespread use of Asian dipping sauces. Since then, the world of Indian chutneys, Middle Eastern sauces and Mexican salsas have given us new flavors and textures to enjoy and broaden our understanding of what a sauce can be.

The most recent culinary movement, Molecular Cookery or Molecular Gastronomy, established by the Heston Blumenthals and Ferran Adriàs of the culinary world, built itself on the earlier foundations of colloidal chemistry and cookery experimenters like Bella Lowe in the 1930s and later Harold McGee in the '80s and '90s. McGee, in his *Food & Cooking* book alone, dedicates 56 pages to the discussion of sauces. The new wave of molecular cooks introduced us to foams, spherification, new jelling agents, airs and dehydrated ingredients created to imitate the look and texture of soils and sands. Although not always meeting the traditional definition of sauces, many of them have taken on the role as sauce replacers.

The information age, which has brought the world into every home via computers and the internet, has given us access to recipes and foods from cultures all across the globe. No longer do we think of sauces as restricted to those from France, Italy, Asia and Europe, but have adopted and included Middle Eastern, African and Mexican sauces in our everyday cooking. Traditional cooks and chefs who have monopolized, claimed and argued that the classics are the only true path to Mastery of the Sauces, have now been confronted by a new wave of modern cooks who reject this and look for recipes elsewhere. We hope this third volume of *The Culinary Library* will provide inspiration for both traditional and modern cooks alike, and reinforce the continued role of the Sauce as one worthy of study and Mastery.

SAUCE TERMINOLOGY

---◆◆◆---

"Doctor Johnson defined a sauce as something which is eaten with food in order to improve its flavor. It would be difficult to believe that a man of the intelligence and culture of Dr Johnson ... had expressed himself in these terms, if we did not know that Dr Johnson was English. Even today his compatriots, incapable of giving any flavor to their food, call on sauces to furnish to their dishes that which their dishes do not have. This explains the sauces, the jellies and prepared extracts, the bottled sauces, the chutneys, the ketchups which populate the tables of this unfortunate people."
—ALBERTO DENTI Di PIRAJNO, *Educated Gastronome*, 1950

DEFINITION ....

The word 'sauce' was brought into popular culture by French chefs describing liquid or semi-liquid preparations, made specifically to accompany other foods. Their purpose is to cook foods in, tenderize, and enhance, balance or contrast the flavor, color or texture of the food they accompany. They are made generally, but not exclusively from a range of foods including meats, vegetables and fats; moisteners like water or wine; flavorings like spices, herbs, fruits; and thickeners like flour, egg yolks, grains or nuts.

History tells us that the word Sauce is derived from the Latin *salsa*, meaning salted, which was the primary flavor of the original *salsa* of Ancient Rome called Garum. The history of sauces however, unlike the invention of the name, is not so simple, rather it is an elaborate game of Chinese whispers, with many claiming a recipe is *the* original or *the* classic version, when in reality ingredients and methods change across time, cultures and chefs. The same sauce recipe given by the French chef Escoffier differs from Carême's, and Larousse's are different from both of these, and so it goes through culinary history. While many sauces retain their classical roots, for practical reasons today, when we say 'stock' we don't mean the 3-day multi-beast reduction of a hundred years ago, but rather we leave it to individual cook to choose the one they are most familiar with. For today's home cook this may mean a reconstituted powder, a pre-prepared commercial stock or a homemade stock made in a few hours.

To identify classic sauces and their uses, we use the following terms to describe them:

– Importance and type: mother (or base), motherless or other, classic, secondary, compound, emulsified.

– Temperature: cold, warm or hot.

– Texture: thin, medium, thick, semi-solid.

– Taste: sweet, sour, bitter, salty and savory, creamy, milky, spicy, herby, buttery or piquant

– Color: brown, blonde, white, neutral, cream, red, orange, pink, yellow, or green.

– Base, if there is one + additional ingredients.

– Other known names.

– Traditional partner: fish, chicken, meats, vegetables, pasta, eggs etc.

Rather than add salt and pepper to each sauce listed, assume that all savory sauces are seasoned, usually at the end of cooking, with both salt and pepper. Many sauces are seasoned twice, once with the making of the mother sauce and again after additional ingredients have been added or before serving. A good general rule of thumb for all cooking, regardless if you are using a recipe or creating as you go, is to taste and re-taste again and again and balance the flavors before serving.

ASIAN SAUCES

The spread and wide acceptance of Asian sauces in the Western culinary world is relatively recent. Asking for soy, chili or teriyaki sauce in Australia 50 years ago was not only unfruitful but positively frowned upon. By the '70s and '80s the three most widely encountered Asian dishes were Beef in Black Bean Sauce and Chicken in either Honey or Lemon Sauce, whereas today there would hardly be a household without several Asian condiment sauces in the cupboard. For cooks who want to make Asian sauces at home, the ingredients are now easily available in every capital city Chinatown precinct, and Asian and mainstream supermarkets. We tend to think of Asian sauces as salty/spicy/savory but there are also interesting sweet sauces based on ingredients like dragon fruit.

BOUQUET GARNI

Also known as 'faggots'. In French cookery, savory sauces and liquids are flavored during the cooking process by the addition of a tied bundle of herb aromats. It is then removed before plating. The traditional Bouquet Garni of Escoffier is made up of parsley, bay and thyme. More modern Bouquets Garnis can include celery and sage.

BUTTER SAUCES ....

Butter is approximately 80% butterfat, 16% water, 2% mineral salts and 2% protein. It is these proteins and salts that brown when butter is heated, and it is the butterfat that turns frothy white. Butter sauces are primarily composed of butter and can be thick or thin, emulsified or compound, and either hot or cold.

Hot Butter: Heating butter until the solids settle makes the simplest of the butter sauces. Skimming the top butter fat from the settled solids is known as clarifying.

Brown Butter Sauce: Further heating turns hot butter brown, which is known as beurre noisette (hazelnut), or brown butter. Traditionally served hot over fish or vegetables. An example of a brown butter sauce is beurre meunière, where butter is heated until lightly brown, then lemon juice, parsley and cayenne pepper are added.

Black Butter: Heating brown butter further turns it dark brown, and is known as beurre noir or black butter. It traditionally has vinegar or lemon juice added along with parsley and is served with meats, scrambled eggs and vegetables.

Compound Butters: Butter that has been softened, had flavoring added, is re-chilled and served in slices on hot food, is also known as a butter sauce. Maître d'hôtel is an example.

CARAMELIZE ....

When we apply heat to food by sautéing, roasting, grilling or broiling, the natural sugars on the surfaces of that food will eventually melt and begin to color, a process known as caramelization. Heating sugar in the same way is also called caramelizing.

CHIFFONADE ....

This is a French term that describes cutting larger leaves like spinach, basil, lettuce, choi etc. into long thin strips or 'little rags'. Rolling them tightly and then slicing across the roll to make thin strips achieves this. Used as a garnish or additive to sauces.

CHUTNEYS ....

The word chutney comes to us from Southern Indian cooking and refers to thick or thin sauces, made mainly from vegetables and/or fruits with added spices, vinegar or lemon, and sugar. Chutneys came to the West via England during the days of the Raj and also via the fusion movement. They can be wet or dry, fine, or coarse and chunky. They differ from relishes because they have less water and are sweeter.

CLASSIC SAUCES ....

Classic sauces originated in 19th Century France in the culinary period known as French classical cooking. This was the time before Nouvelle Cuisine, when master chefs like Carême and Escoffier were undisputed rulers of the culinary world. Carême, who variously cooked for Talleyrand, Napoleon, George IV, Tsar Alexander and the Rothschild's, was the first to introduce to culinary sauces the classification of four mother sauces, Béchamel, Espagnole, Velouté and Allemande. His successor, Escoffier, reclassified these, replacing Allemande with the Egg Emulsions, whose mother he called Hollandaise and secondaries include Mayonnaise, Béarnaise, and Russian salad dressing. Escoffier also introduced a fifth mother sauce, Tomato.

COMPOUND SAUCES ....

Traditionally a compound sauce has meant a sauce made from a mother sauce + additions, usually herbs, spices, vegetables or reductions. Also known as small or derivative sauces. Most but not all of the classic sauces are built on a base of one of the mother sauces with additional processes and ingredients added. The more modern definition of a compound sauce is actually much wider than this traditional definition. Any sauce becomes a compound sauce when, once made, its ingredients can only be divided from each other chemically but not physically. They therefore include not only the classic sauces but tomato ketchup, English sauces, many Asian-style sauces and mayonnaise-based salad dressings. Compounding simply means to combine two or more separate ingredients until they form a single whole, different from their primary ingredients and unable to be physically separated (except by chemistry) back into those individual ingredients.

CONDIMENT SAUCES ....

Condiment, from the Latin condmentum or condmentium, oringially meant 'to season', but its meaning by the Middle Ages had come to mean a relish, vinegar or spice used to pickle or preserve food to prevent it spoiling. Today we use the word loosely, and a condiment sauce is generally thought of as something commercially prepared that you buy off a supermarket shelf. Condiment sauces include things like BBQ, chili, fish, ketchup (tomato), mayonnaise, mustard, soy and Worcestershire.

DASHI STOCK ....

Dashi is a foundation or building block of Japanese cuisine. It is the ultimate carrier of the unique savory flavor we call Umami.

There are several Dashi types, but the classic one is water infused with the flavor of Kombu seaweed and Katsuobushi, which is tissue-thin, dried, shaved bonito fish.

DEGLAZE, DÉGLACER ....

Deglazing is a technique of extracting meat drippings and juices, vegetable crusts, or pieces of caramelized food from the surface of a pan in which they have been fried, by the use of a liquid. When food is fried or sautéed in a stove top pan or in the oven it is usually removed for resting before serving. Adding a liquid such as water, stock, broth, marinade, wine or cream to the residual leavings in the cooking pan serves to loosen and dissolve them from the bottom of the pan, and stirring and scraping brings them into solution. When further heated, the liquid is reduced and the flavor intensified. This process is known as deglazing and results in a pan sauce with intense flavor which can be used in its own right or as a stock or base for more complex sauces.

DEMI-GLAZE OR GLACE ....

Pronounced 'demi-GLASS', this is a rich French reduction sauce, traditionally made from espagnole and veal stock. Used to accompany meat, it has a deep, rich and satisfying flavor.

DESSERT SAUCES ....

It's hard to imagine a dessert that can't be enhanced by the addition of a sweet sauce of one kind or another – and then there are desserts that are only half the story without their saucy partners. Christmas pudding without custard, crème caramel without its caramel, waterfall pudding without the apricot sauce waterfall. The most wonderful thing about dessert sauces is dousing that last spoonful with more sauce than dessert. Dessert sauces by definition are served as partners with the sweet foods traditionally served after the main savory course of a meal, but basically they can be enjoyed anytime of the day.

DIPPING SAUCES ....
Any sauce can become a dipping sauce simply by thinning it down. The original Western dipping sauces were thick gluggy affairs based on sour creams or cream cheeses like French onion dip, but today's dipping sauces, thanks to the influences of fusion food, are thinner, silkier and more sophisticated. They can be hot or cold, spicy, sweet, creamy, astringent, salty, sour, or a mixture of several flavors. Alton Brown, a James Beard Foundation Award-winning chef and Iron Chef America host, suggests that a dip be defined based on its ability to 'maintain contact with its transport mechanism over three feet of white carpet.'

DUXELLES ....
Duxelles is a mixture of finely chopped vegetables, sautéed in butter, that is used as a base for sauces. It contains mushrooms or mushroom stems, onions, shallots and herbs.

EMULSIFIED SAUCES ....
Oil droplets are a lot bigger and slower moving that water molecules, and can act as a thickener when added to and blended with water based liquids. When a liquid's molecules are dispersed and bound 'inside' another liquid, we call it an emulsion. (When air is dispersed and bound inside a liquid we call it a foam.) Some foods are naturally occurring emulsions, such as fat + water in milk, cream and egg yolks, whereas sauce emulsions are usually

created by agitation processes like beating, whipping or stirring. Not all sauces are emulsions but the ones you may be most familiar with include hollandaise, béarnaise and salad dressings that have a mixture of oil and vinegar. When you thicken a sauce with starch, egg yolk, cream or butter it usually becomes and remains stable even with freezing and reheating, but emulsified sauces are different. Emulsions are inherently unstable because oil and water are not normal bedfellows and are always trying to get away from each other and congregate with their own molecules. That's why oil and vinegar dressings, when they have no additional added emulsifiers or stabilizers (like starch, pectin, gum, or plant tissue like tomato paste or mustard), have to be shaken or re-stirred every time before use. Electrical charges keep emulsions stable, but so too do acids like vinegar, lemon and wine, and emulsifiers like egg yolk, milk, cream, Gellan, Gum Arabic and lecithin. Wine, if used as a stabilizer for emulsions, must be reduced and concentrated more than lemon or vinegar because it is a weaker acid. When separation occurs in an emulsion sauce it's called 'splitting'. See Tips & Tricks in the last chapter for rescuing split emulsion sauces.

ESSENCES ....
An essence, as it is used in sauce cookery, is an extract of vegetable, fruit or meat, where the essential flavor of a food is extracted using water, alcohol or oil. Vanilla is an essence created by an alcohol extract; chili, lime or lemon oil are oil extracts, and stock is a water extract, which when reduced further is called a broth or bouillon. Brandy and whisky are also extracts or essences, but are produced by distillation.

FLAVOR CLASSIFICATIONS & COMPONENTS ....
Flavor is a part of taste, a sensation created firstly by the mouth and nose. Food flavors have base notes, much the same as perfume does, but instead of rose or jasmine or violet, taste is classified into five base notes. Sweet, sour, salty and bitter are the first four flavors, easily identified and understood by most people. The fifth and most recent flavor classification is *umami*.

Umami is a more difficult flavor to describe. It is a combination of glutamates + inosinates. Fermenting by yeast, enzymes or bacteria is a common way to produce the umami flavor, which is a savory taste varying from strong to mild with a lingering aftertaste. The quintessential umami flavor is Dashi, the Japanese fish stock made by infusing shaved bonito (fish) flakes and dried kombu (seaweed) in water. It is also found in foods like ceviche (raw fish + lemon + salt), sake, miso, bonito and dried seaweeds like kombu and nori, anchovies, prosciutto, shitake mushroom, matured cheddar cheeses (especially Parmigiano Reggiano), fish and soy sauces, ripe tomato (especially sundried) and the yeast extracts Vegemite, Bovril and Bonox.

Flavor experience is also effected by texture and chemicals that create 'coolness' like menthol or ethanol and 'heat' like capsaicin, found in chili and pepper. Some experts argue that hotness, piquancy or pungency should be classified as a sixth base note flavor in its own right and astringency as the seventh. Other components of taste or flavor include metallicness, fat, calcium, fullness or thickness, aroma and temperature. As you can see, flavor is a subjective experience that differs through the ages, across cultures, and changes with experience. Professional chefs talk about 'balancing your flavors', another subjective term but one that is important. It means adjusting the base notes of flavor to produce a blend or balance that appeals to an experienced palate. It can be specific to, or widely accepted as 'authentic' for, a particular food or recipe. Flavor is influenced firstly by the quality and type of the ingredients used, the quantity of individual ingredients in recipes and with experience through the trial and error of the sauce maker.

FOAMS ....
An edible foam in cooking is made by incorporating air or another gas into a liquid. The purpose is to create a lighter texture and different mouth feel. Foams are intrinsically unstable and prone to loosing their 'lift' unless a 'stabalizer' is added to help them retain their gas. Stabilizing agents include whipped-in additives like agar agar or lecithin. Commonly encountered food-foams include the frothed milk used for coffee, whipped cream and whipped egg whites. Espuma is another name for foam and applies to foams made with a piece of equipment, previously known as a cream whipper and now known as a thermo whip.

A brand of thermo whip canister, the iSi, is a tool of choice for professional chefs for introducing N_2O to a stabalized liquid to achieve the lightest of textures.

FOND ....
Fond is a French word, meaning base or bottom. In cooking it refers to the caramelized particles left on the bottom of a pan after roasting and sautéing. Fond is usually lifted into a liquid suspension by the addition of wine, stock or cream and becomes a pan sauce.

FUMET ....

Fumet is an older cooking term coined in France in the early 1900s where it was used to describe the aroma and then the liquid of a reduced, seasoned fish stock. Later it was broadened to include meat and vegetable stock reductions. A fumet is simply a water-based stock that is reduced to a stronger, more concentrated flavor.

GASTRIQUE ....

A sauce that has both acid and sweet flavors combined is called a Gastrique. It is the 'sweet & sour' of Western cooking. The best known Gastrique is caramelized sugar deglazed with vinegar which can be used as the base for tomato sauce, savory fruit sauces and the classic sweet/sour orange sauce served with duck à l'orange. In Italian cooking a Gastrique sauce is called Agrodolce, *agro* meaning sour and *dolce* meaning sweet.

GELÉE ....

In the 14th Century the French word for a congealed gel was gelée, and it referred to the natural gelatin from meat cookery. Calf's Foot Gelée was probably one of the first well-known gelées. When the English adopted the word they changed it to 'jelly', which instead of conjuring recipes of champagne gels, aspics or sensuous meat gels, became synonymous with sweetened, flavored liquids set to gels using either gelatin or pectin. But today's chefs have reclaimed the original French word and its meaning to re-create and newly-create both sweet and savory gelées that vary in textures from soft, pourable liquids to firm-setting versions of liquids. Because many of today's gelées are savory and not sweet, you're not going to find them in dessert books. They don't really appear anywhere consistently, so finding them in a sauce book is not a big stretch of the imagination. Just think sauces that are softly, luscious, melt-in-the-mouth gels. With an increasing range of jelling agents (hydrocolloids) has come a comparable increase in gel innovation, including: yuzu dashi, cucumber, pomegranate, bacon and sage.

GLACE ....
Glace means a glaze or ice. When Escoffier said 'glace' he usually meant icecream, but when we say 'glace' we mean a brushing or pouring sauce or syrup used to add a shiny coat to fruit tarts and desserts or to savories and meats. Sauces used for glazing other foods are usually not marinades, but rather are brushed or poured on at the last minute before cooking or even afterwards. They tend to be, or add to, a shiny glossy finish and can be both savory and sweet. An old classic French meat glaze is Glace de Viande, a dark brown, highly-flavored viscous base made by reducing brown stock on a slow heat. A more modern example is the citrus/honey/spice glaze used on baked hams. Sweet glazes were used traditionally for finishing cakes, buns and tarts, but are often found today as saucy smears on dessert plates. Some glazes have sweet, sour and salty components, like the Asian glazes used for coating pork and duck.

JUS ....
At its simplest, jus is the residual pan juices and fats rendered from roasting meats like beef, veal, lamb and chicken, but the term also includes these juices flavored by the addition of finely chopped vegetables that are sautéed, deglazed with stock and then strained. Jus is different from a pan gravy because it is served un-thickened. Although not a true jus, when cornstarch or arrowroot are added as thickeners to a brown stock and then simmered to reduce, it is called a jus lié or fond lié.

LOBSTER OR CRAYFISH CULINARY TERMS ....

CORAL: The roe or egg sack of the Female Hen or Paquette. It is deep red in color when raw and lightens to a coral pink when cooked. Used as a sauce thickener and in hot butter and crayfish sauces.

CULL OR PISTOL: Name for a lobster or crayfish that has lost one of its claws.

FEMALE LOBSTER: Hen, or Paquette if carrying fully-formed eggs.

HUMANE DEATH: Laws are currently coming into force around the world for the humane slaughter of crustaceans. Electrocution is seen as the most humane method. Knife slaughter and live boiling are definitely no longer accepted.

MALE LOBSTER: Cock

SIZE CLASSES: Eighth = $1\frac{1}{8}$ lb, Quarter = $1\frac{1}{4}$ lb, Chicken = between 1 and 2 lbs, Large = $1\frac{1}{2} - 2\frac{1}{2}$ lb, Jumbo + or Extra Large = over $2\frac{1}{2}$ lb.

SLEEPER: A lobster that appears asleep; is close to death.

SOFT SHELL: Lobsters, like crabs, molt their shells. When their new shell is soft they are lighter, have less meat and less flavor and make a rattly sound when shaken. Chefs prefer hard shelled lobsters.

TOMALLEY: Lobster liver. It is a green color and should not be wasted or discarded as is used as a sauce thickener and flavor booster.

MASTER STOCK ....

Water flavored with soy sauce + spices + ginger + garlic. Used as a stock to submerse and cook other foods in. Also known as Asian

Master Sauce, 'Thousand Year Sauce', or the ancient 'red cooking' method, Master Sauce is a term used to describe a soy-based stock used as a cook-in braising liquid for meat, vegetables and tofu. Foods are slow cooked in the stock until they become tender or meat falls off the bone, staying very moist, intensely flavored and taking on a red color. A small amount of Master Stock is often reduced to use as a coating sauce and the remainder kept and reused for years with a 'topping-up' of spices. Thought to originate in China, the term has now spread and is used in other Asian countries. There are many cultural and family variations to the ingredients and spices used to flavor Master Stocks, including star-anise, Szechuan pepper, five spice powder, ginger and rock sugar. Use for cooking chicken, veal, beef, pork, tofu, eggs and vegetables.

MIREPOIX
Carême in the 1830s was making a sauce called mirepoix with vegetables, meat and wine, but during his reign the recipe was simplified and the term came to mean a mixture of the three vegetables only. He called these aromatics, a term changed by modern chefs to aromats. Cubed carrot, celery and onion, used raw or roasted but more usually sautéed in butter or olive oil, is used today as a base for sauces, stocks, soups and stews.

MODERN SAUCES
Modern sauces are not really modern and may be older or younger than the classics, so by 'modern' we mean any sauce that has come into wide use and acceptance in Western cookery since the Nouvelle Cuisine movement of the 1960s. They include the lighter sauces, pan juice sauces, fruit and vegetable purées, vinaigrettes, and Asian and Middle Eastern sauces. Some modern sauces may

even have been invented in antiquity, but only recently, in the last 40 or 50 years, have they risen from exotic obscurity to popular notoriety.

MOTHER SAUCES ....

There are hundreds of traditional classic sauces and many of them, probably about three quarters, come from a few basic sauces that chefs traditionally call 'Mothers'. Carême was the first chef to use these names, and he invented or identified four mother sauces. Escoffier later changed the terminology slightly and added a fifth basic sauce. There has never been total agreement amongst chefs about how many there are, but in general it is safe to say that most experts agree with Escoffier, that there are five basic classic sauces and they are classified by color. The Mothers are: White (Béchamel), Brown (Espagnole), Yellow (Hollandaise), Blonde (Velouté), and Red (Tomato). All of the warm or hot mother sauces, except Hollandaise, use stock or liquid in their preparation. These are derived from animal, fish and poultry flesh or bones, tomato purée, vegetable stock, milk, wine or water. In most cases the stock or liquid is thickened with eggs or a roux made from a 1:1 ratio of fat (usually butter or pan juice fat) and flour.

MOTHERLESS ....

A term *The Culinary Library* uses to describe Classic sauces that do not have, as their base, one of the five mother sauces. There will be argument by some traditional chefs against their inclusion in the classic sauce family, but just because they aren't derivatives of the five big Classic Mother sauces it doesn't mean they are not Classic sauces in their own right, and by our definition if they were in common use during the culinary reigns of Carême or Escoffier they qualify.

NEUTRAL SAUCES ....

The traditional meaning of a neutral sauce is one made from a non-meat base. Tomato is an example.

PAN SAUCES ....

When meats are cooked in baking or frying pans in the oven or on the stove top the residue left after the meat is removed is called a 'fond'. When a liquid is added and the fond 'bits' scraped up to flavor it, this is known as deglazing, and the result, with or without additional additives, is known as a pan sauce. When liquid is added to a fond it is sometimes simply brought up to heat and served, but can be further reduced by simmering to intensify flavor, thus becoming a reduced pan sauce. It's always necessary to season pan sauces with salt and pepper, and finishing them with a little butter produces a glossy shine.

There are endless options to garnish or flavor the base fond, either before or after adding the liquid. Flavor enhancers often include shallots or onion, garlic, bacon or pancetta, whole black, pink or green peppercorns, lemongrass, ginger, chili and herbs. Options for the liquid or *déglaçage* are red or white wine, apple cider, cognac, vinegar, water, citrus juices, stock, cream, milk, yoghurt, buttermilk, coconut (in water, milk or cream form), champagne, pomegranate, orange or cranberry juice, verjuice, dashi or master stock reduction. Options for making the *fond* include veal, beef, chicken, fish, pork, roast vegetables.

There are also options to further bind the flavors or thicken the consistency of a pan sauce by using a *liaison* or *finition* (binder).

Common finitions are flour or butter roux, beurre manié, plain butter, corn, rice and wheat flours. They can also be solids like capers, avrils, fruit segments, zests or soft herbs, or mustards, calvados, brandy or cognac.

REDUCTION SAUCES ....

When cooks talk about reduction sauces or 'reducing' a sauce, they mean decreasing its volume. This process is usually done by evaporation, by applying heat and boiling without a lid until it thickens to the desired consistency and the flavors intensify. Care should be taken not to reduce a sauce to the point where its flavor essences have been destroyed, creating bitterness or a burnt flavor.

SALSAS ....

Salsa is the Spanish word for sauce, and the Spanish and Mexican cuisines have the most salsa recipes. Originally made in the Mortar & Pestle, called a 'molcajete' in Mexico, today they are made by finely hand-chopping vegetable or fruit into a uniform size and then adding liquids like citrus juice or oil for wetness and herbs, chili or spices for flavor. Traditional Mexican salsa ingredients include cactus, tomatillo, tomato, cucumber, jalapeño and chipotle chili peppers, black beans, lime juice and corn. More modern salsa ingredients include avocado, radish, mango, watermelon, red and spring onion, peach and lemon juice.

SECONDARY SAUCES ....

In Classic French cookery when additional ingredients are added to a base Mother sauce they are called secondary sauces. They are also sometimes called minor sauces.

SIEVE ....
When we sieve a sauce we pass it through some type of mesh, usually metal or plastic, which strains the sauce to separate solids from liquids. There are several types of sieves available to cooks, including:

CONE SIEVES: A cone-shaped strainer with a larger open end, where a handle is usually attached, that tapers to a pointed or bluntly-pointed end. Also known as Chinoise or China caps. They usually come in three sizes of perforation, large, small and fine.

DRUM SIEVES: Usually round metal or wooden-sided frames with a mesh stretched across one end.

FABRIC SIEVES: An open-weave fabric such as muslin used to sieve foods.

ROUND SIEVES: A straining mesh, either metal or plastic, on a solid round frame where a handle may or may not be attached. The mesh falls or is shaped into a round bottom well below the frame.

SKIM OR DÉPOUILLER ....
Skimming means removing the top layer of fat and/or impurities from a sauce, soup or stock, usually with a spoon but it can also be done with absorbent paper or by decanting.

SLURRY ....
When starch is added to a warm or hot liquid it can form clumps, but mixing it with a cold liquid before adding to warm sauces, soups and stews avoids this. When added to cold liquids and stirred, starch dissolves or disperses evenly and is called a *slurry*. Another word used in cooking, when powder is mixed with water, is *slake*. Recipes using starch as thickeners may say something like 'slake with water' or 'mix to a slurry'.

SOFFRITTO ....
This is the Italian version of the French mirepoix and is used as a base for sauces, especially pasta sauces. Finely diced onion, celery and carrot in a ratio of 1:1:1, sautéed in butter, oil and sugar in a ratio of 1:1:1.

SOILS ....
Culinary 'soils' are associated with the molecular gastronomy movement and are foods, dehydrated by heat or chemicals and then crushed to imitate the texture and appearance of soil or dirt.
Used as replacements for traditional sauces, they don't meet the definition of 'wet' as they are just the opposite, but they do fulfill the role of a sauce and accompanying other foods as partners.

STOCK ....

Stock is water flavored with meat, seafood or vegetables, used as a base for sauces and soups. It means something different today than it did during the Classical period of cookery when it was made from scratch with meats, bones and vegetables. Today the home cook generally purchases stock as a concentrated dehydrated powder or a pre-packaged liquid.

BROWN VEAL OR BEEF STOCK ....

Veal or beef meat and/or bones + water + vegetables. Classically called Fond Brun de Veau/Boeuf, also known as Bouillon. Brown stock is made from browning and then slow simmering beef, veal or lamb meat and/or bones and vegetables in water. The solids are then sieved out. Once seasoned, the stock can be further clarified (made clear), by the addition of an egg slurry (1 egg white beaten with ¼ cup cold water) which coagulates, capturing the fine suspended particles. It is then strained. Clarified stock is bouillion. The same method of preparation applies for white stock.

Brown Stock derivative: Meat Consommé.

Meat Consommé derivative: Meat Glaze or Glace.

COMMERCIALLY PACKAGED LIQUID STOCK ....

Dehydrated stock powder + water. We choose not to buy liquid stock as it is more eco-friendly to buy dehydrated powder. It makes no sense to transport bulky liquids when you can add the water yourself.

GAME STOCK ....

Game meat and/or bones + water + vegetables. Classically called Fond Brun de Gibier

LOBSTER AND SHELLFISH STOCK ....

Lobster, crayfish, prawn or scampi + water + vegatables.

Commercially available shellfish stock powders and essences include Faima shrimp powder, Fergusons lobster oil (from Australia), Mafe shrimp powder and Mecci shrimp cubes. Most Asian shops sell shrimp paste concentrates.

DEHYDRATED STOCK POWDERS ....

There are too many brands of commercially available stock powder for us to cover here but check the labels for artificial color, flavor and MSG. See **TheCulinaryLibrary.com** for a comparative review of the brands available in Australian supermarkets. Our preferred brand is Massell.

WHITE CHICKEN STOCK ....

Chicken meat and/or bones + water + vegetables. Classically called Fond Blanc de Poulet.

WHITE FISH STOCK ....

Fish meat and/or bones + water + vegetables. Classically called Fond Blanc de Poisson.

Fish Stock derivative: Fish Consommé.

Fish Consommé derivative: Fish Glaze or Glace.

Commercially available powdered fish stocks include Dashi powder with bonito, Jumbo, Essential cuisine, Hako and Collage salmon powder.

WHITE VEAL STOCK ....

Veal meat and/or bones + water + vegetables. Classically called Fond Blanc de Veau.

Most home cooks today buy powdered or liquid stocks, some of which are entirely vegetable-based, with added color and flavors. More chefs than you would guess buy powdered Demi-glace, Espagnole, Béchamel, Beef, Chicken, Vegetable and Tomato sauce bases. When a sauce recipe calls for stock you must make your own decisions, based on your finances, time available, animal welfare morals and other important factors known only to you and suited to your individual circumstances. We don't support commercial liquid stocks because of their cost, their bulk and transport costs. Given that you are buying water + stock powder we prefer buying powdered stock and adding our own fresh water. It is possible to easily source good beef and chicken stock powders that are wholly vegetable derived. We live in a fast, convenient world, brought up on fast, convenient tastes, with a myriad of financial and emotional pressures. But one day soon, if time permits, you might find that you want to discover what a classically prepared stock tastes like so you can compare the difference. And if you do find yourself making that brown or white stock, you can have a plan formulated for those left over succulent veal shanks or that whole poached chicken, one that includes making a sauce, one that you've made from their extracted and reduced juices.

TEMPER ....
Tempering in cookery has two general meanings, the first being the precise heating and then cooling of chocolate to stabilize and harden the crystals. The purpose of this is to make the chocolate firm or hard at room temperature. When tempered chocolate is spread into thin sheets and cooled it cracks and shatters when hit with a fork or spoon. The second meaning is adding a hot liquid to a cold one (usually egg based) by blending a little at a time to slowly raise the temperature of the cold one. This allows you to blend without curdling.

THICKENERS ....
A thickener is an ingredient, usually animal or vegetable matter, or any process, such as the application of heat or cooling or the

introduction of air or gas, that serves to reduce the water content or increase the particle size of sauces and thereby create lower viscosity and a greater density on the palate. Thickeners are used essentially to change the textural experience of a sauce, but they can also change the perception of flavor, not only by intensifying it but by bringing it to the front of the palate and holding it there longer than would be the case if left in a more liquid form.

VEGETABLE CUT TERMS ....
The French Classics: a system of culinary terms was devised to assist chefs in cutting vegetables into uniform, precise shapes and sizes. When sauces, soups and food asks for garnishes or sauté bases they can be stipulated by cut type and size. There is some variation of size between chefs but the following list is a general guide.

ALLUMETTE: Another name for Julienne

BATON OR BATONETTE: 'little sticks', 5cm x 5mm x 5mm (2¼-3 x ¼ x ¼")

BOUQUET GARNI : vegetables and herbs cut between Brunoise & Jardinière

BOUQUET MATIGNON: 2mm x 2mm x 2mm ($^1/_{12}$") carrots, celery, and onion. Used as a base for sauces. When Madeira is added it's called a matignon au maigre, when bacon is added it's called a matignon au gras.

BRUNOISE: 3mm x 3mm x 3mm ($^1/_8$") cubes, cut from julienne

BRUNOISE FINE: 1.5mm x 1.5mm x 1.5mm ($^1/_{16}$") cubes, cut from fine julienne

CARRÉ OR LARGE DICE: 2cm x 2cm x 2cm (¾") cubes

CHIFFONADE: long thin very fine slices 1-2 mm thick, used for flat herbs and small leaves that are rolled then finely sliced across.

DEMIDOFF: 2mm ($^1/_{12}$") thick, any shape

JARDINIÈRE: 5mm x 5mm x 20mm (¼ x ¼ x 1")

JULIENNE OR ALLUMETTE: 3mm x 3mm x 7cm ($^1/_8$ × $^1/_8$ × 2½")

JULIENNE FINE: 1.5mm x 1.5mm x 5cm ($^1/_{16}$ × $^1/_{16}$ × 2")

JULIENNE ROUGH: 2mm x 2mm x 5-7cm ($^1/_{12}$ × $^1/_{12}$ × 2-3")

MACÉDOINE: small dice, 1cm x 1cm x 1cm (¼") squares

MIREPOIX: 2mm x 2mm x 2mm ($^1/_{12}$"), cubed carrot, celery and onion, cooked slowly in butter until soft. Used as a base for sauces.

PARMENTIER: 12mm x 12mm x 12mm (½") cubes

PAYSANNE: 1cm x 1cm x 3mm (½ x ½ x $^1/_8$") thin squares

PRINTANIÈRE: tiny whole baby spring vegetables used as a garnish

TOURNEY OR TURNED: seven sided oval or olive shape, 1 - 3" long

VINCHY: 2mm ($^1/_{12}$") thick slices

ZEST ....
Zest refers to the outer skin of citrus fruit, generally removed with a five-holed zesting tool, grater, peeler or micro-plane. Used as a flavor additive, garnish or textural element.

ASIAN SAUCES

"I buy soy sauce and flavor it five different ways: with sake, mirin, sugar, kombu and bonito flakes. I use them on lots of dishes at home."
—MASAHAU MORIMOTO, Japanese Iron Chef

BLACK BEAN ....

2 tablespoons black beans, softened and crushed
1 tablespoon each garlic and ginger, minced
1 tablespoon light soy
1 tablespoon cornflour, slurried with a little water
100 ml mirin
150 ml chicken stock
oil for frying
2 spring onions, white and green parts sliced

Sauté the garlic and ginger in oil then add the remaining ingredients and stir until it thickens and comes to the boil. Add to sautéed beef, chicken or fish with bamboo shoots.

BROWN GARLIC ....

½ cup soy sauce
½ cup chicken broth
½ cup rice wine
3 tablespoons sugar

1 tablespoon sesame oil
pinch white pepper
2 tablespoons cooking oil
1 tablespoon minced garlic
1 tablespoon minced ginger
2 tablespoons corn-starch or cornflour dissolved in ¼ cup water
Sauté ginger and garlic in oil, add the rest of the ingredients and stir until sauce thickens and comes to a boil. Add to any stir-fry.

CASHEW GINGER ....

In a Mortar & Pestle, food processor or blender, crush/blitz together 2 cups toasted/sautéed cashew pieces, 2 teaspoons grated ginger, 2 teaspoons tamari, a pinch of salt and 3 cups of milk or coconut milk until smooth. Serve with grains, vegetables, meat, chicken and curries.

CHILI LIME ....

3 long green or red chilis
3 tablespoons fish sauce, Megachef or Red Boat brands if you can source them
3 tablespoons mirin
2 limes, juice and zest
1 garlic clove, crushed or finely sliced
1 tablespoon caster sugar
Season, taste and adjust flavors to your palate. For salads, seafood, all meats and poultry.

CORIANDER ....

1 small bunch coriander, finely chopped
1 garlic clove, minced

4 tablespoons olive oil
2 tablespoons each red wine vinegar and sherry vinegar
2 small blocks or half rounds palm sugar (2-3 oz)
Dissolve the palm sugar in a small saucepan with a dash of water and cook until it turns to golden brown syrup. Grind with the rest of the ingredients in a Mortar & Pestle or blitz in a blender. For salads, seafood, soba noodles.

CURRY ....

Curry is an English term originally used to describe the cook-in gravies of Indian cookery, though today it has broadened to include Thai, Malaysian and other Asian dishes with both thin broths and thick gravies. Curry sauces usually combine ingredients like oil, powdered and whole spices, herb seeds, onions, chili, lemongrass, ginger, garlic, water or coconut milk. There are too many curry sauces to include in this small sauce book, literally hundreds exist and a whole book is needed to cover them all. There are many good books already on the market with information on their origins and regional histories.

DASHI ....

Water + kelp + dried fish flakes. If you're going to make Japanese dipping sauce you'll need to know how to make Dashi. Dashi is made in two strengths.

Ichiban Dashi or 'first fish stock' extracts the best flavor and nutrients from kombu (kelp or seaweed) using heat and then infuses the flavor of katsuobushi (bonito flakes) by steeping. The very short cooking time prevents the stock from becoming strongly flavored or yellow. Ichiban dashi is used in preparations for which a more refined flavor and weaker color are required. Add 4 cups of water and 1 piece of kombu (about 5-6" long) in a saucepan and sit for 30 minutes. If your kombu has a whitish surface do not wash this off as it intensifies the umami flavor. Slowly bring to a simmer for 10-15 minutes but do not allow it to boil. Remove the kombu then bring your dashi base up to a boil. Turn off the heat, skim any impurities, cool for a couple of minutes then add 2 handfuls of bonito flakes and allow to steep for a few minutes without stirring. Strain through a muslin lined sieve without pushing or forcing, as this will cloud the stock. This deep golden colored clear stock is your Ichiban Dashi.

Niban Dashi or 'second fish stock' requires a return to the saucepan of the kombu and katsuobushi used for the Ichiban preparation. Add to them another 4 cups of water and bring slowly to the boil then turn heat off and add another fresh handful of bonito flakes. Steep for 5-10 minutes then strain, squeezing as much liquid as you can from the ingredients. This is your Niban Dashi; not as colorful or fragrant as Ichiban but wonderful as a stock for cooking and sauce making.

Kombu kelp comes in different qualities as follows:
Ma-Kombu: the most popular, highest quality, its wide thick leaves make a clear stock with delicate sweet overtones.
Rishiri-Kombu: sweeter, saltier, harder than ma-kombu, it makes a rich, savory and clear stock.
Rausu-Kombu: fragrant and soft, makes a rich stock with the characteristic kombu-color.
Naga-Kombu: the most common kombu kelp produced, its dashi needs additional flavor from sake, soy and sugar and it is then used as a simmering stock for other foods (dishes known as Nimono).

Saomae-Kombu: a rare type of kombu often growing near naga-kombu but harvested earlier when it is very soft. It has a very light subtle and delicate flavor.

A simple and delicious Dashi sauce for all purpose use is to mix Dashi, light Japanese soy sauce, olive oil and rice vinegar in a ratio of 2:2:2:1

DIPPING SAUCES ....

While there are hundreds of Asian dipping sauces, we have chosen a representative dipping sauce from each culture.

CHINESE: PEKING STYLE: Mix together 3 tablespoons each of light soy, dark soy, rice or red wine vinegar, 1 teaspoon of chili oil, 1 teaspoon each of minced garlic and ginger and sugar to taste.

FILIPINO: To ½ cup rice wine or white wine vinegar add 2 tablespoons of soy, 2 tablespoons each of finely chopped garlic, red onion and spring onion then add salt, pepper, chili flakes and sugar to taste.

INDIAN: MINT YOGHURT: Blitz together 1 bunch fresh mint leaves (but not the stalks, which are bitter) with 2-3 tablespoons plain yoghurt, 2 tablespoons sugar, juice of 1 lemon and a pinch of flaked salt. Can also be made using cream as a substitute for yoghurt, as the lemon juice will curdle the cream and make it taste like yoghurt.

INDONESIAN: CHILI SAMBAL: After chopping, sauté in oil 4 spring onions or shallots, 2 cloves of garlic, 2 long red chili, 5 long green chili, 2 white ends of lemongrass, 1 teaspoon of powdered or 2cm fresh turmeric, 1 tablespoon sugar. Blitz in a food processor with 1 large tomato, juice and zest of 1 lemon or 2 shredded kaffir lime leaves and a pinch of salt.

JAPANESE: TEMPURA DIPPING SAUCE: Mix 1 cup dashi Ichiban stock with ¼ cup each of mirin and Japanese soy then add a pinch of sugar. Grated daikon radish is also a traditional addition if you have it.

KOREAN: Mix 4 tablespoons each of soy sauce and rice wine vinegar to 1 tablespoon each of sesame oil, chili flakes, finely chopped garlic and sliced spring onions.

NONYA: To 4 tablespoons of fish sauce add 2 tablespoons of rice wine vinegar then 1 tablespoon each of lime juice, sugar, finely chopped red chili, grated baby carrot and grated daikon radish.

THAI: Dissolve ½ cup of sugar in ½ cup water and ½ cup rice wine vinegar and add a finely shredded baby carrot. Stir through finely chopped red chili or a little chili sauce.

DOUBANJIANG ....

Fermented soybeans + fermented broad beans + rice + spice + salt (+ optional chili). A salty Chinese sauce that can be made plain or spicy by adding chili. Doubanjiang is an essential base note in Sichuan cookery and in many Asian brands of instant packaged noodles. Also known as Hot Bean Paste, Chili Bean Sauce or Gochujang. Doubanjiang is traditionally prepared from broad beans, also known as fava beans. Fresh red chilies are pulverized and fermented for a few months in earthenware containers then cooked mashed broad beans, soy beans, salt and wheat flour are added and the mix left to ferment up to a year. It is used in stir-fries, with tofu and to flavor noodles.

To try making your own: Mix 250 grams of malt flour with a liter of warm water in a bowl and set aside for an hour. Tip off the surface liquid into a saucepan and discard the residual solids. Add 250 grams of wheat flour to your malt water and simmer for half an hour or more until it reaches a glue like consistency. Add 250 grams of fermented soybean or broad bean flour and chili powder to taste. The paste can be stored for months and thinned for sauce making.

DRAGON FRUIT CACTUS ....

Dragon fruit + coconut milk + lemon + sugar.

Dragon fruit + mayonnaise.

Also known as strawberry pear or pitahaya, dragon fruit is a strangely shaped and colored fruit popular in Thailand, Mexico and South America. It is a member of the cacti family and grows on a climbing vine or tree. It is mild, sweet, crunchy and has an amazingly subtle but complex flavor, being a cross between honey melon, nashi pear and kiwi fruit. Its white flesh, speckled with small black edible seeds inside a bright pink or lime green skin, is visually interesting.

Cold Sauce 1: Dragon fruit + mayonnaise. For fish

Cold or warm Sauce 2: Dragon fruit + lemon + milk. Blend together ½ pink dragon fruit, peeled, zest and juice of ½ lemon, 1 teaspoon sugar and enough coconut milk to make a sauce consistency.

DUCK ....

See also PLUM Sauce. Duck sauce is another name for sauces served with duck. It is usually Plum Sauce or Plum + hoisin. An alternative to serve with duck is to boil in a saucepan, for 15 minutes:

4 cups of fresh mixed chopped fruit e.g. apple, peach, plum, pear

1 cup of water or cider

¼ cup each of cider vinegar & light brown sugar

2 teaspoons tamari, a pinch of salt and 1 crushed garlic clove.
Serve chunky or mash with a potato masher.

FISH ....

Fermented fresh fish (usually anchovy) + sea salt + water.
Thin, clear, amber through to ochre or deep brown in color, umami flavor.

Fish sauce is to South-East Asian cuisine what soy is to China and salt is to the West. It is a used as a dipping sauce base, added to soups, stews and other sauces, and for kimchi. As with many foods there are natural products and there are those that are chemically enhanced with artificial flavors and colors. With fish sauce there are also those whose fermentation process has been hastened from a year down to 2 days by the addition of enzymes. Short or artificial fermentation usually results in a strong fishy flavor while long natural fermentation will give a sweet, nutty, rich flavor.

The strength of the natural protein or umami taste in fish sauce is graded by numbers which indicate the nitrogen content per liter. When a bottle is labelled °N/L, it indicates the concentration of fish protein in each drop. The higher the number the more fish protein and the bigger the umami taste.

50 and 43°N/L = highest protein, highest umami flavor, first extraction.

40, 30, 20 and 15°N/L indicate subsequent extractions, after additional water (usually seawater) has been added. We recommend Red Boat, Blis and Megachef because their long, natural fermentation gives them a big umami punch. Experiment and add to everything that needs more salt and savory. There is supposedly a 60°N/L fish sauce made by New Town although we have never been able to source it. See also in Cold Sauce chapter.

HOI SIN ....

Fermented soy + garlic + vinegar + chili + sugar.

Also called Chinese barbecue sauce, hoisin has a fragrant, pungent, salty, sweet flavor and is dark and thick. It tastes something like a spicy and sweet mixture of soy sauce, garlic and peanut butter. Use as a glazing, dipping and additive sauce with duck, poultry, tofu or vegetables and in Pho or Vietnamese noodle soup.

HONEY GINGER ....

6 tablespoons light soy sauce
3 tablespoons spring onions, finely sliced
3 tablespoons honey
2 tablespoons peanut oil
2 tablespoons lemon or lime juice
1 tablespoon ginger, minced
1 tablespoon garlic, minced
1 tablespoon long red chili, finely sliced
Blend all ingredients together.

JAPANESE MAYONNAISE OR KEWPIE ....

Egg yolk + rice vinegar + yuzu juice + mustard + sugar + salt + dashi powder.

Japanese mayonnaise (Kewpie) was invented in Japan in 1925 and is widely available in Asian grocers in the West. It comes in a small plastic squeeze bottle with a Kewpie doll on the front and the flavor is smooth with a creamy, tangy, sweet, umami taste reminiscent of the mayonnaise the Dutch serve with their chips or French fries. Don't be fooled by the cutsie packaging, Kewpie is well worth using and has a world-wide fan base but because the commercial brand is not MSG free why not try making your own version at home.

In a small mixing bowl or mortar mix 2 tablespoons of yuzu juice (use ½ lemon, ½ lime if you don't have yuzu), 1 tablespoon of rice vinegar and 1 tablespoon sugar, ½ teaspoon each of hot Japanese mustard, salt and dashi powder. Add 2 eggs (yolks only) and blend together. Slowly drizzle in 1 cup of rice-bran oil, mixing continuously until it thickens to an emulsion. Then beat in another tablespoon of rice vinegar, and hot water by the tablespoon until it is the consistency you require. Use with all seafood, salads, steamed vegetables (especially potatoes), greens, sushi and rice.

LEMON ....

Chicken stock + lemon + sugar + thickener.

This is the sauce traditionally used for lemon chicken or pork. It is sweet and sour and also pairs well with battered fish, prawns and tempura vegetables.

1 cup chicken stock

3 tablespoons lemon juice

3 thin slices of lemon, peeled

3 tablespoons sugar

1 tablespoon thickener (cornstarch or arrowroot)

pinch finishing salt

Heat stock, sugar, and lemon and add the thickener, made into a slurry with a little water. Season with salt. Serve warm over chicken or pork pieces that have been marinated in soy, then dipped in batter, fried and sprinkled with sesame seeds.

LIME CARAMEL ....

Sugar + rice vinegar + chili + ginger + fish sauce.

1 cup sugar, half white, half brown

1 tablespoon good quality fish sauce

1 tablespoon mirin or rice wine vinegar
1 long red chili, finely diced or sliced
1 tablespoon fresh ginger root, grated
Add the fish sauce and mirin to the sugar and stir until it melts, then cook until it just begins to color. Take off the heat and add the other ingredients. Serve warm or cold.

MANGO ....

Mango + honey + vinegar.
To each cup of ripe mango, puréed, add 1 teaspoon each of honey and cider vinegar. For chicken, meats, curries, desserts, custards etc. To make a sweet and sour mango sauce add to this base 1 tablespoon each of chili sauce (we use Linghams), oyster sauce and light soy. Taste, adjust and season.

MASSUMAM ....

Coconut milk/cream + fish sauce + stock + vegetables (onion, potato, green pepper, tomato) + spices (ginger, garlic, red, green or yellow chili, lemongrass, turmeric, coriander, cumin, cinnamon, cardamom, tamarind or lime juice, shrimp paste, palm or brown sugar) + basil and/or coriander + peanuts.
Also known as Mussaman or Massaman
Sauté one sliced onion in oil, add one teaspoon each of the spices and cook the paste, then add 2 tablespoons fish sauce, ½ cup stock and 400ml coconut milk or cream*, roughly chopped tomato, red pepper and potato. Simmer approximately 20-30 minutes or until soft and cooked through and the sauce thickened. Garnish with fresh herbs and peanuts.
* Finely sliced raw chicken breast or thigh, beef, lamb or pork, fish or whole prawns can be also added at this stage.

MASTER SAUCE OR STOCK ....

Chinese Master Sauce: Also known as Lushui Zhi, Lo Shui (old water), Lu Shui or Loo Shui (steeping water), is a spice infused soy-based stock used to poach or simmer meats, vegetables, fish, eggs and especially chicken. Master stock differs from other stocks because it is not discarded after use but is stored, renewed and reused to deepen and enhance its flavor. Chinese cooks have been renewing and reheating their Master Stocks year after year, for hundreds of years some of them, a practice that has now been embraced by Western chefs. Home cook can strain, refrigerate or freeze their master stock for reuse. Chinese Master Stock (and its derivative reduction sauce) have captured the imaginations of modern chefs with a few now claiming copyright of their variation of the recipe. This is just elitist nonsense of course, as Chinese Master Stock can never be 'owned'. It has been used for thousands of years by thousands of cooks, with endless 'tweeeking' of the flavor additives. Adding an extra clove, star anise or garlic clove does not equate to originality, invention or ownership.

Master stock is water + soy sauce + Shaoxing or rice wine + rock sugar + a variety of other spices and flavorings such as spring onions, shallots, star anise, coriander seed, dried citrus peel, cassia bark, ginger, galangal, Szechuan pepper, garlic, ginger, dried mushrooms.

For 3 liters of water add 1 cup light soy sauce, 2 cups Shaoxing wine, ½ cup yellow rock sugar, crushed, ⅓ cup sliced ginger, 5 sliced garlic cloves, 6 sliced spring onions, ½ teaspoon sesame oil, 4 star-anise, 4 whole cloves, 4 split green cardamom pods, 2-3 cinnamon sticks, 3-4 shavings of dried or fresh mandarin peel, 1 teaspoon each of peppercorns, fresh or dried red chili, coriander seeds, cumin seeds and fennel seeds.

MISO ....

Fermented soybeans + fungus + salt. Also made with fermenting rice or barley. Miso is a traditional Japanese flavoring paste used for sauces and stocks. Traditionally made from fermenting soybeans, rice or barley, with added salt and a natural fungus. There are three main types:

White Miso: also known as Komi, Dashi (white miso + bonito), Shiro or Rice Miso, this is the most widely used variety. It is the least fermented and made from rice and barley with a smaller amount of soybeans. If a greater quantity of soybeans is added, the miso becomes red or brown. White Miso tastes sweet, soft and lightly umami.

Red Miso: also known as Mami, Mame or Akamiso Miso, is aged longer than white miso, 12 months or more, and has a greater quantity of soybeans. Its flavor is salty and astringent with strong umami.

Mixed Miso: also known as Awase Miso, is as it sounds, a mix of Mame and Kome and has a flavor between the two.

Try all three and use the one you prefer in the following recipes:

Mushroom Miso Sauce: Sauté 2 cups of sliced mushrooms, add a tablespoon each of miso paste and light soy sauce, then add cream and salt to taste.

Mustard Miso Cream sauce: Fry seafood, meat or vegetables, remove from pan, deglaze with white wine then add miso, mirin, soy sauce, sugar and a splash of water. Bring to a boil then add cream and mustard.

Greens in Miso Sauce: Sauté greens like asparagus, broccoli, kale, mustard greens, Chinese cabbage, bok choy in sesame or peanut oil with garlic, chili and ginger then add white miso, soy and mirin.

Miso glazed Eggplant*: Also known as Nasu Dengaku. Halve lengthwise then deeply score eggplant in a cross-hatch and slowly fry or bake cut side down until the flesh is soft and golden. Serve with either of the following sauces.

Sweet Miso sauce 1: In a small saucepan mix 3 tablespoons of white Miso paste, 4 tablespoons of Mirin (or 2 each of Mirin and Sake), 1 tablespoon Japanese or light soy sauce, 1 teaspoon sugar, 1 teaspoon sesame oil and 4 tablespoons of Dashi stock or water with a little Dashi powder added.

Sweet Miso sauce 2: In a small saucepan mix 2 tablespoons of white Miso paste, two tablespoons of red Miso paste, 2 tablespoons of sugar, 1 tablespoon of Mirin and 1 teaspoon of either Dashi or bonito powder. Stir until it comes to a simmer, but do not boil.

* Recipe from **TheCulinaryLibrary.com**

NAM JIM ....

Chili + ginger + coriander + sugar + fish sauce + lime.

This classic Thai sauce is hot, sour and spicy and is perfect with red meat, chicken or shellfish. Best made in a Mortar & Pestle but can also be made in a food processor. Chop and crush 2 long red and 2 long green chili, 1 garlic clove, a small bunch of coriander roots, stems and leaves and 100 grams of palm sugar. Then add 3-4 tablespoons each of a good fish sauce and lime juice. Taste and adjust the balance of sweet, salty and sour by adding more sugar, fish sauce or lime juice if required.

OYSTER ....

Oyster essence + caramelized sugar + salt + water + cornstarch.

Cold, thick, dark, salty, sweet. Oyster sauce is a dark brown Asian sauce that also comes in a vegetarian version made with shiitake mushroom instead of oyster extract. Because of its strong flavor, oyster sauce is often thinned with soy and water then added to stir-fries, used as a marinade for meat or chicken, or used as a dipping sauce.

PAD THAI

Tamarind pulp + fish sauce + palm sugar + paprika or Thai chili powder.

Sour, sweet, salty and spicy. Two cups of sauce will make about 6-8 portions of Pad Thai. To make two cups of Pad Thai sauce, heat in a saucepan ½ cup of tamarind pulp, 2 cups of water, ½ cup fish sauce, $^1/_3$ cup palm or brown sugar until dissolved. Then add a dash of rice vinegar and chili powder, a little at a time, depending on your taste. Don't add salt, as the fish sauce will be salty enough. Simmer, taste and adjust the flavor to your palate and reduce a little.

PLUM

Plum jam + water + vinegar + onion + allspice + ginger + salt.

Cold or warm, sweet, sour and spicy. Chinese style Peking duck is served with Hoisin sauce in China but our Western palate often finds this too strong a flavor. An alternative is plum sauce. You'll have to track down 1 cup of plum jam, dilute it with half a cup of water, add 1 tablespoon each of white vinegar and onion powder then add a pinch each of allspice, ginger and salt. Bring to a slow boil before using. Spread on Peking duck pancakes or use as a dipping sauce for spring rolls.

PONZU

Soy + citrus + rice wine + sugar + dashi.

Thin or medium thickness, hot, salty, spicy, citrus. Ponzu is a Japanese sauce used for fish, shellfish, vegetables and chicken, as a raw vegetable slaw dressing, for stir fries, marinades or adding to pan juices.

For a quick no-cook Ponzu: Mix $1/3$ cup soy, $1/4$ cup orange juice, a squeeze of lime or lemon juice, 1 tablespoon each of rice wine vinegar and castor sugar and $1/3$ cup of dashi.

For a traditional cooked Ponzu: In a saucepan put the juice and zest of 1 lime, lemon or orange, 2 tablespoons sake, 1 tablespoon sugar, 1 tablespoon soy and boil until reduced by half. Then add a pinch of cayenne pepper, $1/2$ teaspoon sesame oil and thicken with $1/2$ teaspoon cornflour slurried with water. If using as a dipping sauce add some finely sliced spring onions.

SATAY ....

Peanuts + coconut milk + sugar + aromats.

There are many versions of Satay sauce but our recipe is fresh, intense and one of the easiest to make.

1 cup peanuts, unsalted, dry roasted
1 small or $1/2$ large can coconut milk or cream
2 cloves garlic
2 tablespoons brown sugar
2 tablespoons fish sauce
2 tablespoons light soy or 1 of regular soy
1 teaspoon sesame oil
1 teaspoon lime/lemon juice or tamarind paste
$1/2$ teaspoon cayenne pepper

Simply blitz the ingredients together in a blender or food processor and serve warmed.

SESAME ....

Tahini + soy + mirin + rice vinegar +sugar + chili + water.

Mix together in the following order: 3 tablespoons of sesame paste, also known as tahini (purchase the organic, water-hulled, pale colored one if you can find it), 2 tablespoons hot water, 1 tablespoon each of soy sauce, rice vinegar, mirin, brown or caster sugar and a small dash of red chili paste. Finish with 1-tablespoon sesame seeds, chopped spring onion and chopped long red chili. For fish, vegetables baked eggplant, red meat, chicken or drizzle over sautéed or salad greens.

SOY ....

Fermented soy beans + roasted wheat + aspergillus mold.

Cold, thin or medium thick, salty, sour, brown. Occasionally sweet as in kecap manis.

There are many types and names for soy sauce including Chinese, Japanese, Indonesian, Vietnamese, Filipino, Taiwanese, Thai, Burmese, Malaysian, Korean and Singaporean. The Japanese company Kikkoman is the world's largest producer. Used for meats, vegetable, chicken, fish, and tofu.

Soy sauce comes in both light and dark styles.

Light soy sauce is obtained from the first pressing of the fermented beans and is a lighter color and softer taste than the dark soy. For this reason it is used for dipping and for sauce making. Dark soy is best kept for cooking. It is thicker and darker due to the addition of caramel and molasses, starch and sometimes MSG. *Shoyu* on the label means wheat and *Tamari* means wheat free. Soy sauce quality is highly variable and graded as follows:

1. Traditional, artisan or craft made: traditional, centuries-old artisan recipes made with non-GM whole soya beans, natural

fermentation and chemical free, wood barrel ageing. Time to make: 18 months - 3 years. Brands include Megachef, Clearspring, Osawa Orgainc Nama Shoyu unpasteurized, Eden Shoyu, Yamasa, Red Boat, Blis.

2. Naturally brewed: natural fermentation speeded up with high temperature heating in steel or plastic tanks for 3+ months and the use of de-fatted soya protein meal rather than whole soya beans. When thin flakes of soya bean are percolated with a petroleum-based hexane solvent to extract its soya oil, the remaining by-product soya meal is the base used for naturally brewed soya sauce production. Time to make: 3-6 months. Colour is transparent light to medium amber with a sweet-salty flavor and delicate smell. Brands include Kikkoman, Pearl River Bridge, Lee Kim Keep. Avoid naturally-brewed soy sauces with added caramel color, high added salt and hydrolyzed soy protein like La Choy and the Chinese Superior brand.

3. Non-brewed or artificial: Most sauces on supermarket shelves labeled 'soy sauce', either light or dark, are non-brewed. They are mass produced, cheap and nothing like traditional soy sauce. They use de-fatted soya flour and rapid acid hydrolysis with hydrochloric acid, high temperature, and high pressure to create hydrolysed vegetable protein (HVP), then add corn syrup, salt, caramel, artificial preservatives, thickeners and flavorings. Time to make: 2-3 days. The toxic chemical 3-MCPD is sometimes a problem with non-brewed soya sauce. Color is opaque, dark with an intense, overpowering, chemical taste and strong smell. Due to possible health risks, non-brewed soy sauce should not be given to children.

SRIRACHA ....
This hot Thai chili sauce is delicious and so simple you find it served by many Asian food stalls and restaurants. In cheaper establishments it's usually the hot thin sauce in a plastic squeeze bottle and with table service comes in small white bowls for dipping spring rolls or adding to Pho. It's hot, thin and pungent, and made simply by mixing Thai hot chili paste (labeled as thai chili paste, nam prik pao chili paste with soya beans or sambal oelek), garlic, sugar, salt and distilled vinegar until the flavors are balanced. See our second recipe under Dipping Sauces.

SWEET & SOUR ....
Heat together 1 cup of pineapple juice, 4 tablespoons each of white vinegar, sugar and tomato sauce, add 1 tablespoon of cornflour mixed with 1 tablespoon of soy and when thickened add a dash of chili oil.

TAMARIND ....
Sour, tangy, spicy, slightly sweet. Tamarind sauce is made from the podded fruit of the Tamarind tree and is an ingredient in Pad Thai, Worcestershire and HP sauces. Tamarind sauce recipes are often called gojji e.g. gojji rice, gojji chicken or gojji vegetables. Vinegar and lime can be used as replacements when tamarind is unavailable. To make a thin tamarind sauce, pop 1 teaspoon of black or brown mustard seeds to 1 tablespoon of heated oil, then add 1 teaspoon of asafoetida, a few curry leaves and 4 long green chilis cut into slivers or rings. Blend together ½ cup tamarind paste, ¾ cup water, 1 tablespoon grated ginger, ½ cup powdered jaggery* and a pinch each of turmeric and salt. Add to the spice mix, being careful of hot spatter from the oil. Bring up to a boil

then turn off and cool. Traditionally served with Pongal (rice) or added to Pad Thai and fish dishes.

* Although they are not the same, palm sugar can be used as a substitute for jaggery, and while palm sugar is easily sourced in Asian grocers, jaggery is more likely to be found in Indian grocers. Jaggery has a richer flavor and is a more concentrated sweetener made from boiling and then solidifying raw cane juice, date palm sap or coconut tree sap.

TERIYAKI ....
In a blender mix 1 cup corn syrup, ½ cup soy, ¼ cup each of mirin and pineapple juice, 1 garlic clove, a few sprigs of coriander (stalk & leaves), 2 tablespoons each of sugar, corn flour, honey, rice wine vinegar and pineapple juice. Add a pinch each of chili powder/flakes, ginger and black pepper. Heat gently or sit for 30 minutes until it thickens a little.

THAI CURRY ....
Red, green or yellow Thai curry paste + coconut cream + fish sauce + palm sugar.
Warm or hot, sweet, spicy, salty, floral. In our opinion, Thai red, green and yellow curry sauces are a 'must have' skill and are required knowledge for all cooks. They are so simple to make from scratch in the Mortar & Pestle*, or you can use a pre-prepared commercial Thai curry sauce paste. The concentrated tubs of paste at your Asian grocer have a far superior taste to the supermarket jar brands, and for the quantity they make are 10 times cheaper and keep for months in the fridge. Always use the best quality coconut cream and not coconut milk when making Thai curry

sauces and at the last minute add a little extra palm sugar and an additional splash of fish sauce for that authentic flavor.

Red curry paste: color is created with dried red chili and has more garlic and onion than the green or yellow. Thai red curry sauce is Massuman curry sauce made with red chili and red chili peppers, with the potato replaced with zucchini and the cinnamon and cardamon replaced with red chili powder and tomato paste. Use with fish or prawns, garnish with coriander and sliced red pepper.

Green curry paste: color is created with fresh green chilies and it has a fresher, greener flavor than the others. Thai green curry sauce is Massuman curry sauce made with green chili and green chili peppers, with the potato replaced with green beans and the cinnamon and cardamon replaced with coriander and basil. Use with chicken, garnish with coriander and basil or finely shredded kaffir lime leaves.

Massuman curry sauce: made with yellow chili and yellow peppers with the potato replaced with spinach leaves and the cinnamon and cardamon replaced with yellow curry powder and extra tumeric. Usually with beef added. Garnish with spinach and sliced yellow peppers.

Yellow curry paste: color is created with turmeric, coriander and cumin and it tastes of lemongrass. Thai yellow curry sauce is Massuman curry sauce made with yellow chili and yellow peppers with the potato replaced with spinach leaves and the cinnamon and cardamon replaced with yellow curry powder and extra tumeric. Use with beef, garnish with spinach and sliced yellow peppers.

* See The Culinary Library's first volume, *Alchemy of the Mortar & Pestle*, for the full recipes

TOM YUM ....

Tom Yum is a popular Thai soup that is easy to make but with complex layers of flavor. With a little modification, it is easily converted into a wonderful hot sauce for seafood, chicken and vegetables.

Simply add 1 tablespoon of Tom Yum paste and 1 teaspoon or less of sambal oelek (chili paste) to ½ liter of water. Simmer gently and add 1 block (around 1-2 teaspoons) of palm sugar, 2 finely sliced garlic cloves, a knob of sliced ginger, 1-2 tablespoons red and green chilis, 1-2 tablespoons grated carrot, 4 quartered baby tomatoes, black pepper and 1 cup of coconut cream. Simmer and reduce by about a third to a half. Turn off the heat and balance the flavor by adding a small splash of fish sauce (salty), a small splash of lime juice (sour) and additional sugar (sweet). Keep tasting and adjusting these three additives slowly until the flavor is balanced. For noodles, chicken, stir fry, meats, soups. Use as a spoon over sauce or immerse raw fish, prawns, chicken or tofu in the sauce and poach gently until they are just cooked.

TONKATSU JAPANESE BBQ ....

For anyone who loves the fruity flavor of Bull-Dog brand Japanese BBQ sauce or can imagine making a thick Worcestershire, we have these simple 2 minute mix-together recipes for a home made version. Tonkatsu sauce is traditionally served with fried fish, crumbed or grilled meat, especially crumbed pork accompanied by raw finely shredded cabbage and steamed rice. Ground allspice, pomegranate molasses, garlic powder and sugar are optional flavor additives.

Recipe 1: 2 tablespoons Worcestershire, $1/3$ cup tomato sauce/ketchup, 1 tablespoon each of soy sauce, mirin, sugar and a teaspoon of Dijon mustard.
Recipe 2: ¼ cup Worcestershire, 1 cup tomato sauce/ketchup, ¼ cup light soy, 1 teaspoon dry mustard powder.

TOSA

Light soy + dashi + bonito + mirin + sake + spring onion + ginger.
Tosa sauce is essentially a soy-based sauce flavored with bonito flakes. It comes from Japan and is popular with sashimi, cooked fish and vegetables. To each ½ cup Japanese soy, add 1 cup each of dashi and bonito flakes, ¼ cup each of mirin and sake, some chopped spring onion and grated fresh ginger.

VINAIGRETTE ASIAN STYLE

Olive oil + rice vinegar + light soy sauce + sugar + sesame oil + lemon juice + 5 spice powder + pepper.

WASABI

Hot, mustard-peppery, made from the root of the wasabi plant. The flavor and heat experience of Wasabi is felt and tasted in the nose rather than on the tongue and its heat sensation is short and doesn't linger. This is because it contains an enzyme, rather than an oil base like in chili, that carries its heat experience. Also known as Japanese horseradish, Wasabi is commercially available as either a powder or paste and both can be used as the basis for wasabi sauces if the fresh root is unavailable. Try the following Wasabi sauces:
Wasabi Joyn: wasabi + soy sauce.
Wasabi Mayonnaise: wasabi + water + mayonnaise.

Wasabi Ginger: wasabi + soy + sherry or mirin + sesame oil + sesame seeds + garlic + fresh ginger.

Wasabi Tzatziki: wasabi + yoghurt or sour cream + chopped or grated cucumber + lemon or lime juice + salt and pepper.

Wasabi Vinaigrette: wasabi + soy sauce + rice vinegar + oil + sugar.

Wasabi Cream: wasabi + onion or shallot + ginger + vinegar + rice wine (simmered and reduced) + cream + soy sauce (simmered and reduced) + butter (whisked in).

XO ....

Dried fish & crustacean + chili + onion + garlic + oil.

XO sauce was invented in the 1980s in Hong Kong. See it mentioned also in the Quirky Characters chapter.

2 tablespoons palm or brown sugar

2 tablespoons Chinese sausage

2 tablespoons dried scallop

2 tablespoons dried shrimp

2 tablespoons dried crabmeat

2 tablespoons sesame oil

3 tablespoons fermented bean paste

3 tablespoons mirin

3 tablespoons soy sauce

4 tablespoons minced ginger

4 tablespoons minced shallot

4 tablespoons minced garlic

4 tablespoons crushed red pepper

Reconstitute the dried seafood in a little boiling water. Sauté the Chinese sausage until golden brown, remove excess fat and add red pepper then the rest of the ingredients, except the oil, and cook a few minutes. Blitz with the seafood in a food processor then put back into the pan to caramelize the paste for about 20 minutes in the sesame oil. Check seasoning. Add half a cup of water, cook for an additional 5 minutes. Transfer to a clean jar and pour the remainder of the oil on top. Keeps in the refrigerator for a few weeks.

YAKISOBA ....

¼ cup Japanese soy + 2 tablespoons Worcestershire sauce + 1 tablespoon each of the following ingredients: Japanese rice vinegar, sake, mirin, brown sugar, tomato sauce, oyster sauce, chili sauce, ginger.
For stir fries, especially noodles.

YAKITORI ....

To each ½ cup of thick Japanese soy, add 3 tablespoons each of mirin, sake and dashi. For skewered grilled chicken as both a marinade and an accompanying sauce.

BUTTER SAUCES, COLD COMPOUNDS

"In the orchestra of a great kitchen the sauce chef is a soloist."
—FERNAND POINT

DEFINITION ....

A compound butter is a butter mixed with one or more other substances to infuse flavor. The term applies to butter prepared in 5 different ways:
- cooked butter
- simple compounds of one or two ingredients
- complex compounds where the butter is used to extract flavors e.g. shellfish
- hot butter sauces like beurre blanc
- butter sauces with cream added

The most usual compound butter preparations are the cold ones. Usually solid butter is softened to room temperature and then pounded until it is light and creamy in texture before the additives are mixed in. Once compounded, the butter can be placed on cling film or foil, rolled into a log shape, and frozen or refrigerated; scooped soft into a piping bag for use on canapés, hard-boiled eggs, decoration, etc.; used as a spread; or molded or cut into shapes. We usually set aside in the fridge or freezer for future use. Lozenge-sized rounds are then cut from the log and are available as a supplement to other sauces and cooked dishes or as a garnish on hot foods where they melt and become the sauce.

Compound butter is also known as beurre composé, finishing butter or flavored butter. Their exact origin is unknown, but compound butters were probably invented in France in the late 1700s in the time of the first celebrity chef, Marie-Antoine Carême, or his predecessor, Savart.

Carême specialized in inventing soups and so it is from him, and his successor Auguste Escoffier writing in the 1930s, that we get our first comprehensive recipes for compound butters. They were intended for use primarily as Sauces. We have taken this selection of compound butter recipes from *The Culinary Library*, Volume 1, *Alchemy of the Mortar & Pestle*, where a whole chapter is dedicated to compound butters.

All recipes below are for use with 250 grams of softened, unsalted butter (approximately thirty one-inch-lozenge-sized servings.) If this is too much for you, use half the butter and, where recipes have ingredient amounts listed, halve these as well. I have purposefully left the measure and balance of additive ingredients to your own taste buds, except where the recipe is more complex, well known, or traditional.

It is recommended you mix the flavor additives together first and incorporate the butter last. Taste and adjust additives. Incorporate salt if necessary at the end. Don't worry if you get the flavor balances wrong a few times to begin with, as continual tasting is still the best way to train your palate to know what flavors you like rather than robotically accepting someone else's ideas.

ANCHOVY BUTTER ....
Simply use as many anchovies as suit your taste, grind them with butter in a mortar and pestle until soft and creamy, and adjust the taste to your preference by the addition of one or several of the following: lemon juice, pepper, mustard or curry powder, cayenne or mace. Great with steak.

CAFÉ DE PARIS BUTTER ....
To softened butter add the following ingredients:
1½ tablespoons tomato sauce or ketchup
1 teaspoon Dijon mustard
1 teaspoon small capers
1 shallot or ½ teaspoon onion
1 tablespoon fresh chopped parsley
1 tablespoon fresh chopped chives
1 tablespoon fresh chopped French tarragon
1 teaspoon fresh chopped marjoram
1 teaspoon fresh chopped dill
1 teaspoon fresh chopped thyme
½ teaspoon fresh chopped rosemary
1 garlic clove
2 anchovies

1 teaspoon brandy
1 teaspoon Madeira
¼ teaspoon Worcestershire sauce
¼ teaspoon sweet paprika
¼ teaspoon curry powder
1 tablespoon each lemon and orange zest
pepper, salt

CAPER TARRAGON BUTTER ....
2 cups fresh tarragon leaves (no stems), ½ cup capers, zest and juice from 1 lemon, salt and white or black pepper to taste.
For fish and pasta. For variety you can also add ½ to one teaspoons of smoked paprika.

CAVIAR BUTTER ....
4 tablespoons of caviar. For fish, seafood, and crustaceans.

CHAMPAGNE BUTTER ....
2 cups of pink champagne reduced to ¼ of original volume, seeds from 1-2 vanilla pods or ½ teaspoon extract, 1 tablespoon chervil or tarragon. Pink and green peppercorns left whole and added at the end are optional. Try and get the fresh vanilla, as the black seeds and green of the herb look great suspended and dispersing in a light consommé or flavored broth. Serve with poached chicken, white fish, fresh steamed artichoke hearts, or white asparagus. Serve also with seafood and crustaceans.

CHERRY BUTTER ....
1 cup pitted fresh or bottled cherries, 1 tablespoon balsamic or cider vinegar, 1 tablespoon castor or powdered sugar, 1 tablespoon

orange zest, 1 teaspoon pomegranate powder or pomegranate molasses. Serve with red meat, poultry, and game, or hot fruit desserts. Other red fruits can be added or substituted in season, such as cranberries, red currants, or pomegranate arils (seeds).

CHILI LIME BUTTER ....

4 tablespoons long red and/or green chilies, seeded, 2 tablespoons lime zest, and 2 tablespoons lime juice. Use wild limes if you have them.

CHOCOLATE HAZELNUT BUTTER ....

8 tablespoons ground hazelnuts + 4 tablespoons melted or grated dark chocolate.

CHOCOLATE ORANGE JAFFA BUTTER ....

½ cup dark bitter-sweet (at least 70% cocoa) chocolate, chopped, melted and cooled, 1 tablespoons cocoa powder, 2 tablespoons grated orange zest, 2 tablespoons powdered/confectioners sugar

CRANBERRY SAGE BUTTER ....

½ cup fresh sage leaves or 1 cup lightly fried sage leaves, 1 clove garlic, 1 cup cranberries or thick cranberry sauce, salt and pepper. For thanksgiving or Christmas celebrations.

CRÊPES SUZETTE BUTTER ....

4-6 tablespoons orange, mandarin, or tangerine zest, 2 tablespoons juice from same, 4 tablespoons powdered or icing sugar; 2 tablespoons White Curaçao is optional. Spread on warm crepes, then fold into quarters and reheat in the pan or oven with orange juice or syrup to moisten. Dust with powdered sugar. Crêpes can be spread and folded the day before being used but need to be reheated longer until the compound butter melts. Flame with spirits if desired. You can also add a little maple syrup to this compound butter and spread on hot waffles.

FIG ORANGE BUTTER ....
4 or 5 roughly chopped fresh figs or diced dried figs (soaked until soft), zest and juice of 1 orange, pinch of cinnamon, 2 tablespoons castor or powdered sugar, 1 teaspoon vanilla extract or seeds from 1 vanilla pod.

GARLIC BUTTER ....
5 garlic cloves, 1 tablespoon grated parmesan cheese.

HERB BUTTER ....
Spring onion or shallots, garlic, 2 tablespoons lemon juice, fresh soft herbs of your choice (e.g. parsley, tarragon, coriander, sage, chervil, chives, mint).

HONEY PECAN BUTTER ....
½ cup honey, cinnamon, 1 cup pecan nuts.

HORSERADISH BUTTER ....
⅓ cup fresh grated horseradish or 2 tablespoons of preserved horseradish. Add a little cream if you want it softer.

KEY LIME BUTTER ....
Finely grated zest and juice of 2 limes, salt and pepper to taste.

LEMON DILL BUTTER ....

Finely grated zest and juice of 2 lemons, 1 cup dill fronds, salt and pepper to taste.

LEMON MUSTARD BUTTER ....

Finely grated zest and juice of 1 lemon, 2 tablespoons prepared mustard of your choice, salt and pepper to taste.

LIQUEUR CHERRY BUTTER ....

2 cups of Morello cherries or 1 cup of maraschino cherries, the red ones if you want almond flavor or the green ones if you want peppermint flavored butter.

MAÎTRE D'HÔTEL BUTTER ....

½ cup chopped Italian leaf parsley, juice of 1 lemon, salt and pepper.

MONTPELLIER BUTTER ....

2 garlic cloves, 2 shallots chopped, 4 anchovy fillets, ½ cup chopped mixed herbs (e.g. parsley, chervil, chives and tarragon), ½ cup chopped rocket, ½ cup cooked spinach, 1 tablespoon capers, 2 hard-boiled egg yolks, 2 small chopped gherkins, 2 tablespoons olive oil, salt and pepper.

NUT BUTTERS ....

Nut butter usually refers to butter that has been heated to a light nut-brown color. Here we mean incorporating the actual nuts into the butter. Use your favorite nuts (walnut, pecan, almond, macadamia, hazel, Brazil, pine, peanut) with garlic, salt/pepper or mustard for savory butter, or orange, lemon or lime zest and sugar for sweet butter.

PESTO BUTTER ....
Basil leaves, pine nuts and/or walnuts, garlic, salt, pepper.

PRINTANIER BUTTER ....
To warmed, creamed butter, add a mixture of cooked vegetables and grind smooth. Vegetables can include any in season, e.g., carrot, turnip, parsnip, pumpkin, beans, peas, asparagus and artichoke. An old French compound butter used as a garnish for hot soup or meat entrees that are served with baby vegetables. It is usually balled with a melon baller or cut into small dice and placed on top of the food at the time of serving. It is a good way to use up leftover roasted vegetables and roasting fats that impart an even richer flavor to the butter. After making the butter, let it cool down before balling or dicing it, or freeze as normal in a rolled log and slice off thin lozenges to float on hot soup.

PROVENÇALE ....
Garlic butter without the parmesan cheese. Work as much or as little garlic as you like into softened butter.

RED WINE BUTTER ....
Reduce 2 cups of good red wine with some chopped shallots over heat to ¼ of its original volume. Add lemon zest and a little juice and chopped parsley. Place in the mortar and work in the butter and flaked salt.

SAFFRON BUTTER ....
Infuse a large pinch of saffron threads in the 1 teaspoon of warm champagne vinegar or apple cider and mix with the created butter. Season with salt and pepper to taste.

SNAIL BUTTER ....
Crush together in your mortar & pestle: 2 tablespoons minced shallots, 2 garlic cloves, 1 tablespoon each finely chopped celery and parsley. Then add salt, pepper and lemon juice and mix in the softened butter.

TRUFFLE BUTTER ....
As much chopped/sliced fresh truffle as you can afford.

WALNUT BUTTER ....
2 cups walnuts, 1 teaspoon cinnamon, 1 teaspoon powdered sugar, 1 teaspoon of lemon or lime juice, 1 pinch of finishing salt. This can be used for both sweet and savory dishes.

WASABI BUTTER ....
1-2 tablespoons wasabi.

WHISKEY BUTTER ....
4-8 tablespoons whiskey or cognac, powdered sugar to taste.

BUTTER SAUCES, HOT

"With enough butter, anything is good."
—JULIA CHILD

BUTTER SAUCE FAMILY ....
Although Butter sauces don't have a 'mother' in the classic Carême or Escoffier sense of classification, many of the hot butter sauces are derivatives of the basic beurre blanc and for that reason we have classified it as a mother sauce.

BEURRE BLANC ....
Hot, thin or thick, emulsified or compound, sweet. Beurre blanc is a sauce where butter is simply flavored with a shallot/white wine reduction. Originating in the Loire Valley in France this is the simplest of the hot emulsified sauces, although it can also be beaten less and left thin as a compound sauce rather than beaten to an emulsified sauce. Both the thicker emulsified and the thinner compound versions of beurre blanc can be used as a base for additional flavor ingredients. Shallots are chopped finely and sautéed, and vinegar and/or white wine added in a ratio of 1:4 (e.g. 1 tablespoon of shallots to 4 tablespoons of wine, ¼ cup shallots to 1 cup of wine). When reduced by half, the liquid can be sieved or used with the onion pieces left in. Pieces of butter are then added and whisked in, a few at a time and simmered at medium heat, but

not boiled. The modern beurre blanc is left thin, whereas the classic one, where more butter is added, is continuously beaten until it is the texture of thick cream. The sauce is then seasoned with salt and pepper and served. If additional flavors are to be added, pepper and salt should be added and balanced after this step and before serving.

All of the butter sauce recipes below can be made using either a thin or a thick creamy beurre blanc depending on your preference. Quicker melted butter sauces are also made today by simply sautéing flavor additives like onion, shallot, herbs, or mushroom in a pan reduction of the cooked food's essences, deglazing with wine or stock and then melting and whisking in salted or unsalted butter.

Hot butter sauces are traditionally used for fish but today we use them with any foods, especially with premium cuts of meat and seafood, chicken & duck breast, ravioli and tortellini pastas, gnocchi, vegetables, pork, veal, lamb, beef steaks and crustaceans.

BEURRE BLANC'S CHILDREN

ALMOND OR AMANDINE BUTTER SAUCE ....
Beurre blanc + chopped parsley + lemon juice + cayenne pepper + toasted almond slices or slivers = Meunière sauce + almond.

ARMAGNAC OR COGNAC BUTTER SAUCE ....
Beurre blanc + Armagnac or Cognac + caramelized shallots + parsley + pepper. For steak.
Beurre blanc + Armagnac or Cognac + powdered sugar + vanilla bean seeds. For crêpes.

BERCY BUTTER ....

Unstrained and thick beurre blanc + parsley. For each ¼ cup thick beurre blanc add 1 heaped teaspoon of finely chopped parsley.

BEURRE D'ÉCREVISSES ....

Warm, medium thick, savory, salty, slightly sour, pink. Also known as Shrimp butter.
Beurre blanc + coral + cognac + shrimp stock reduction. (Pulverized shrimp/prawn shells + mirepoix of carrot, celery, onion, shallots, garlic + white wine + bouquet garni + water or stock.)

BEURRE DE HOMARD ....

Warm, medium thick, savory, salty, slightly bitter, pink.
As above but made with lobster instead of shrimp/prawn shells. Also known as Lobster butter.

BEURRE MANIÉ ....

Butter + flour. See Thickeners.

BEURRE NOIR OR BLACK BUTTER ....

Hot, thin, sour, nutty, buttery, deep brown. For fish.
Butter heated till brown + acid (vinegar or lemon).

BEURRE ROUGE ....

Hot, thin, rich, deep red. For fish and meat.
Red wine + red wine vinegar + shallots + butter in a ratio of 4:2:1:4. E.g. 1 cup wine, ½ cup vinegar, ¼ cup chopped shallot, reduced by ¾ and then 1 cup cold chopped butter whisked in and seasoned.

BROWN BUTTER ....
Beurre blanc + heat.

CAPER BUTTER SAUCE ....
Beurre blanc + capers.

CORIANDER & LIME BUTTER SAUCE ....
Beurre blanc + lime juice & zest + chopped coriander.

DILL BUTTER SAUCE ....
Beurre blanc + finely chopped dill + lemon juice.

FRENCH & ENGLISH BUTTER SAUCE ....
French Butter Sauce: roux (butter + flour) + water + egg yolks +
cream + butter + salt.
For a roux made with 2 tablespoons each of butter & flour, add salt
and thin and cook for a few minutes, with enough water until it just
coats the back of a spoon. Take off the heat, whisk in 2 tablespoons
of cream and one egg yolk and then gradually add and whisk in
pieces of softened butter until smooth and creamy.
English Butter Sauce is the same as above but without the egg yolk.

GARLIC & HERB BUTTER SAUCE ....
Beurre blanc made with minced garlic + lemon juice and zest +
chopped herbs.

GINGER SOY BUTTER SAUCE ....
Beurre blanc (unstrained) + minced fresh ginger + soy sauce +
honey + lemon juice & zest.

LEMON BUTTER SAUCE ....
Beurre blanc + lemon + cream + parsley.

MANGO BUTTER SAUCE ....
Beurre blanc + mango purée.

MARINARA ....
Secondary, hot, thin to medium, savory, salty, herbal, blonde. Also known as Marinière Sauce. For pasta, poached fish, vol-au-vent, timbales and mussels. Bercy Butter, (Butter + white wine + parsley + shallots), + egg yolk + poached mussels and their reduced liquor.

MEUNIER BUTTER SAUCE ....
Beurre blanc + chopped parsley + lemon juice + cayenne pepper. Also known as Beurre a la meunière. Traditionally used for fish, seafood and chicken.

MISO BUTTER SAUCE ....
Beurre blanc + white soy bean paste + mirin + sugar + sesame seeds.

ORANGE BUTTER SAUCE ....
Beurre blanc + sugar + orange juice and zest + lemon juice.

PARMESAN BUTTER SAUCE ....
Beurre blanc + finely grated Parmesan + lemon juice.

PINOT NOIR ....
Beurre blanc + red wine (pinot noir) + shallots.

POLONAISE SAUCE ....

Beurre blanc + lemon juice + chopped parsley + cayenne pepper + chopped hard-boiled egg = Meuniere + hard-boiled egg.

RUM BUTTER SAUCE ....

Beurre blanc + brown sugar + cream + rum.

SAFFRON CREAM BUTTER SAUCE ....

Beurre blanc + infused saffron + cream.

TERIYAKI TABASCO BUTTER SAUCE ....

Beurre blanc + Tabasco sauce + teriyaki sauce.

TOMATO BUTTER SAUCE ....

Beurre blanc + puréed sautéed tomato + puréed sautéed onion + finely chopped herbs or finely grated Parmesan or both. Sauté the onion and tomato together until soft and caramelized then purée in the blender.

TRUFFLE BUTTER SAUCE ....

Beurre blanc made with minced garlic & sherry instead of shallot and white wine + thyme + cream + shaved truffle and/or truffle oil.

TUSCAN BUTTER SAUCE ....

Beurre blanc + chopped chervil + parsley + tarragon + chives.

VÉNITIENNE SAUCE ....

Beurre blanc + chopped chervil + tarragon + tarragon vinegar + shallots + white wine.

CHUTNEYS & RELISHES

"All Chatneys should be quite thick, almost of the consistence of mashed turnips or stewed tomatoes, or stiff bread sauce. They are served with curries; and also with steaks, cutlets, cold meat, and fish."
—ELISA ACTON, *Modern Cookery for Private Families*, 1845

DEFINITION ....

Chutneys, also known as Chatneys or Chatnis, in Sanskrit means 'to lick', probably because they are a bit sticky and definitely because you won't want to leave any on the plate. They come to us from South Indian cuisine and are thick or thin sauces, made mainly from vegetables and/or fruits with spices, vinegar or lemon and sugar. Chutneys can be wet or dry, coarse or fine and they differ from relishes because they have less water and are sweeter. Chutney has a shelf life of a few months and relish up to one.

The word 'relish' first appeared in English cookery in 1798, derived from the Old French word *reles* meaning 'something remaining'. Relish recipes therefore tend to be made from a wide range of ingredients, often ones readily on hand. Relishes come to us from many cuisines around the world, including the USA, Europe, the Pacific Islands and Asia. For most cooks, chutneys and relishes are so similar they are interchangeable.

When chutney or relish is to be stored it must be sealed in sterile jars. Sterilize heat-proof jars and vinegar-proof lids by boiling gently in hot water then draining on paper towel. Add warm chutneys and relishes when jars are still hot and as they cool they will form a partial vacuum and seal the lids.

APPLE RELISH ....

2 cooking apples like granny smith, peeled, cored, and chopped
2 tablespoons light brown sugar
2 tablespoons water
2 tablespoons cider vinegar
Cook together until soft.

BLACK OLIVE CHUTNEY ....

1 cup large, pitted kalamata olives
4 anchovy fillets, drained and chopped
1 tablespoon capers
1 garlic clove, minced
¼ cup olive oil
Blitz together for a few seconds, making sure to leave some texture.

CHOW-CHOW RELISH ....

Chow-Chow, a sweet, tangy and spicy vegetable relish based on cabbage and similar to Piccalilli relish, was probably introduced to America from Nova Scotia. It's made from chopped green tomatoes, cabbage, mustard (seed or powder), onions, hot peppers, sweet peppers and vinegar. Other optional ingredients include cucumbers, celery, corn and cauliflower.

In a large saucepan bring to the boil 2½ cups of cider vinegar, 1 cup brown sugar, 1 tablespoon yellow mustard seed, 2 minced garlic cloves, 1 teaspoon celery seeds, ½ teaspoon red chili flakes and simmer 5 minutes. Add 4 cups each of chopped cabbage and green tomatoes, 1 large chopped onion and 1 cup each of chopped red and chopped yellow peppers or capsicums. (The vegetables must be chopped, salted well, allowed to rest and then rinsed before adding to the pickling brine.) Cook on simmer for 15-20 minutes then bottle the vegetable and spice, pouring in the liquid. Leave ¼" space, fit lids and they will form a vacuum seal as they cool. Refrigerate after opening.

COCONUT CHUTNEY ....

One cup of fresh coconut, grated

1 cup roasted gram or chana dal soaked for 20 minutes (Dalia/pottu kadalai - available in Indian stores)

2-3 green chilies (or as per taste)

½ cup curd (buttermilk) salt to taste

optional: 1 teaspoon grated ginger

Mix together in the blender until smooth, adding a little water or more buttermilk if needed. Heat some oil in a pan, add 1 teaspoon of mustard seeds, 1 teaspoon of split black gram dal (urad dal), 1 red chili, some fresh curry leaves and a pinch of asafoetida. Part cover with a lid and cook until the mustard seeds pop. Stir through the coconut mix.

CORIANDER CHUTNEY ....

Also known as green chutney or chaat, this is one of India's favorite daily accompaniments to food. Even if you add no other chutneys to your regular arsenal of cooking, add this one. Just blitz the ingredients together in a blender or food processor and keep in the fridge.

2 cups coriander leaves, stalks included
2 cups mint leaves, no stalks
optional: ½ cup coconut cream
1 red onion
2 or more long green chilies, de-seeded
2 tablespoons lemon juice
1 tablespoon sugar
For samosas, pakoras, roti, curries, chicken, crumbed foods, fish, and meats.

CRANBERRY RELISH ....
2 cups dried cranberries
2 cups pineapple juice
1 orange, juice and zest
1 lemon, juice and zest
½-cup light brown sugar
Bring all ingredients to a boil then simmer until soft and reduced.

CUCUMBER RELISH ....
Cut 1 continental or 2-3 Lebanese cucumbers, ½ long green or red chili* and 3-4 shallots (or one small onion) into Macédoine (small dice, 1 x 1 x 1 cm or ¼" cubed). Make a pickling syrup of ¼ cup each of boiling water, sugar and white wine vinegar. Add a pinch of finishing salt and chopped coriander and then the Macédoine. Great with everything!
* Use red capsicum or radish if you prefer it milder.

EGGPLANT CHUTNEY ....
Brunoise, Brunoise Fine, Carre or Macédoine 3 large aubergines and salt them in a colander. Leave for a few minutes, rinse and

drain. Add 2 chopped onions, 1-2 chopped long red chilis, a chopped piece of root ginger about an inch long and 3 garlic cloves, minced or cut fine. Make pickling syrup by dissolving 2 tablespoons of tamarind paste and 1 cup brown sugar in 2 cups of cider vinegar. Then sauté 2 teaspoons each of cumin seed, coriander seed, black mustard seed and ½ teaspoon fenugreek in hot oil until the mustard seed pops then add the drained eggplant until it softens and colors. Add the pickling syrup, simmer for 10-15 minutes then store in sterilized jars for 4 weeks before use. Refrigerate after opening.

JALAPEÑO RELISH ....

1 kilogram or 2 pounds each of jalapeños (seeds removed) and tomatoes, diced brunoise or Macédoine.
1 large onion, diced
4 garlic cloves, minced or sliced
2 tablespoons dried oregano or 4 of fresh
2 cups cider or white wine vinegar
1 cup balsamic vinegar
1 cup water + salt
½ cup sugar
Bring all ingredients to a boil then reduce to a simmer for a few minutes until the sugar dissolves and it reaches a consistency you like.

LEMON CHUTNEY ....

8 lemons quartered and quartered again or finely sliced in a food processor
1 onions, roughly chopped or sliced
½ cup plump golden sultanas

½ cup raisins

1 tablespoon black mustard seed

1 tablespoon chopped fresh ginger

2 cups soft brown sugar

2 cups white wine or cider vinegar

2 teaspoons celery or nigella seeds

1 teaspoon chopped garlic

½ teaspoon each of black peppercorns, mace, clove, allspice, cinnamon

4 bay leaves

1 cinnamon stick

Salt the cut lemons and onion and leave covered for a couple of days, then drain and rinse. Add the raisins and sultanas. In a large pan, add spices and cook till the mustard seeds pop. Add the fresh garlic and ginger and stir till it cooks a little. Add the lemon mix, sugar, vinegar, bay leaves and cinnamon. Simmer for an hour or more, stirring occasionally. Taste and adjust flavor before sealing in hot jars.

FIG & BALSAMIC CHUTNEY ....

2 kilograms of fresh or dried figs, stems removed and quartered

2 cups of seedless red grapes

12 pitted black Kalamata olives, halved

12 pitted green olives, halved

1 orange, flesh chopped, skin peeled finely and cut in fine strips

3 garlic cloves, minced

2 cups water

1 cup cider vinegar

2 spring onions, sliced

2 generous tablespoons aged Balsamic vinegar

salt & pepper
Sauté garlic in oil, add onion, then grapes and olives then orange peel strips and flesh. Add the rest of the ingredients and simmer until figs are soft. Cool and seal in jars.

GREEN TOMATO CHUTNEY ....

1 kilogram or 2 pounds of green tomatoes, chopped
2 tablespoons of fresh ginger, chopped
2 garlic cloves, minced
1 cup each of honey and cider vinegar
1 teaspoon each of ground cumin, coriander and turmeric
salt and cayenne or black pepper to taste
Bring all to a boil then reduce to a simmer for 40-50 minutes and cool slightly before placing in sterilized jars.

LIME CHUTNEY ....

8 ripe limes, quartered and quartered again
1 onion, roughly chopped
½ cup plump golden sultanas

½ cup raisins

1 tablespoon fresh ginger root, chopped

1 teaspoons each of powdered cumin, coriander, black mustard seeds and chopped garlic.

½ teaspoon each of chili powder or cayenne, ground black pepper, salt

2 cups cider vinegar

2 cups soft brown sugar

Salt the cut limes and onion and leave, covered, for a couple of days then drain and rinse. Add the raisins and sultanas and chop finely, in batches, in a food processor. In a large pan add spices and cook till the mustard seeds pop. Add the fresh garlic and ginger and stir till it cooks a little. Add the lime mix, sugar and vinegar and simmer for an hour or more, stirring occasionally. Taste and adjust flavor as required before sealing in hot jars.

MAJOR GREY'S CHUTNEY ....

The original recipe is attributed to an English army officer in the Bengal Lancers in India in the 1800s, but there is some argument about who first made it commercially. It was either the Sun Brand Poonjiaji brothers in Bombay, or Crosse & Blackwell (now American and European owned). We prefer the sun brand because it's spicier and not so sweet. Both are still available for sale today (see Amazon), or you can easily make your own:

1 kilogram green cooking mangos*, peeled and cubed Parmentier (½") or Macédoine (¼")

1 large onion, peeled and chopped

1 cup each of white sugar, light brown sugar, apple cider vinegar and plump golden raisins

2 tablespoons each of lemon juice and fresh ginger, finely chopped

½ teaspoon each of ground cloves, black pepper, minced garlic, cinnamon, cayenne or chili powder, nutmeg and salt

Bring all ingredients to the boil in a large saucepan then simmer for 1-2 hours until it reaches the thickness you prefer. Taste, adjust flavor and seal in jars. It is sweet and spicy and served with chicken, meat and vegetables, especially curries.

* Use only green cooking mangos from your Asian grocer, not the ripe yellow ones.

MANGO CHUTNEY

2 raw green cooking mangos*, peeled, shredded or cubed Parmentier (½")

2 tablespoons plump golden raisins

1 good tablespoon fresh ginger, sliced

4 dry red chili, sliced or chopped finely

1 teaspoon nigella seeds (or onion seeds)

1 cup sugar, white or brown

½ cup cider vinegar

salt, pepper, oil

Sauté nigella seeds and chili in the oil, add raisins, stir, and then add the rest of the ingredients. Cook until the mango is soft. Allow to cool, then jar.

* Use only green cooking mangos from an Asian grocer, not ripe yellow ones.

MINT CHUTNEY

1 cup mint leaves, no stems as they are bitter

½ cup coriander leaves and stems

1 red or green long chili, deseeded and roughly chopped

2 tablespoons red onion, roughly chopped

4 tablespoons lemon juice or brown vinegar
6 tablespoons water
salt and pepper
Blend all ingredients together in the blender on medium speed until smooth (but still with some texture). Taste, add more lemon if needed. For meats and vegetables or dipping pakoras and samosas.

MUSTARD PICKLE RELISH ....

4 cups cucumbers, chopped Macédoine or Parmentier
2 cups onions, chopped Macédoine or Parmentier
1 cup each green and red bell peppers, Macédoine or Parmentier
3 cups sugar
2 cups white wine or cider vinegar
1 tablespoon each of celery and mustard seeds
Salt the cucumber, onion and peppers and let stand a couple of hours. Rinse and drain. Heat the spices in a pan before adding the rest of the ingredients. Bring to a boil then simmer for 10-15 minutes. If you like your mustard pickle relish thicker, add a slurry made from a little arrowroot slaked with vinegar.

PICCALILLI CAULIFLOWER RELISH ....

1 large cauliflower and 2 large onions, sliced/cut into small pieces, sprinkled with salt and left overnight.
Bring 1 liter of white or cider vinegar to a boil. Mix 2 tablespoons plain flour with 4 tablespoons prepared mustard or 1 tablespoon mustard powder, 4 tablespoons sugar, 1 tablespoon turmeric, a teaspoon of cayenne pepper and enough water to make a paste. Add to the vinegar and then add the cauliflower. Simmer until tender, around 20-30 minutes.

PINEAPPLE CHUTNEY ....

1 fresh pineapple, peeled, cored and cubed Parmentier (½")
1 cup each of pineapple juice, cider vinegar and castor sugar
1 cinnamon stick
1 teaspoon each of curry powder and chopped fresh ginger
½ teaspoon each of cardamom seeds and ground cloves
Bring all to the boil then simmer until cooked to your preferred consistency.

RED ONION CHUTNEY ....

10 red onions, peeled and sliced
1 cup raw cane sugar or light brown sugar
2 cups Muscovado or dark brown sugar
1 cup each of cider or red wine vinegar and balsamic vinegar
2 bay leaves and ½ long red chili, left in the piece
Sauté the onions in a little oil until soft, add the cane sugar and melt in for a few minutes to caramelize the onions, then add the rest of the ingredients. Bring to the boil and simmer about 10 minutes, stirring occasionally, or until it is the consistency you prefer. Remove the bay and chili. Gets better with age.

SWEETCORN RELISH ....

5-6 fresh sweet corn cobs, kernels removed with a sharp knife
2 celery stalks, de-strung and chopped Brunoise
1 red capsicum pepper, chopped Brunoise
1 onion, peeled and chopped Brunoise
1 long red chili, deseeded and chopped Brunoise Fine
½ cup caster sugar
1 cup cider or white wine vinegar
2 tablespoons flour

1 teaspoon each of English mustard powder and ground turmeric
½ teaspoon each of celery seeds and salt
Make a slurry paste of the flour, mustard, turmeric and a splash of
the vinegar. Sauté everything else in a little oil then add the slurry.
Simmer for 10 minutes or until it thickens and reduces.

TOMATILLO CHUTNEY ....

4 cups fresh tomatillos, husks removed, quartered, salted, rested
and rinsed
1 tablespoon black mustard seed, toasted
2 star anise and 1 teaspoon fenugreek seeds, toasted
6 long red or green chilies, finely chopped
2 inch piece of fresh ginger, skin removed and grated
1 cup sugar, brown, white or mixed
Cook all ingredients together until boiling, then reduce heat and
simmer for five minutes before cooling a little and bottling.

TOMATO & APPLE CHUTNEY ....

4 tomatoes, chopped
4 cooking apples, peeled, cored and chopped
1 cup each of honey & cider vinegar
1 garlic clove, minced
1 tablespoon chopped fresh ginger
½ cup orange juice
1 teaspoon each of ground cinnamon, cloves and salt
cayenne or black pepper to taste
Bring all to a boil then reduce and simmer for 30-40 minutes
before storing in a jar.

CLASSIC SAUCES & THEIR DERIVATIVES

———◆———

"Sauce, the one infallible sign of civilization and enlightenment. A people with no sauce has one thousand vices; a people with one sauce has only nine hundred and ninety-nine. For every sauce invented and accepted a vice is renounced and forgiven."
–AMBROSE BIERCE

THE BROWN SAUCE FAMILY

MOTHER ESPAGNOLE ....
Hot, thin to medium thick, savory, brown.
Rich meat stock (bones + mirepoix vegetables (onion, carrot, celery) + herbs) + brown roux.

Basic Espagnole recipe for 2 liters:

4 tablespoons each of butter and flour, cooked to a brown roux, light brown color and nutty smell

3 liters of brown stock*, whisked into the roux off the heat.

salt and pepper

2 tablespoons tomato purée

white wine is optional

Espagnole is begun by making a rich brown meat stock, traditionally either Beef or Veal flavored. Just imagine you're making a beef or veal braise and then straining out the solids. To make at home, brown some beef and/or veal shin (Ozzo Bucco), along with some fresh-diced belly of pork or a ham shank. Leave any skin on, cut all into small chunks, and sauté in some oil and butter in a big pot. Add whole peppercorns but do not add salt. Once colored or browned, remove for a minute and add some chopped carrot, onion and celery, allow to color a little, then return the meat and add enough water to cover well. Add a tied bunch of herbs like parsley, bay or thyme. Bring it up to a boil, skim, reduce to a gentle simmer and cook for an hour and a half with a lid half on until it reduces by at least half. Top up the water if you need to. (Restaurants use whole chunks of meat and cook theirs for 12 hours). Sieve and cool the liquid then remove any fat on the top. Clean the pot and brown only the cooked meat again in hot fat, add the strained stock and reduce to half. Strain and skim off any visible fat. Taste and reduce further if you want an even more intense flavor. Aim for 2 liters. It needs to be the color of amber and as clear as you can strain it.

* Commercial brown stock powders and liquids are now available for cooks but it is always good to try making a real one, even if only once, so you can compare flavors and make an informed choice.

One of the most popular and widely used mother sauces, Espagnole is the base for: demi-glace and its derivative Madeira, and Madeira's derivative Périgueux; Bordelaise and its derivative Rouennaise; Chasseur, Piquante; and Poivrade and its derivative Grand Veneur. Classically this sauce is paired with grilled, roasted and pan fried meats like beef, duck, lamb and veal.

ESPAGNOLE'S CHILDREN ....

AIGRE-DOUCE ....
Hot, sweet-sour, acid, thin, citrus.
Espagnole + sugar + red wine vinegar + orange + butter + herbs.
It's best to make Aigre-douce as a pan reduction sauce after sautéing chicken or duck and setting aside. Simply add 1 tablespoon of brown or raw sugar to the pan, and melt to a caramel before adding 60 ml of red wine vinegar and 125 ml of espagnole. Reduce by simmering and add 60 ml of orange juice, some zest and segments. When it begins to thicken and turn glossy, whisk in 20 grams butter, chopped parsley and/or thyme, salt and pepper.

BERCY ....
Rich, brown.
Demi-glace + white wine + parsley + shallots + bone marrow.
For meat.

BIGARADE ....
Hot, thin, sweet-sour, piquant, citrus, brown.
Espagnole + orange zest + orange juice + lemon juice.
For duck: roasted, braised or poeled (roasted covered, sitting on stock-moistened vegetables).

BORDELAISE OR BORDEAUX ....

Medium thick, savory, deep brown-red.

Demi-glace sauce + red Bordeaux wine + shallots + bay + parsley + thyme.

Bordelaise sauce is Burgundy sauce made with red Bordeaux wine instead of red Burgundy wine.

For all meats.

BURGUNDY OR BOURGUIGNONNE ....

Medium thick, savory, deep brown-red.

Demi-glace sauce+ red Burgundy wine + shallots + bay + parsley + thyme.

Bourguignonne sauce is Bordelaise sauce made with red Burgundy wine instead of red Bordeaux wine.

For meats.

CHAMBERTIN ....

Hot, medium thick, winey, citrus.

Demi-glace + red wine + citrus + spice.

2 tablespoons cornflour or arrowroot slaked with some of the wine

1 cup red wine

2 ounces granulated sugar

1 lemon and 1 orange, zest and juice

1 whole cinnamon stick

8 mint leaves

1 whole clove

Heat all together, then add the slaked cornflour or arrowroot and stir until it thickens. Sieve before use.

CHAMPAGNE ....

Hot, thin, savory, sweet.

Champagne sauce is made using either an Espagnole or a Velouté sauce, being a derivative sauce of both mothers. For every 2 cups Espagnole Sauce add 2 tablespoons mushroom liquor, ½ cup champagne and 1 tablespoon sugar.

CHARCUTIÈRE ....

Hot, medium thick, pale gold, tart.

Demi-glace + onions + mustard + white wine + chopped cornichons.

For pork and rich meats. Best made as a pan reduction sauce. To ½ small onion sautéed add 1 cup white wine, 6-8 tablespoons demi-glace, 2 tablespoons chilled unsalted butter diced and whisked in, 1 tablespoon Dijon mustard, and 6 cornichons julienned or chopped. Season with salt and pepper. Spoon over meat and garnish with baby cornichons.

CHASSEUR ....

Hot, thin to medium thick, savory, earthy, brown.

Espagnole + white wine + mushroom + shallot + tomato sauce or purée + parsley.

For braising chicken or meat.

CHATEAUBRIAND ....

Espagnole + white wine + shallots + lemon juice + tarragon or thyme + butter + cayenne pepper.

Originally invented to accompany Chateaubriand (beef fillet) steaks until replaced by Béarnaise sauce.

CHEVREUIL ....
Hot, medium thick, complex and pungent with rich sweet, sour and salty notes.

Chevreuil Sauce is attributed to English chef Charles Elmé Francatelli, author of *The Cook's Guide and Housekeeper's & Butler's Assistant* (1861). Working at the Reform Club during Victorian times he made a poivrade (pepper) sauce base then added French red wine, Harvey's sauce (anchovies + vinegar + India soy + mushroom ketchup + garlic + cayenne + cochineal powder), anchovy essence, wafer-thin slices of gherkin, lemon juice, cayenne, nutmeg and redcurrant jelly. As you can imagine we thought seriously about putting this sauce in the Quirky Characters chapter.

Sauté in a couple of tablespoons of butter 2 slices of chopped ham or bacon, 1 carrot and 1 onion both chopped, 1 bay leaf, 1 sprig thyme, 10 black peppercorns and 1 blade of mace. Fry until well browned. Add 150 milliliters of vinegar, 75 milliliters of mushroom catsup and 1 teaspoon of anchovy essence. Stir to a boil and continue cooking, stirring frequently, until reduced by half. Now stir in 300 milliliters of brown Espagnole sauce along with 4 tablespoons of strong stock and 150 milliliters of sherry. Bring to a gentle boil again for about 10 minutes or until all the fat has risen to the surface. Skim then sieve. Return to the pan; add 150 milliliters of a big red wine, 75 milliliters of Harvey's sauce, 2 heaped tablespoons of redcurrant jelly and a few small gherkins sliced into thin wafers. Boil, stirring until the redcurrant jelly has dissolved and cooking for five minutes. Serve with grilled meat.

COLBERT ....
Glace de Viande + butter + parsley + Madeira.

Heat ¼ cup of Glace de Viande (or 1 tablespoon of concentrated jellied beef extract) with 1 tablespoon of hot water and gradually add ½ cup soft butter, whisking in a little at a time. Then add 1 tablespoon of finely chopped parsley, 2 tablespoons each of lemon juice and Madeira and a small pinch each of nutmeg and cayenne pepper. For meat and chicken.

CURRY ....

Hot, spicy, peppery, salty, yellow.

Also known as Indienne sauce.

In butter, sauté vegetables and herbs, (onion, celery, parsley, thyme, bay, chives, mace etc.), add flour, curry powder and white stock. Bring to a long, slow boil and then sieve. For fish, shellfish, chicken, eggs.

DEMI-GLAZE OR GLACE ....

Demi-glaze, also known as demi-glace, is made traditionally by reducing, to half its volume or less, an equal quantity of basic Espagnole and veal stock. Escoffier's recipe for Demi-glace was: Espagnole + veal stock + fat (dripping, duck fat, oil or clarified butter) + flour + tomato purée + chopped mushroom and a small dash of sherry traditionally added at the end.

He made a pale or blonde roux with 1 ounce of fat and 1 ounce of flour. Added 2 pints of Espagnole slowly, whisking to avoid lumps then added 2 pints of veal stock, 1 teaspoon of tomato purée and 3-4 chopped mushrooms. It was stirred while coming to the boil then simmered gently, skimmed, and reduced by half until it reached a silky, syrupy texture. Then a dash of sherry was added before it was strained through a fine strainer. Glace is also made today by replacing the veal stock with chicken stock.

Examples of Escoffier's traditional veal Demi-glace derivative sauces include:

Bigarade: Demi-glace + vinegar + duck stock + cognac + orange zest

Bordelaise: Demi-glace + red wine + thyme + shallots + bay + lemon + black pepper

Champignon: Demi-glace + mushroom essence + button mushrooms

Chasseur: Demi-glace + white wine + mushroom + shallots + cognac + chervil + tarragon

Chevreuil: Demi-glace + red wine + venison stock

Diable: Demi-glace + white wine + shallots + vinegar + cayenne pepper

Diane: Demi-glace + thick cream + truffles

Duxelles: Demi-glace + mushrooms + onions + shallots (chopped and sautéed)

Financière or Périgeux: Demi-glace + truffles

Fine Herbs: Demi-glace + white wine + fine herbs (chervil, tarragon, parsley)

Godard: Demi-glace + mirepoix + white wine + mushroom + ham

Grand Veneur: Demi-glace + cream + currant jam

Hussarde: Demi-glace + white wine + tomato purée + garlic + horseradish + shallots + ham

Italiene: Demi-glace + tomato purée + duxelles + ham + parsley + chervil + tarragon

Lyonnaise: Demi-glace + white wine + vinegar + sautéed onions

Madeira: Demi-glace + Madeira

Meurette: Demi-glace + red wine + thyme + shallots + parsley + bay + mushroom

Piquant: Demi-glace + shallots + white wine + gherkins + parsley
Poivrade: Demi-glace + white wine + mirepoix + pepper
Porto: Demi-glace + port
Regency: Demi-glace + mirepoix + white wine + truffles
Robert: Demi-glace + onions + mustard
Romaine: Demi-glace + white wine + raisins + pine nuts
Salamis: Demi-glace + mirepoix + white wine + meat essence

DEVIL
Hot, thin to medium thick, spicy, brown.
Demi-glace + Worcestershire + sautéed shallots + brandy + tomato purée + chervil + cayenne.
Also known as Diable sauce.
For chicken and grilled meat.

DEVILLED
Warm, medium thick, piquant, spicy, brown.
Escoffier's version of Devil sauce: Diable + softened butter at the ratio of 1:1
Traditionally for chicken, pigeon, and cold meat.

DIABLE
see Devil sauce

DIANE
Thin to medium thick, hot, savory, spicy, pale brown, creamy, peppery.
Poivrade + cream + butter.

FINANCIÈRE ....

Classic, secondary, hot, thin, brown, winey, earthy.

Madeira sauce (=Demi-glace + Madeira) + mushrooms + ham + truffle.

Madeira sauce flavored with black truffle essence. An old 1868 recipe from *The Housekeeper's and Butler's Assistant* says sherry can be substituted for Madeira and adds a pinch of cayenne pepper.

GENEVOISE ....

Hot, thin, rich, salty, reddish-brown, fishy.

Also known as Genoise or Geneva sauce.

Espagnole + fish stock + mirepoix + red wine + anchovy essence* + butter. Sieve and use on fish.

* Escoffier used a fish essence reduction made from the head and bones of salmon but anchovy sauce or fillets are substituted today.

GODARD ....

Espagnole + Champagne + mushroom + carrot + onion + ham.

For Chicken and sweetbreads.

GRANDE VENEUR ....

Hot, medium thick, savory, peppery, sweet, creamy, spicy, brown.

Poivrade (= Espagnole + mirepoix + white wine + pepper) + game stock + gooseberry or red currant jelly + cream.

For venison and game and any meat that pairs well with fruit, e.g. duck, pork, turkey.

ITALIENNE ....

Classic, secondary.

Demi-glace + duxelles + tomato purée + ham + chervil + parsley + tarragon.

It also has two variants with other mothers.

Variant 1: Velouté + shallots + parsley + mushrooms + white wine reduction.

Variant 2: Mayonnaise + calf brain purée + fine herbs.

LYONNAISE ....

Classic, secondary, brown,

Espagnole + Onion sauce + white wine + butter + vinegar.

Alternatively, Demi-glace + white wine + vinegar + sautéed onions

Also known as Lyon Sauce.

For cold meats, ragout, braised or boiled meat, chicken or fish.

MADEIRA ....

Classic, secondary, hot, thin, savory, brown.

Demi-glace + Madeira.

MOSCOVITE ....

Classic, secondary, hot, thin to medium thick, hot, savory, peppery, spicy, brown.

Poivrade (= Espagnole + mirepoix + white wine + pepper) + juniper berries + marsala

PÉRIGUEUX ....

Classic, secondary.

Demi glace + shallots + garlic + madeira + cognac + black truffle + fois gras + butter.

For fillet steak.

PIGNON ....
Classic, secondary, compound, thin to medium thick, hot, savory, peppery, spicy, piquant, brown.
Poivrade (= Espagnole + mirepoix + white wine + pepper) + juniper berries + fir apple kernels + raisins + Madeira.
For venison and game.

PIQUANTE ....
Classic, secondary, brown, tart, fresh, astringent, herbal.
Demi-glace + shallots + white wine + vinegar + gherkin + caper + fresh herbs (chervil, parsley, tarragon).

POIVRADE ....
Thin, hot, savory, peppery, spicy, brilliant-clear.
Also known as Poivre Sauce.
Espagnole + mirepoix vegetables + white wine + pepper.
For grilled or pan fried meats and ragu.

PORT WINE ....
Classic, hot, savory, red.
Demi-glace + port or red wine reduction + butter.
For red meat, especially fillet and game.

REFORM ....
Semi-solid, hot, savory, peppery, spicy, meaty, brown.
Demi-glace + Poivrade at ratio of 2:1. Garnished with small julienne of diced mushroom, pickled or salted tongue, truffle and sliced hard-boiled egg white.
Attributed to Chef Alexis Soyer, Reform club, London 1830.

REGENCY ....

Demi-glace + mirepoix + white Rhine wine + truffle.

There is also a classic secondary Velouté derivative sauce called Regency sauce.

ROBERT ....

Demi-glace + sautéed onion + white wine + mustard. This is a very, very early sauce; Robert was around long before Carême wrote of it. A document called *Le Grand Cuisinier* in 1583 mention a sauce called Robert, as does an even earlier document, *Le Viandier* where there is a sauce for rabbit called *taillemaslée* which was basically a demi-glace + fried onions + verjus + vinegar + mustard. But it was an even earlier Renaissance-period intellectual called François Rabelais (1484-1553), who was the first author to record Sauce Robert. He is also attributed with the saying, "Do what thou wilt, eat, drink and be merry."

Use Robert for all meats and eggs.

ROMAINE ....

Warm, chunky, brown, fruity, sweet, and nutty.

Demi-glace + sugar + white vinegar + game stock + currants + sultanas + pine nuts.

THE WHITE SAUCE FAMILY

MOTHER BÉCHAMEL ....

Mother, classic, compound, hot, thick, sweet, salty, white.

White Roux + flavor infused milk.

Named after the Marquis Béchamel, by Louis XIV of France. Also know as the King of all sauces.

Basic Béchamel Recipe for 2 cups:

4 tablespoons each of butter and flour

2 cups milk, infused with herb and sauté mirepoix vegetables

salt, white pepper and a grate of nutmeg

Simmer milk with herbs and vegetables until their flavors infuse, strain and whisk in to a warm Roux made with half butter, half flour. Whisk continuously on low-medium heat until thick and creamy.

Some chefs take a short cut by adding cream to Chicken or Veal Velouté and calling it Béchamel, but it's actually Supreme sauce which does not have the depth or complexity of flavor of a true Béchamel. Escoffier used to also infuse some cubed raw veal in his milk for more flavor and also because the chefs of his time were obsessed with meat flavor extraction. Salt is not normally added until the end in both Béchamel and Cream sauces as it can curdle the sauce, as can too little stirring. High heat is not used either as it may separate solids from the milk and give an uneven, lumpy or separated sauce. Béchamel is classically paired with eggs, fish, green vegetables, pasta, poultry and veal.

BÉCHAMEL'S CHILDREN..

ADMIRAL ....

Hot, thick, salty, sour, buttery, creamy, white.

Cream sauce (Béchamel + Cream) + lemon juice and zest + capers + parsley + butter.

If you like Béchamel you'll love Admiral. To one cup of thick Cream sauce add the grated zest and juice of half a lemon, two tablespoons each of capers, chopped parsley and butter. Blend and re-heat but do not boil. Season and serve with fish, pasta, chicken and vegetables.

À LA KING ....

Secondary, emulsified, hot, thick, sweet, savory, white.

Cream sauce (Béchamel + cream) + finely diced hard boiled egg yolk + meat + sweet pimento + green pepper + mushroom.

Also known as Long Island sauce. For chicken.

ALBERT ....

Warm, savory, cream, spicy

Béchamel + shallot + horseradish + mustard.

Sauté 2 finely chopped shallots in 2 tablespoons butter, add 1 tablespoon each of Dijon mustard, horseradish, vinegar and sherry. Add to a Béchamel.

AURORE ....

Warm, savory, creamy, pink.

Béchamel + tomato purée + sherry.

Add 2 tablespoons each of tomato purée and sherry to a basic béchamel.

AVIGNON ....

Warm, thick, pungent. Also known as Sauce Avignonaise.

Cream sauce (Béchamel + cream) + garlic + onion + grated parmesan cheese + egg yolk + chopped parsley.

2 cups Béchamel sauce

1 cup finely diced onions + 1 crushed garlic clove, sautéed in 2 tablespoons butter

½ cup each of cream and grated Parmesan cheese

1 egg yolk

2-3 tablespoons chopped parsley

Sauté onion and garlic in butter, build the Béchamel on top, add cream, parmesan and beaten egg yolk. Check seasoning and finish with parsley. Thin with a little stock or milk if too thick. Serve with meats, chicken, game, fish, vegetables and pasta.

BOHEMIAN ....

Hot or cold, spicy, salty, savory, creamy, pink.

Cream Sauce, (Béchamel + cream), + horseradish + paprika + lemon juice + salt.

BRANTOME ....

Warm, creamy, spicy.

Cream sauce (Béchamel + cream) + sautéed shallots + white wine + oyster liqueur + crayfish butter + cayenne pepper + grated truffle.

BREAD ....

Hot or warm.

Béchamel or Supreme (Chicken Velouté + cream) + fresh breadcrumbs.

Also known as Sauce au Pain à l'Anglaise. Milk heated with an onion (cut in half and stuck with a clove) + grated fresh breadcrumbs. Onion is removed before seasoning with salt, cayenne, and nutmeg and finishing with cream, and a little butter.

CARDINAL ....
Hot, sweet, creamy, pink. Also known as Sauce Cardinale.
Béchamel + fish stock + truffle essence + cream + red lobster butter + cayenne.
For shellfish, braised and baked fish.

CELERY ....
Hot, thick, salty, earthy, buttery, creamy, white.
Cream sauce (Béchamel + Cream) + celery diced and sautéed in butter + lemon juice and zest + parsley or chervil .

CHAMPAGNE ....
Hot, thick, sweet, creamy, white.
Cream sauce (Béchamel + Cream) + champagne + shallots sautéed in butter + chervil.

CHANTILLY ....
Warm, sweet, creamy, citrus.
Cream sauce (Béchamel + cream) + lemon.
Add 4 tablespoons of thick whipped cream into a Béchamel and finish with the juice and fine zest of 1 lemon.

CREAM (CRÈME) ....
Classic, secondary, compound, hot, savory, sweet, salty, creamy.
Béchamel + cream.

To a basic béchamel add 2 or 3 tablespoons of cream. For boiled or poached chicken, fish, eggs, corned beef, vegetables, pastas, brains, tripe.

DILL ....
Hot, thick, anise, creamy, white.
Cream sauce (Béchamel + Cream) + lemon juice and zest + capers + dill + butter.

DUXELLES ....
Hot, creamy, earthy.
Cream sauce (Béchamel + cream) + duxelles.
Sauté 2 finely chopped onions in 2 tablespoons butter, add 1 cup finely chopped mushrooms. Set aside. Mix 1 egg yolk with 2 tablespoons cream and add with the mushroom mix to a basic béchamel.

HORSERADISH ....
Hot, thick, spicy, creamy, white.
Cream sauce (Béchamel + cream) + horseradish.

LEEK OR LYONNAISE ....
Hot, thick, salty, sour, buttery, creamy, white.
Cream sauce (Béchamel + cream) + sautéed leeks.

MORNAY ....
Hot, thick, cheesy, creamy.
Cream Sauce (Béchamel + cream) + cheese + egg yolk.
Beat 1 egg yolk with 3 tablespoons of cream and add to a basic béchamel with 1 cup grated cheese. Heat gently to melt the cheese.

MUSHROOM ··

Hot, medium-thick, creamy, earthy.

Béchamel + mushroom.

Sauté 2 cups of sliced mushrooms in butter until sweet and caramelized. Set aside. Make a Béchamel. Mix together 1 egg yolk and 2 tablespoons of cream and stir through the warm sauce then add the mushrooms.

MUSTARD OR MOUTARDE ·····························

Hot, medium-thick, creamy, spicy.

Cream sauce (Béchamel + cream) + Mustard

When making a Béchamel add 1 tablespoon of dry mustard or 2 tablespoons of Dijon mustard to the melted butter and when the sauce is made add 2 tablespoons of cream before serving.

NANTUA ··

Hot, medium-thick, creamy, pink.

Cream sauce + crayfish butter and tail.

PARSLEY ··

Béchamel or Cream sauce (Béchamel + cream) + chopped parsley. Also known as Persil sauce.

For boiled meat, chicken, fish, rabbit, veal.

PIEDMONT ··

See Soubise. Hot, thick, creamy.

Béchamel + sautéed onion

POULETTE ··

Hot, medium-thick, creamy, earthy. Béchamel + mushroom.

QUENELLE ....
Warm, creamy, pale yellow.
Cream sauce (Béchamel + cream) + sherry + egg yolk
To a basic Béchamel blend in 2 tablespoons of thick whipped cream, 1 egg yolk and 2 tablespoons of sherry.

SAFFRON ....
Hot, medium-thick, creamy, yellow.
Béchamel + infused saffron.

SOUBISE ....
Hot, thick, creamy.
Cream sauce (Béchamel + cream) + sautéed onion.
Sauté 2 cups of finely chopped onions with 1 teaspoon of sugar in 2 tablespoons butter then continue to build the Béchamel sauce on top. Add 2 tablespoons cream before serving. You must try this sauce; it is one of our favorites.

TALLEYRAND ....
Classic, secondary, compound, warm, thick, herbal, savory, white.
Béchamel + egg yolk* + lemon juice + parsley.
For one liter of Béchamel, off the heat whisk in 2 egg yolks, 1 teaspoon of lemon juice and then reheat gently, being careful not to curdle. Taste, season, and then add 1-2 teaspoons of chopped parsley. Excellent with grilled meats, especially veal. Also for mashed potato, fish, chicken, vegetables, lasagna, moussaka and all oven-cooked braises.
* Whisking egg into white sauce and oven baking makes a softer and fluffier topping than using white sauce alone.

THERMIDOR ....
Béchamel + mustard powder + brandy + tarragon.
For each cup of béchamel add ½ teaspoon dry English mustard powder, 2 tablespoons brandy and some chopped tarragon. Parsley can be substituted if you don't have tarragon but make sure you chop it finely. For spreading on top of lobster/crayfish in the half shell and then optionally topping with parmesan cheese before coloring under a grill flame.

THE BLONDE SAUCE FAMILY

MOTHER VELOUTÉ ....
Mother, classic, warm, thin, savory, silky, blonde.
Blonde roux (flour and butter) + white stock (chicken, fish or veal).
Velouté is from the French *velour* meaning velvet, and Velouté sauces are creamy and silky but lighter than Béchamel. Stock is made from unroasted fresh bones and this is then thickened with a blond roux (butter and flour in a ratio of 1:1). There are three different Velouté bases:
CHICKEN Velouté: chicken stock + roux (Flour + butter)
FISH Velouté: fish stock + roux (Flour + butter)
VEAL Velouté: veal stock + roux (Flour + butter)
Velouté is Classically paired with Eggs, Chicken, Crustacean, Fish, Green and white Vegetables, Mollusks, Pasta, Shellfish, Veal.
In the Velouté family is a sauce called Allemande that is a thickened Velouté. It was so popular in the days of Carême as the base for making Velouté derivative sauces and Velouté based soups, that the famous Classic chef classified Allemande as a Mother Sauce. This classification was rejected by and reversed by

Escoffier. For the same reason, he felt that Demi-glace is a derivative and not a mother sauce.

BASIC VELOUTÉ RECIPE ....
Recipe for 2 cups:
4 tablespoons each of butter and flour
2 cups chicken or veal stock
salt, white pepper and a grate of nutmeg
The following sauces are derivatives of Velouté and by definition are all classic, secondary sauces.

VELOUTÉ'S CHILDREN ....

ALLEMANDE* ....
Hot, savory, cream. Also known as Carême's sixth Mother Sauce.
Velouté + cream (= Supreme) + lemon juice + egg yolk (+ optional mushroom liquor).
* Allemande is Velouté sauce thickened with egg yolks and heavy cream, and seasoned with lemon juice. Escoffier also used mushroom liquor. To make Allemande, in a large saucepan mix together 1 cup white stock (chicken, veal or fish), 2 large egg yolks, juice of ¼ lemon and 2 cups Velouté. (Optional: ¼ cup mushroom liquor). When reduced by a third, add ¾ cup cream.

ALBUFERA ....
Hot, medium thick, savory, silky, ivory white.
Chicken Velouté + cream (=Supreme) + glace de viande.
Also known as Ivory sauce.
For eggs, chicken and sweetbreads.

AMERICAINE ....

Version 1: Hot or warm, medium thick, creamy, spicy, orange-pink. Lobster shells + lobster Velouté + shallot + tomato + cream + herbs. A French classic attributed to Parisian chef Pierre Fraise in the 1860s. Sauté one broken lobster shell or the equivalent in prawn shells in about 5 tablespoons of butter or butter + oil for a few minutes then season. Add 2-3 chopped shallots, 2 chopped tomatoes, 1 cup of white wine or lobster Velouté and a splash of cognac. Simmer for a few minutes to extract the flavor then sieve. Whisk in 2 tablespoons of butter, 5 of cream and some chopped tarragon and/or chervil. Spoon hot or warm over fish, lobster and shellfish. If a little spice is preferred, a pinch of a good smoked paprika or cayenne pepper can be added to sauce.

Version 2: Hot or warm, medium thick, creamy, spicy, white. Velouté + lobster meat pieces sautéed in butter + white wine + burnt brandy + shallots + garlic + parsley + cayenne + brown butter.

Also known as a L'Américaine or American. For lobster and fish.

ANCHOVY ....

Warm, thick, compound, salty, piquant, pinky-white.
Normande (fish Velouté + cream + egg yolks + mushroom liquor) + anchovy.

AURORA ....

Hot, thick, compound, creamy, bright pink-orange.
There are several classic recipes and variations for making aurora sauce, including:
Velouté + tomato purée, in a ratio of 1:1 + butter.

Supreme (= Chicken Velouté + cream + reduced mushroom liquor) + tomato purée in a ratio of 4:1.
Allemande (= Velouté + cream + lemon juice + egg yolk + optional mushroom liquor) + tomato purée, in a ratio of 4:1.
For pasta, fish, shellfish, vegetables.

BERCY ....
Hot, thin to medium, savory, sweet, herbal, blonde.
Bercy for Fish = Fish Velouté + white wine + parsley + shallots + egg yolk.
Bercy for Chicken = Chicken Velouté + white wine + parsley + shallots + egg yolk.

BONTEMPS OR CAPER ....
Hot, thin or medium, sweet, spicy, salty.
Velouté + sauté onion + cider + mustard + capers + paprika.
For red meat.

BORDELAISE OR BONNEFOY ....
Hot, thin, savory, herbal, white. Also known as Bonnefoy sauce.
Velouté + white Bordeaux wine or Sauterne + shallots + tarragon + butter.

BRETONNE ....
Hot, thin, earthy.
Velouté + Julienne vegetables + cream + white wine.
Vegetables can include mushroom, leek, celery and onion.
For seafood, especially poached fish and shellfish.

CELERY ....
Warm, fresh.
Velouté + sautéed & puréed celery + onion.
For chicken, dumplings, eggs, fish, pasta, veal or vegetables.

CHIVE ....
Warm, onion, pale with green flecks.
Velouté + sautéed & puréed onion + chopped chives
For chicken, dumplings, eggs, fish, pasta, veal or vegetables.

CHIVRY ....
Hot, savory, creamy, very rich.
Allemande + chopped herbs (like tarragon, parsley, chervil) +
lemon juice + egg yolk + mushroom liquor + herbs.

DIPLOMAT ....
Compound, thick to semi-solid, hot or warm, savory, sweet, white
to palest pink, very rich and creamy.
Normande (Fish Velouté + cream + mushroom liquor + egg yolks)
+ brandy + truffle + lobster butter.

GRANDVILLE ....
Creamy, pungent.
Supreme (Chicken Velouté + cream)+ white wine + anchovies +
shallots + cream.
Sauté 2 finely diced shallots with 4-6 anchovy fillets in their oil
until soft, mash a little then add 4 tablespoons of sherry, ½ cup of
cream, salt, pepper and nutmeg. For fish.

GRAPE ....

Chicken Velouté + sautéed shallots + seedless green grapes + cognac + cream.

For each cup of Velouté: 2 sautéed shallots, 12 grapes halved, 2 tablespoons cognac or brandy, ½ cup cream.

HERB ....

Hot, thin to medium thick, savory, silky, green-flecked blonde.

Velouté + shallot + beurre manié (butter + flour, 1:1) + mixed fresh herbs (parsley, chervil, tarragon, chives) + stock.

For poached, boiled, grilled and pan-fried fish.

HUNGARIAN ....

Hot, medium thick, silky, spicy, salty, blond pale pink.

Velouté + sautéed onions + white wine + salt + paprika + butter.

For lamb, veal, eggs, chicken, fish.

INDIAN ....

Hot or warm, medium thick, citrus, silky, spicy, pale beige.

Chicken or Fish Velouté + lemon juice + mace.

IVORY ....

Hot, medium thick, savory, silky, ivory white blonde.

Chicken Velouté + cream (= Supreme) + glace de viande.

Also known as Albufera sauce.

For eggs, chicken and sweetbreads.

JOINVILLE ....

Hot or warm, savory, sweet, creamy, blonde pale pink. For fish.

Version 1: Normande (Fish Velouté + cream + egg yolks + mushroom liquor) + shrimp butter + crayfish butter.
Version 2: Normande (Fish Velouté + cream + egg yolks + mushroom liquor) + prawn butter + crayfish butter + mushroom + truffle.

LOBSTER ....
Warm, medium thick, sweet, creamy, pink.
Normande (Fish Velouté + cream + mushroom liquor + egg yolk) + coral.

MAÎTRE D'HÔTEL ....
Hot, thick, buttery, herbal, blonde.
Chicken or Veal Velouté + demi-glace + maître d'hôtel compound butter (= butter + parsley, lemon juice, salt & pepper).

MUSHROOM ....
Hot, savory, earthy, rich, creamy
Allemande (=Chicken Velouté + cream + egg yolks) + sautéed mushrooms + their cooking liquor.

NORMANDE ....
Hot or warm, savory, sweet, creamy, off-white.
Fish Velouté + cream + mushroom liquor + egg yolks.
For fish.

OYSTER ....
Fish Velouté + cream + mushroom liquor + beurre manié (butter + flour, 1:1) + egg yolk + shallot + parsley + finely diced oyster meat. When made in quantity Oyster Velouté is served as a soup.

PARSLEY ....
Warm, creamy, herbal.
Velouté + cream + egg yolks (= Normande) + parsley

POULETTE ....
Creamy, earthy, herbal.
Velouté + mushrooms + chopped parsley + lemon juice.

RAVIGOTE ....
Creamy, spicy, citrus.
Velouté + cream + egg yolks (= Normande) + onion/shallot + mustard + white wine vinegar or lemon juice.

REGENCY ....
Supreme + mushroom + truffle + white wine.

ROYALE ....
Velouté + cream + egg yolk + truffle.
For poached chicken and eggs.

SORREL ....
Velouté + cream + egg yolks + chopped sorrel.

SUPREME ....
Chicken Velouté + cream (+ optional reduced mushroom liquor)

VENETIAN OR VÉNITIENNE ....
Allemande + vinegar + chervil + tarragon + parsley + shallots.
Larousse named this sauce Vénitienne in honor of the city of Venice. 1 chopped shallot is cooked with ½ cup of vinegar and 2

tablespoons of chopped chervil and parsley until reduced by two-thirds then strained. Make 1 cup of Velouté, add strained reduction, 2 tablespoons melted butter and some finely chopped tarragon and chervil. For eggs and white meat.

VÉRON ....

Creamy, piquant and herbal.

Fish Velouté + cream + egg yolks (= Normande) + shallots + white wine + herbs (tarragon and chervil) + fresh tomato + anchovy + cayenne or black pepper.

This is a complex old sauce to make. The name Véron suggests it originated in Verona, northern Italy, best known as the city of love, the setting of Shakespeare's *Romeo and Juliet*, but it was actually named after a Dr Véron, a gourmande and manager of the Opéra-Comique in Paris. Suitable for fish and white meat.

VILLEROI ....

Allemande + truffle + ham.

2 cups Allemande + 2 tablespoons each of truffle essence + ham essence.

WHITE WINE ....

Hot, thin, savory, silky, blonde.

Velouté + white wine reduction + butter.

THE YELLOW SAUCE FAMILY

MOTHER HOLLANDAISE ....

Warm, emulsified, thick, buttery, savory, light and creamy blonde.
Butter + lemon juice + egg yolk + seasoning.
It is the most delicate of all the sauces and splits (curdles) if
overheated. It is never cooked at over 82°C/180°F because the eggs
coagulate at 88°C/190°F. Used for dressing vegetables like
asparagus, cauliflower, broccoli, fish, eggs.

BASIC HOLLANDAISE RECIPE ....

For 1 cup:
1 cup clarified butter
4 egg yolks, room temperature
1 dessertspoon vinegar or lemon juice
(1 tablespoon of boiling water will thin hollandaise or 1 teaspoon
lemon juice will stabilize its thickness)
Melt a good tablespoon of the butter in a pan, add salt and pepper
and a dessertspoon of vinegar or lemon juice. Over a slow heat or
bain-marie add 3 of the egg yolks, one at a time, whisking
continuously until thick and smooth. Then add the clarified butter
a teaspoon at a time, whisking continuously. An average egg will
take a maximum of 7 teaspoons butter before splitting or seizing.
Season again and serve warm. For poached and hard-boiled eggs,
poached chicken, fish, shellfish, steak, vegetables.

HOLLANDAISE'S CHILDREN ....

ANCHOVY OR ANCHOIS ....
Warm, thick, emulsified.
Hollandaise + anchovy.
Add 1 tablespoon of anchovy paste to a basic hollandaise.

BAVAROISE ....
Classic, warm, thick, emulsified, buttery, spicy, salty, hot.
Hollandaise + horseradish + shrimp butter + nutmeg.
Also known as Bavarian sauce.

BEARNAISE ....
Classic, secondary, warm, thick, emulsified, buttery, savory, sour, sweet.
Hollandaise + shallots (cooked in white wine with chopped tarragon, chervil, thyme and bay).
Made first at the Henri IV Pavillion after his death, and named after the province of his birth.

CAPER OR CAPRES ....
Warm, thick, emulsified.
Hollandaise + capers. Add 2 tablespoons nonpareil or surfine capers* to a basic Hollandaise.
* See under the recipe for Gribiche in the Modern Sauces chapter for the caper size classifications.

CHAMPAGNE ....
Hot, thick, sweet, creamy, white.
Hollandaise + Champagne + shallots sautéed in butter + chervil.

CHANTILLY ....
Classic, secondary, warm, thick, savory, salty, smooth, milky.
Hollandaise + whipped cream, in a ratio of 2:1.

CHORON ....
Béarnaise + tomato paste.
2 cups béarnaise, 2 tablespoons tomato paste.

CITRON ....
Hollandaise + juice and zest of 1 lemon.

DIVINITY OR DIVINE ....
Chantilly (Hollandaise + cream) + sherry or liqueur muscat.
Add 3 tablespoons of sherry (reduced by half from 6) or 3 of
liqueur Muscat to Chantilly.

MALTESE OR MALTAISE ....
Classic, secondary, emulsion, warm, thick, buttery, sweet, citrus,
yellow.
Hollandaise + blood orange juice and zest.
Also known as Maltase sauce. For boiled vegetables, fish.

MOUSSELINE ....
See Chantilly

NOISETTE ....
Classic, secondary, warm rather than hot, thick, emulsified, sweet,
savory, nutty, blonde.
Hollandaise + hazelnuts sautéed in butter.
For boiled fish, especially salmon and trout.

CLASSIC SAUCES & THEIR DERIVATIVES

THE RED SAUCE FAMILY

MOTHER TOMATO

Escoffier's classic tomato sauce involved sautéing a fatty, salted, breast of pork. Today we use bacon, either in the piece or sliced. Vegetarians and non-pork eaters can omit the meat. In an ovenproof pot, sauté 2 chopped bacon strips or rashers in butter with 1 chopped onion and 1 chopped carrot until colored, then add 2-3 crushed garlic cloves and 1 tablespoon flour and cook. Add 2 liters chicken stock, 8 chopped tomatoes, salt, pepper and thyme and bring to the boil. Cover and cook for 1½ hours either in oven or on stovetop. Reduce and sieve before using. Yields about 2-3 cups.

Classically paired with pasta and gnocchi, chicken, fish, poultry, pulses, red meat, shellfish, veal, vegetables.

TOMATO'S CHILDREN

CREOLE

Tomato sauce + sautéed mirepoix (onion, celery, carrot) + green capsicum + minced garlic + bay leaf + oregano + lemon zest and juice.

Simmer 10-15 minutes. Remove bay and season with salt, pepper and cayenne. Serve hot or cold.

FRANÇOISE

Tomato sauce + herbs + cream.

To 2 cups of fresh tomato sauce add 1 cup cream and 1 tablespoon each of chopped fresh basil, oregano, tarragon and thyme.

HUSSARDE ....

Tomato sauce + ham + parsley + horseradish.
Simmer 10-15 minutes, season with salt, pepper. Serve hot or cold.

MARINARA ....

Napoletana sauce + seafood or fish.
Simmer 10-15 minutes. Remove bay and season with salt, pepper and cayenne. Serve hot or cold.

MATRICANA ....

Napolitana sauce + bacon + chili.
Sauté 4 strips or rashers of bacon, add to 2 cups of Napolitana sauce with your favorite type and quantity of chili (fresh, dry flaked, powder or oil).

NAPOLETANA ....

Tomato sauce + tomato purée + basil + bay.
Simmer 10-15 minutes. Remove bay and season with salt and pepper. Serve hot or cold.

PRIMAVERA ....

Napoletana + Macédoine cubed vegetables.
Simmer 10-15 minutes, season with salt and pepper. Serve hot or cold.

PARMIGIANA ....

Tomato sauce + chopped Roma tomatoes + chiffonade cut basil + grated parmesan cheese
Simmer 10-15 minutes, season with salt and pepper. Serve hot or cold.

PROVENÇALE ....

Tomato sauce + mushroom + garlic

Simmer 10-15 minutes. Remove bay and season with salt, pepper and cayenne. Serve hot or cold.

SICILIANA ....

Tomato sauce + eggplant + capsicum + anchovy + olive + caper + parsley.

Sauté chopped eggplant, add all ingredients and simmer 10-15 minutes. Season with salt and pepper. Serve hot or cold.

MOTHERLESS CLASSICS ....

BREAD ....

Boil 2 cups milk, add 6 tablespoons fresh white bread crumbs, 1 small whole onion with 1 clove stuck in it, 2 tablespoons butter and a pinch of salt. Simmer gently for 10-15 minutes then remove onion and clove and whisk until smooth, adding a few tablespoons of cream and salt & pepper. Serve with feathered game and roast chicken.

GRAVY ....

Fond + thickener + flavor additives.

Gravy is a pan sauce flavored with the fond of meat or vegetable juices and fats left in a pan after roasting. A thickener like flour and additional flavoring agent is usually added and cooked before stock or water and the whole stirred until it thickens. Flavoring agents can include giblets, onions, caramel, herbs like sage, parsley, tarragon or thyme, salt or pepper. Color can be deepened by caramelizing a little sugar with the fond. Traditional gravy is light or medium brown in color and intense in flavor. Commercially prepared, mass produced, gravy powders are available today that replace fond. Well-known brands include Bisto, Gravox, Hain, Orgran, Marigold and Massell, although you can easily make your own by mixing flour, sugar, stock powder, dried herbs, pepper and salt. Traditionally served with all roast meats and vegetables, sausages, crumbed meats like schnitzels, sautéed onions, chips or mashed potato.

PIQUANTE ....
Fine herbs + garlic + shallot + mustard + vinegar + pepper.
Sauté 2 shallots and 2 crushed garlic, add 1 tablespoon mustard and black pepper and ½ cup vinegar. Blitz with a tablespoon each of parsley, tarragon, chervil and chives.

WHITE ITALIENNE ....
Simmer 1 tablespoon oil, 1 tablespoon chopped truffles, 2 cloves garlic, parsley, peeled lemon slice and a cup each of white wine and chicken stock.

CLASSIC SAUCE & FOOD PAIRINGS

———◆———

"What is sauce for the goose may be sauce for the gander but it is not necessarily sauce for the chicken, the duck, the turkey or the guinea hen."
—ALICE B. TOKLAS, 1877-1967

DEFINITION ....
The general rule for food pairing today is that there are no rules, because there are always new frontiers to be explored by innovative and experimental cooks. Food and pleasure are subjective experiences and tastes vary. We learn what we like by educating our palates through tasting and by reading and reproducing the recipes of successful cooks and chefs. Professional chefs adjust the base notes of their flavors to produce a blend or balance that appeals to a broad range of palates. It should be remembered however that the time of Classic cookery and chefs was more than a hundred years ago and our tastes and palates have changed. The following food pairings apply primarily to the classic sauces as a guide for both beginner and professional cooks.

DUMPLINGS & QUENELLES ....
Admiral (Velouté + mushrooms), aurore, bercy, bordelaise (white), morney, nantua, soubise, tomato

EGGS ....

HARD BOILED, WARM OR HOT: allemande, alicante, aurore, béarnaise, béhamel, curry, devil, duxelles, Indian sauce, lyonnaise, mornay, soubise, tomato.

HARD BOILED, COLD: aioli, mayonnaise, mornay, ravigote, rémoulade, soubise, verte, vinaigrette, white sauces, tartare.

POACHED: américaine, andalouse, aurore, béchamel, béarnaise, bourguignone, bretonne, chasseur, chateaubriand (petit duc), chivry, choron, cream sauces, tarragon, hollandaise, Hungarian, Indian, ivory, mornay, nantua, Portuguese, printanière, provençale, rouennaise, royale, soubise, supreme.

Eggs Florentine: poached eggs + hollandaise, + spinach

Eggs Hemingway: poached eggs + hollandaise + salmon

Eggs Mornay: poached eggs + béchamel + cheese

Eggs Provençale: poached eggs + béarnaise

Eggs Russian: poached eggs + béchamel, flavored with mustard, lemon and black caviar

OMELETS: Asian sauces like ginger soy, béchamel, butter, chasseur, chili, madeira, mushroom, normande, reform, soubise, tomato.

FISH ....

BRAISED OR BAKED: alicante, américaine, bourguignone, bonne femme, bretonne, bourguignone, cardinale, chambertin, wine sauce, chambord, compound butters, diplomate, crayfish sauce, genoese, grandville, greek sauce, gooseberry sauce, Hungarian sauce, Italian, joinville, meurette, normande, newburg, veron, white wine and red wine sauces.

DEEP-FRIED & PAN FRIED: aioli, alicante, allemande, banquière, beurre noisette, bretonne, compound butters, grandville, hot butter sauces, Hungarian, ivory, meurette, ravigote, soubise, supreme, sweet & sour, tartare.

SMOKED FISH: aioli, cream sauce, cucumber sauces like raita, gribiche, horseraddish.

GRILLED FISH: aioli, alicante, anchovy, bercy butter, compound butters, batarde, béarnaise, cardinale, choron, colbert, fennel sauce, herb sauces, Italian, mustard sauce, pesto, salsas, tapenade.

MARINATED FISH: Italian sauce, tomato sauce.

FISH COOKED 'MEUNIÈRE': brown butter, bonnefoy sauce.

FISH ROE: Brown butter, tartar sauce.

POACHED OR STEAMED FISH, SERVED HOT: allemande, beurre blanc, brown butter, black butter, anchovy sauce, batarde sauce, béchamel, bercy sauce, white sauce or fish velouté, caper sauce, chervil sauce, cream sauces, grandville, green curry sauce, hollandaise, Indian, oyster sauce, maltaise, mariniara, mornay, mousseline, mustard, nantua, parsley sauce, poulette, sorrel sauce, thermidor, truffle, vénitienne.

POACHED OR STEAMED FISH, SERVED COLD: aioli, alicante, anchovy sauce *(served cold)*, gribiche, mayonnaise, oriental sauce, ravigote, rémoulade (mayonnaise *with Dijon mustard)*, Russian sauce, sorrel sauce cold, tartar, tomato sauce, verte sauce, vinaigrette, vincent.

FROGS LEGS ....
Aioli, garlic butter, poulette, Allemande + mushroom + parsley + lemon juice.

FRUIT ....
Armagnac, caramel, chocolate, coulis, crème anglaise, berry, hot apple purée, hot apricot purée, hot orange butter, hot prune purée, redcurrant and blackcurrant, rum, sabayon, saffron cream.

GAME, FEATHERED ....
Bread sauce, moscovite, port wine sauce, and salmis sauces. Salmis is a classic name for feathered game sauces made as rich pan reductions. The pan juices and fond are deglazed using red or white wine, a little brandy, cognac or stock and reduced before adding rich flavorings like foie gras, shallots, herbs, bacon, mushrooms or truffles. Bread sauce is also a classic for game birds.

DUCK: Bigarade, muscovite, orange, plum, port wine.

GEESE: Apple, bread, cider gravy, Cumberland (red currant + port), Madeira.

GROUSE: Bread sauce.

GUINEA FOWL: Bread, Madeira, red wine sauce, supreme.

PARTRIDGE: Apple, cranberry, elderberry, red wine with juniper.
PHEASANT: Apricot, cumberland, port wine, red wine with chestnut, sherry.
QUAIL: Fig, grape.

GAME, FURRED ....

Apple, bread, cherry, cumberland, demi-glace, grand veneur, jus, muscovite, napoletana, onion (soubise), pepper (poivrade), perigourd, reform, port wine and red wine sauces.
GOAT: Curry, yoghurt, mint.
HARE: Juniper.
RABBIT: Albert, chasseur, mustard, robert, sorrel, white or red wine.
VENISON: Diane, cumberland, pepper, red wine.
WILD BOAR: Tomato, red wine.

GRATINS ....

Béchamel, white sauce, bolognaise, duxelles, mornay (béchamel with egg yolk and cheese).

MEAT ....

BEEF: Albert, béarnaise, bordelaise, compound butters, demi-glace, horseradish, mushroom, red wine, yoghurt sauces like raita.
LAMB: Demi-glace, gravy, jus, mint sauce, mushroom, perigeux, reform, satay, yoghurt sauces.
MINCED OR BOILED: Devil, minced sauce, Italian, lyonnaise, bread sauce, poor man's sauce, piquant, robert, verjus.
HAM: Cumberland, Madiera, sherry, Yorkshire.

LARGE CUTS FOR ROASTING OR BRAISING: Jus, cooking liquid (braised meat), Albert, English cream sauce, breadcrumb sauce, Godard, Madera, pepper sauce, Russian sauce, Talleyrand.

MUTTON: Harrissa (Moroccan chili paste sauce), Cumberland, Indian, mint jelly and mint yoghurt, onion sauce.

SMALL CUTS, SERVED PANFRIED OR SAUTÉED: Sweet and sour, béarnaise, bordelaise, bourgignone, chasseur, choron, duxelles, tarragon sauce, financière, Hungarian, hussarde, Italian, Madiera, Portuguese, provençale, Talleyrand, tomato, sherry wine.

PORK: Apple, chili, cumberland, ginger-soy, pineapple salsa, rémoulade, sambal, satay, sweet and sour, charcutière, piquante, Robert, sage, yoghurt.

WHITE MEAT: Aurore, bretonne, cream sauce, Hungarian, Italian, parsley, romaine, saffron cream, soubise, tarragon, truffle sauce.

COLD MEAT: Aioli, anchovy, avocado, Cambridge, chutneys, dijonnaise, horseradish, mayonnaise, mint, parsley, ravigote, rémoulade, tarragon, tomato sauce.

GRILLED: Anchovy butter, barbecue, béarnaise, bercy butter, bonnefoy, bontemps, bordelaise, chateaubriand, chivry butter, choron, chutneys, colbert, foyot, harrissa, maître d'hôtel, mustard, ravigote, robert.

CRUMBED, DEEP-FRIED: Chutneys, salsa, sweet and sour, tomato, villeroi, worcestershire.

CRUMBED, PAN-FRIED: Diablo, diane, mushroom, mustard, pepper, Worcestershire.

OFFAL ....
BRAISED, DEEP-FRIED OR PAN-FRIED: Sweet and sour, allemande, beurre noisette, bretonne, chicken velouté, Hungarian, ivory, meurette, ravigote, soubise, supreme, tartar, villeroi.

OX TONGUE: Piquante, tomato sauce.
PIG TROTTERS: Devil, mustard.
BRAISED SWEETBREADS: Albufera, aurore, chantilly, tarragon, financière, foyot, godard, nantua.
KIDNEY, GRILLED OR PAN-FRIED: Madiera, Portuguese sauce.
VEAL HEAD: Gribiche, mayonnaise, parsley sauce.

PASTA ....

Al fungi, arrabbiata, pesto, bolognese, duxelles, financière, ketchup, poulette, vinaigrette, alfredo, carbonara, tomato, napoletana. Specific pasta shapes lend themselves to particular sauce types:
ANGEL HAIR: Butter, cream, cheese, pesto, seafood, tomato.
SPAGHETTI: Tomato.
FARFALLE: Butter, cream, cheese, meat, pesto, seafood, tomato, vegetables.
FETTUCCINE: Butter, cream, meat, seafood, tomato.
LASAGNE: Cream, meat, tomato.
LINGUINE: Butter, cream, cheese, meat, pesto, seafood, tomato, vegetable.
MACARONI: Butter, oil, cream, cheese, meat, tomato, vegetable.
ORECCHIETTE: Meat, pesto, tomato.
PAPPARDELLE: Meat.
PENNE: Cream, tomato.
RIGATONI: Cream, meat, tomato.

PASTRIES, SAVORY ....
PAKORAS: corriander chutney, green goddess, Indian mint yoghurt, tamarind, dipping sauces,

PASTIES, PIES, SAUSAGE ROLLS: chili, chutneys, mushroom, red pepper, tomato.
SPRING ROLLS: Asian dipping sauces, coriander chutney.
VOL AU VENTS : Allemande, béchamel, financière, marinière, normande, soubise, supreme.

PASTRIES, SWEET

CHOUX: Coulis, crème anglaise, caramel, crème pâtissière, chocolate, custard, fruit sauces.
CROISSANTS & DANISH: Almond cream, brandy cream, caramel, chocolate, coulis, raspberry, strawberry.
FRUIT TARTS: Crème anglaise, coulis, lemon, orange, passionfruit, raspberry, redcurrant.
STREUSEL: Chocolate, crème anglaise, custard, fruit coulis.

POTATOES

Aioli, any of the hot or cold butter sauces, cream sauces, gravy, mayonnaise, parsley, vinaigrette and any yoghurt sauce, especially mint.

POULTRY

BRAISED: Albufera, celery sauce, duxelles, financière, Godard, onion sauce.
DUCK: Apple, bigarade, cherry, chutneys, dipping sauces, orange, pineapple salsa, muscovite, plum, port wine, redcurrant, sweet and sour, soy.
GOOSE: Apple sauce, sage sauce.
POACHED OR PAN-FRIED DISHES: Albufera, allemande, aurore, cold avocado, bretonne, chervil, chantilly, chivry, cream sauce, tarragon sauce, mixed herb sauce, Indian curry sauces, ivory,

mayonnaise, mornay, nantua, perigueux, parsley sauce, ravigote sauce, royale, supreme, thai green curry, thai red curry, vénitienne.
GRILLED CHICKEN: Bontemps, devil, paloise (béarnaise with tarragon replaced by mint).
ROAST POULTRY: Sweet and sour, cranberry, English sauces like mint or red currant, bread sauce, jus, gravy.
SAUTÉED POULTRY: Bourguignone, chasseur, duxelles, Hungarian, Indian.

RICE ....
HOT: Chasseur, duxelles, Indian, mustard sauce, tomato sauce.
COLD: Mayonnaise, tartar, vinaigrette.

SHELLFISH, CRUSTACEANS & MOLLUSCS ....
ABOLONE: Asian dipping, cream, creole, green goddess, lemon, mayonnaise, mushroom.
COLD DISHES : Gribiche sauce, mayonnaise, remoulade, verte (green sauce).
HOT DISHES: Américaine, prawn sauce, lobster sauce, Indian, nantua, Newburg, Victoria, thermidor.
LOBSTER/CRAYFISH: Newburg, thermidor.
MUSSELS: Butter, herb, garlic, lemon, marinière, poulette, provençale, ravigote, tomato
OYSTERS: Shallot, tartar, mignonette, vinegar.
PRAWNS/SCAMPI/SHRIMP: Asian dipping sauces (if battered and deep fried), garlic butter, mayonnaise, seafood.
SEA URCHIN: Hollandaise.

SNAILS ....
Aioli, bourguignonne, garlic butter, ginger lime, poulette, tomato.

SOUPS ....

Fresh herbs, sour cream, grated cheese and croutons are common garnishes for soups but did you know sauces can also be used to garnish soups? Traditional sauces added to soups include aioli, pistou, rémoulade and rouille.

VEGETABLES ....

ROOT, VINE AND LEAF: Aioli, alicante, anchovy, allemande, aurore, béarnaise, béchamel, bretonne, chantilly, cheese, hollandaise, curry, hot and cold butter sauces, horseradish, lyonnaise, maltaise, mayonnaise, mornay, mousseline, parsley, rémoulade, salsas, tomato, truffle sauce, vinaigrette, yoghurt sauce.
GREEN LEAF: Caesar, colbert, cream sauces, mayonnaise, supreme, tomato, vinaigrette.

COLD SAUCES

———◆◆◆———

"Mayonnaise: One of the sauces which serve the French in place of a state religion."
—AMBROSE BIERCE, 1842-1914

AIOLI

Thick, emulsified, piquant, salty, sour, yellow.
Mayonnaise + garlic + lemon juice.
Also known as Provence Butter.
For vegetables, salads or cold meats.

ALICANTE

1 cup thick mayonnaise, use whole egg or soy
1 orange, zest and juice
2 egg whites, beaten to soft holding peaks
a pinch of paprika or cayenne, pepper & salt
Mix all gently together and use immediately.

ANDALOUSE

Thick, salty, spicy, sour, creamy, pink.
Mayonnaise + Worcestershire + tomato paste + red pimento + lemon juice.

To 1 cup of mayonnaise, add 3 tablespoons of tomato paste, 2 tablespoons diced red pimentos, 1 teaspoon of lemon juice and ½ teaspoon Worcestershire sauce. Goes well with meats and poultry.

AVOCADO ....
Thick, smooth, creamy, pale green.
Avocado + oil + white wine or cider vinegar + basil, parsley, tarragon, chive.
Blitz 2 ripe avocados, ½ cup oil, and ¼ cup vinegar. Season and add 1 cup finely chopped herbs. Thin with a little liquid of your choice (water, cream, coconut milk). For fish, chicken, vegetables or bread.

BARBECUE ....
Barbecue sauce has many different recipes and flavors but in general it is spicy, thick, sweet and savory. Vinegar and mustard are often paired as a foundation as are Tomato and molasses. If you want to try making it yourself here are a couple of variations.

BBQ Sauce 1 (for marinades and use as a cooking-in sauce):
Sauté half a finely chopped onion and 3 cloves of crushed garlic in olive oil until soft and then add:
2 cups of tomato sauce or ketchup
2 good tablespoons of brown sugar
1 tablespoon each of tomato purée, Worcestershire sauce and cider vinegar
1 teaspoon hot mustard powder
a pinch each of cayenne pepper, smoked paprika, salt & pepper.
Simmer 15-20 minutes.

BBQ Sauce 2 (for an accompanying sauce for cooked meats):
 2 cups tomato sauce or ketchup
1 cup of tomato paste
1 cup each of applesauce and red wine vinegar
$\frac{1}{3}$ cup each of honey, molasses, butter and maple syrup
$\frac{1}{2}$ teaspoon each of garlic and onion
$\frac{1}{2}$ teaspoon each of chili powder and smoked paprika
$\frac{1}{4}$ teaspoon each of cinnamon, cayenne, salt & pepper
Simmer 20 minutes.

BASIL ....
Cold, thick, savory, creamy, light green.
Mayonnaise + basil + cream.
For chicken, vegetables, pasta. There are several types of Basil sauce. See also Pesto.

CAMBRIDGE ....
Mayonnaise + hard boiled egg yolks + anchovy + mustard + fresh herbs (parsley, tarragon, chive).

CEASAR SALAD ....
$\frac{1}{2}$ cup olive oil
4 anchovies, mashed
4 garlic cloves, crushed
1 egg yolk
2 tablespoons each of vinegar and grated Parmesan cheese
1 tablespoon each of lemon juice, and Dijon mustard
1 teaspoon Worcestershire sauce
salt & pepper

CHANTILLY ....

Thick, savory, salty, smooth, milky.

Mayonnaise + whipped cream in a ratio of 2:1.

Also known as Mousseline Sauce. For fish and boiled vegetables.

CHIMICHURRI ....

Thick, green, garlicky.

Garlic + parsley and/or coriander + onion + lemon + vinegar.

This Latin American green sauce or salsa verde is traditionally served with grilled meat in Argentina, but is also good with fish, chicken and vegetables. Just blitz everything together in a food processor, blender or mortar & pestle. For each cup of fresh parsley and/or coriander, use 2-3 cloves of peeled garlic, 1 tablespoon chopped onion, 1 tablespoon each of vinegar and lemon or limejuice, salt and pepper. Add some fresh oregano leaves as an addition if you have them.

CHIPOTLE ....

Mayonnaise or sour cream + chipotle (sauce or crushed, reconstituted dried peppers) to your taste.

CUMBERLAND ....

Hot or cold, thick, savory, sweet, piquant, deep red.

Orange juice + cornflour + red wine vinegar + mustard + red current jelly + port + cayenne.

Also known as Oxford sauce. Mix the juice and zest each of an orange and lemon with ½ cup red currant jelly, ½ cup port, 1 tablespoon of red wine vinegar, ¼ teaspoon of dried mustard powder and a slurry made from ½ teaspoon of cornflour mixed with 2 teaspoons water. Bring to a slow boil, stirring until it thickens. Season with salt and pepper and a touch of cayenne (optional). If you can't find red currant jelly in the jam section, substitute cranberry jelly or similar red berry conserve. For game, ham, and lamb.

DIJONNAISE ....
Creamy, savory, blonde.
Hard-boiled egg yolks + Dijon mustard + oil + lemon juice.

GREEN ....
Also known as Chimichurri, Gremolata, and Salsa Verde. Green sauce is a simple sauce to make where herbs are blended with oil and aromats like garlic, chili, anchovy, chili or lemon.

GREMOLATA ....
Semi-solid, cold, herbal, citrus.
Parsley + garlic + lemon.
A version of salsa verde. For each bunch of flat-leaf Italian parsley, use 2 garlic cloves and the zest and juice of 1 lemon. Blitz in the food processor or macerate in the Mortar & Pestle.

GRIBICHE ....
Classic, motherless, cold, thick to semi-solid, herbal, salty, sharp, pale green.
Hard-boiled egg yolks + oil + vinegar + chopped capers & gherkins + fresh parsley, tarragon and chervil + thin julienne hard-boiled egg whites.
For cold fish, shellfish, vegetables.

HORSERADISH ....
Horseradish + mayonnaise + sour cream + mustard + onion.
For every cup of mayonnaise add ¼ cup prepared horseradish, ½ cup sour cream + 1 teaspoon Dijon mustard, 1 tablespoon finely chopped onion.

HORSERADISH AND SOUR CREAM ....
Horseradish + sour cream + lemon + mustard + honey.
For every cup of sour cream add ¼ cup prepared horseradish, 2 tablespoons lemon juice or cider vinegar, 1 teaspoon honey or sugar, 1 teaspoon Dijon mustard, pepper and salt.

HORSERADISH AND APPLE ....
Horseradish + mayonnaise + yoghurt + apple + mustard.
For every cup of mayonnaise add ¼ cup prepared horseradish, ½ cup plain yoghurt, ½ grated peeled apple, 1 teaspoon Dijon mustard, salt and pepper.

HUMMUS ....
Chickpeas + garlic + tahini + olive oil + lemon juice + parsley.
Blitz 1 cup of cooked chickpeas with 1 or 2 garlic cloves, 2 tablespoons of tahini sesame seed paste, ¼ cup oil, ¼ cup lemon juice, some fresh parsley, salt and pepper. Taste and adjust the flavors then thin with a little water or coconut milk.

MINTED SPICY YOGHURT ....
Other, compound, cold, runny, sweet & sour, spicy, minty, creamy, pale green.
Curry paste + mint sauce+ yoghurt + milk + chili + sugar + salt.

Sauté a finely chopped medium onion in oil/butter or ghee until soft, add 1-2 teaspoons of cumin powder then blitz in a blender with a cup or more of fresh mint leaves (not stalks as these are bitter), 2 cups of Greek yoghurt, salt and a pinch of sugar to taste. Before serving sprinkle with hot smoked paprika, chili powder or cracked black pepper. Use with pakoras, samosas, all meats and fowl, Indian curries, dolmades, spring rolls, or anything and everything.

MAYONNAISE ....
The Mother of the Cold Emulsified Sauce family, mayonnaise is cold, thick, semi-solid, creamy, spicy.
Eggs + vegetable oil + acid (lemon or vinegar).
For each cup of Mayonnaise, whisk 2 egg yolks in a bowl or blender with 1 tablespoon Dijon mustard, and 1 tablespoon of fresh lemon juice or vinegar until blended then add 1 tablespoon of oil at a time, making sure to blend each in well before adding the next. Once you have a good emulsion going after 4-5 tablespoons you can add a little quicker. Stop when it is the thickness you desire. It can be thinned with water or lemon juice if you make it too thick.
* Basic mayonnaise can be flavored with curry powders, spices, herbs, chopped dill pickles, capers, etc.

MINT (ENGLISH) ....
Other, cold, thin, sweet & sour, green.
Mint + sugar + vinegar.
For roast meats especially lamb.
Dissolve caster sugar with finely chopped mint leaves, vinegar and water in a ratio of 1:2:3:4, i.e. 1 tablespoon of sugar to 2 tablespoons of mint to 3 tablespoons of vinegar to 4 tablespoons of

water (or use the 1:2:3:4 ratios in ounces, grams or cups). Season with salt and pepper to taste.

OXFORD ....
See Cumberland.

PESTO ....
Basil + parmesan cheese + pine nuts.
Everyone has his or her favorite pesto recipe; this one is simple and delicious. Just crush or blitz together 3 cups of fresh basil leaves, 1 cup each of grated parmesan cheese and pine nuts. Add a splash of oil, pepper and salt. If you like a little more punch add a clove of garlic and a squeeze of fresh lemon juice. For everything, especially pastas.

PIRI PIRI OR PERI PERI ....
This traditional cold chili sauce is very hot both in taste and popularity and could equally have been placed in the Dipping Sauces or Modern Sauces chapters. It is an old, very simple to make, Portugese sauce that has been rediscovered and become popular in the West in the last 20 years or so. Simply finely chop a small handful (10-15) bird's-eye chili and stir in 2 tablespoons of garlic powder, juice of 1 lemon, a pinch of salt and enough olive oil to give a consistency you like.

RANCH ....
Mayonnaise + sour cream + garlic + herbs.
1 cup mayonnaise
½ cup buttermilk or sour cream
1-2 garlic cloves

1 cup fresh mixed herbs (Italian parsley, chives, oregano, tarragon, chervil)
salt & pepper
Blitz together until smooth. Serve with salads, pastas, meats, and cold chicken.

RAVIGOTE ....
Vinaigrette + mustard + caper + parsley + onion.
3 tablespoons extra virgin olive oil
2 teaspoons each of Dijon mustard and chopped parsley
1 teaspoon red wine vinegar
1 teaspoon capers, chopped
1 tablespoon tarragon, chopped
1 shallot, finely chopped
salt & pepper

RÉMOULADE ....
Thick, salty, herbal, and creamy.
Mayonnaise + anchovy + French mustard + caper + gherkin + herbs (chervil parsley and tarragon).
Pronounced: ray-muh-lahd. For cold seafood, chicken and meat. For each cup of mayonnaise add 1 teaspoon each of french mustard, chopped gherkins and chopped capers, 1 tablespoon of chopped fine herbs like parsley, tarragon and chervil, then finish with a few drops of anchovy essence.

ROMESCO ....
Nuts (almonds) + garlic + oil + bread + red peppers.
This is a classic Spanish Catalan sauce. In a food processor blitz a handful each of blanched almonds and hazelnuts, 1 slice of stale

bread fried into croutons, and 1 large tomato. Add 2 large roasted red peppers or capsicums, 1 onion and a few cloves of garlic that have been roasted until sweet, 1 cup of olive oil, a splash of vinegar to taste and a pinch each of red pepper flakes and sweet or smoked paprika. Taste, adjust flavors and serve with meat, fish, poultry or vegetables.

ROUILLE ....

Other, cold, bread thickened, garlicky, Mediterranean flavor.

1 red capsicum pepper, roasted, de-seeded, peeled

2 garlic cloves, crushed

1 slice white bread, crusts removed, torn into pieces

1 egg yolk, free range

1 tablespoon Dijon mustard

1 lemon, juice only

salt and pepper

½ cup olive oil

Blitz everything together in a food processor or crush in a large mortar & pestle adding the oil last. For fish, stuffing or topping shellfish before grilling and garnishing soups, especially Bouillabaisse.

RUSSIAN ....

Thick, creamy, tangy, light pink color.

½ cup each of mayonnaise and thick, plain yoghurt

2 tablespoons tomato sauce or ketchup

2 tablespoons chopped dill pickle or mustard pickle relish

2 tablespoons lemon juice

1 tablespoon Worcestershire sauce

salt and pepper

SEAFOOD ....

Other, emulsified, cold, medium thick but runny, spicy, sour, creamy, pink.

Mayonnaise + Worcestershire + tomato + tabasco + lemon juice.

For cold seafood especially shellfish like shrimp, prawns, crayfish.

SUEDOISE ....

Mayonnaise + apple + horseradish.

To each cup of mayonnaise add 1 cup of homemade applesauce and 1 tablespoon of horseradish. Great with pork, chicken and all cold meats.

TAPENADE ....

Olive + capers + anchovies + olive oil.

Although credited today to the French and eaten as a dip or spread, the original tapenade was a sauce, an invention of the Ancient Romans, who ate it with their roasted meats. The recipe for *Olivarum Conditurae* was first mentioned in the First Century AD in *De Re Rustica of Columella*.

Black Olive Tapenade Sauce: Blend 1 cup pitted kalamata olives, 5 or more tablespoons olive oil, 1 tablespoon each red wine vinegar, capers, lemon juice and chopped shallot, 1 teaspoon unseeded Dijon mustard, 1-2 anchovies, salt & pepper.

Green Olive Tapenade Sauce: Blend 1 cup pitted manzanilla olives, 5 or more tablespoons olive oil, 1 tablespoon each white wine vinegar, capers, lemon juice, chopped coriander and chopped shallot, 1-2 anchovies, salt & pepper.

TARTARE ....
Mayonnaise + vinegar + spring onion or chives + chopped
cornichon (or dill pickle).
For each cup of mayonnaise add 2 tablespoons each of vinegar,
mustard, finely chopped spring onion and pickle.

THOUSAND ISLAND ....
Thick, creamy, salmon pink colour.
Mayonnaise + tomato + onion + pickle + sugar + vinegar.
To each cup of mayonnaise add a ¼ cup of tomato sauce or
ketchup, a tablespoon each of finely chopped minced onion,
mustard pickle relish, sugar and vinegar, then season with pepper
and salt.

VERDE, SALSA ....
Acid, fruity, green, thin to medium depending on how course or
fine the parsley is chopped.
Parsley or green soft herbs + garlic + onion + capers + anchovy +
oil + vinegar or lemon juice.
Salsa verde is a cold peasant sauce with variations used in Italian,
French, South American, Mexican, African and Island cuisines.
Used as a condiment or dipping sauce for grilled or stewed fish,
meats, poultry or vegetables. One well-known salsa verde is
gremolata, the usual accompaniment to ossobuco.

VINAIGRETTE ....
Oil + vinegar.
The traditional ratio of oil to vinegar is 3:1 and any good oil and
vinegar can be used. Optional flavor additives can be added to the

basic emulsion including lemon juice, herbs, mustard, salt and pepper, garlic.

WALNUT ....
2 onions and 2 garlic cloves, sautéed in oil
2 cups of walnuts
1 pinch each of powdered cinnamon, clove, fenugreek, marigold or saffron, coriander, chili pepper and salt
1 tablespoon of vinegar or lemon juice
Blitz all ingredients in a food processor then slowly add water to thin to a sauce consistency. Taste and balance flavors. Serve cold or at room temperature with vegetables, chicken, meats, and pasta.

DESSERT SAUCES

"Always serve too much hot fudge sauce on hot fudge sundaes, it makes people overjoyed and in your debt."
—JUDITH OLNEY

APPLE ....
Fruit, compound, cold, warm or hot, acid, sweet, greenish-brown.
Apple flesh & juice + sugar + lemon juice + cinnamon + mixed
spice + butter.
Peel core and roughly chop 4 granny smith apples, add ½ cup
brown sugar, ¾ cup apple juice, a squeeze of lemon juice, and a
pinch each of cinnamon and mixed spice. Simmer until soft, strain
or purée and add a knob of butter. For pork, meats, poultry, pies
and deserts.

APPLE BRANDY ....

Liqueur, compound, hot, sweet, creamy.

Apple brandy + sugar + cream + vanilla.

Heat, melt and simmer for five minutes ¼ cup each of white and brown sugar, vanilla, 2 tablespoons corn syrup, ½ cup heavy cream and 3-4 tablespoons Calvados apple brandy or apple schnapps. Optionally, a few drops of lemon juice or a few grains of salt can be added before serving.

For steamed pudding or bread and butter pudding.

BRANDY CUSTARD ....

Alcoholic, compound, warm or hot, egg cream.

Crème anglaise + brandy (2 cups:2 tablespoons)

BUTTERSCOTCH ....

Warm (too hot will burn the tongue), sweet, light caramel color.

Cream + brown sugar + butter + vanilla.

Heat and melt together, 1 cup of cream, ¾ cup of brown sugar, 2 tablespoons of butter and 2 teaspoons of vanilla. Boil for 5 minutes or until it thickens slightly.

For puddings, cakes, ice cream, parfaits.

CARAMEL ....

Warm, sweet, light caramel color.

Sugar or sugar + butter + cream (salt, nuts and chocolate optional).

Next time you're tempted to reach for a bottle of store bought caramel sauce, made from corn syrup, dozens of chemicals and artificial vanilla flavor, why not take 10 minutes to make the best caramel sauce on the planet?

Spread 1 cup of white sugar evenly in a heavy bottom pan, heat gently until it begins to melt around the edges and just pull the melt gently into the center to prevent burning. If you stir too hard it will clump. As soon as it is all melted and the color you want you have several options:

1. Pour into or around molds for desserts like crème brulée or crème caramel.
2. Use as a glazing sauce for fruit flans.
3. Make praline by adding a cup of nuts (the praline ratio of sugar to nuts is 1:1). Add a few grains of good salt, pour onto a greased baking sheet, cool and crush.
4. Use as a dipping sauce for profiteroles or fruit such as strawberries.
5. Take off the heat and carefully put the bottom of the pan onto a tray of ice to stop the cooking. Dip in a fork and make spun sugar. Grease the outside of round molds or cups and spin some cages or spin over fruit tarts or around profiterole stacks.
6. Make a caramel pouring sauce by taking off the heat and adding ½ cup each of unsalted butter and then cream. (Cold into hot = spitting + bubbling so be careful)
7. Make a salted caramel pouring sauce by adding 1 teaspoon of finishing salt to #6 after its made.
8. Add some chopped dark, milk, white or Toblerone nougat chocolate to #6 or #7 above for a chocolate caramel sauce.
9. Even if making salted caramel, use unsalted butter for the cooking process or your caramel may get a slightly bitter flavor.

Serve with tarts, fruit crumbles, pancakes, custards, yoghurts, waffles, milky desserts, icecreams and cakes. Makes 1 cup. Recipe can be doubled. Keeps in fridge for 7-10 days.

CHERRY ....
Classic Fruit sauce, thin to medium thick with semi-solids, hot or cold, savory, sweet, acid, bright red.
Sweet Cherry sauce: Stewed cherries with syrup + red current jelly + kirsch. For desserts and cakes.
Savory Cherry sauce: Stewed cherries with syrup + red current jelly + orange juice + spices (ginger powder, cinnamon, nutmeg, mace) + port + lemon juice + arrowroot or cornflour fécule (slurry).
For roast duck, pan fried duck breast, baked ham, game, chicken, and pork.

CHOCOLATE ....
Other, warm or cold, sweet, thick, dark.
Chocolate solids + sugar + vanilla + water.
Add 1 cup of water, ½ cup white sugar and ½ cup light corn syrup or glucose to a heavy-bottomed pan. Bring to a simmer, then take off the heat and stir in ½-¾ cup Dutch unsweetened cocoa powder and 55 grams of dark chocolate. Cool a few minutes and serve warm. Makes 2 cups. Keeps in the fridge for 7-10 days.

CHOCOLATE (HARD CRACK OR HARD SHELL) ....
Melt your favorite plain dark, milk or white chocolate or a flavored chocolate in a double boiler with 1 tablespoons of coconut oil for every 100 grams of chocolate. Cool or use warm. When served on cold desserts like ice cream it will set to a hard shell. Use for

dipping cold fruit, e.g. strawberries, marzipan stuffed prunes and dates or for dipping balls of ice cream, truffles or confection.

CHOCOLATE MINT ....

Melt 200 grams dark chocolate in a double boiler, then add 1 can of sweetened condensed milk until hot. Thin with ½-¾ cup of hot, but not boiling, water and add a small pinch of salt. Stir in peppermint oil a few drops at a time, tasting as you go until it is to the desired mint flavor.

CHOCOLATE TOBLERONE ....

For a new take on traditional chocolate sauce why not try Nigel Slater's idea. Toblerone chocolate melted + cream + butter.

COCONUT ....

Boil together 400ml coconut cream with 1 cup brown or palm sugar until it reduces by about half and begins to thicken. Add a few drops of vanilla and a few grains of salt. For hot and cold fruit desserts, rice or chocolate desserts, hot steamed puddings, baked custards and cheesecakes.

COCONUT CREAMS ....

Other, compound, hot or cold, thin or thick, sweet or savory, cream.

Mirepoix + roux + coconut cream + stock + cream.

Coconut Cream + curry powder + milk = coconut curry sauce

Coconut Cream + reduced sugar syrup + whipping = coconut caramel sauce

Coconut Cream - watery liquid + whipping = fluffy coconut sauce

COFFEE ....

Heat, melt and simmer ½ cup brown sugar, 1 cup heavy cream, 1 teaspoon vanilla extract, 1 tablespoon unsalted butter, and 2 tablespoons strong black coffee. It will begin to thicken after five minutes.

COULIS ....

Most cooks think of Coulis as dessert sauces because many are fruit based. Coulis, from its root word derivative, means 'strained' and in classical culinary terms refers to a sauce made by blending or puréeing either cooked or uncooked fruit or vegetables and then passing them through a sieve or strainer. This process makes sauces that are thick, silky, soft and smooth, without chunks, skins or seeds. The term is used loosely today by chefs and cooks, and many Coulis recipes are simply purées that have not been strained. Vegetable coulis, like red capsicum coulis, are usually served with savory dishes. Fruit coulis can be used as sauces for sweet dishes like desserts, cakes, pancakes and ice creams or can be frozen and forked into granitas. Coulis can also be added to other sauces to thicken their texture or enhance their flavor. Almost any seasonal fruit or vegetable can be cooked, puréed and sieved to make a Coulis, so the field is limited only by your imagination. Tart fruits generally have sugar added and are simmered to soften and sweeten them before puréeing and straining. Common dessert coulis include apple, apricot, blackcurrant, blackberry, mango, peach, raspberry, redcurrant and strawberry.

CREAM CHEESE ....

Blend together 2 tablespoons of well-softened cream cheese, 1 tablespoon lemon juice, $^2/_3$ cup powdered or confectioners' sugar,

¼ cup thick/heavy cream and a few drops of vanilla. Use milk a little at a time to thin to the desired consistency. For rich fruit puddings, baked apples, stewed fruit, parfait and berries.

CRÈME ANGLAISE ....

Warm, semi-thick but thin enough to pour, sweet, creamy.
Sugar + eggs + milk + vanilla.
Also known as English cream or English custard.
Whip 4 egg yolks and ½ cup sugar together until the yolk is almost white. Slowly add 2 cups of warmed milk (hot milk will curdle the eggs) and continue whisking. Add seeds from 1 vanilla bean pod or 1 teaspoon of vanilla paste or extract. Apply a low heat and stir constantly until it is thick enough to coat the back of a spoon then remove from the heat. For saucing cakes or fruit, used with meringue in floating islands, a base for ice cream and crème brulee.

When modified, crème anglaise is a base for many desserts:
Crème Anglaise + starch = Crème patissière.
Crème Anglaise + additional eggs + cream = Egg custard.
Crème Anglaise + starch + crème + fruit + baked= Clafouti.
Crème Anglaise + gelatin = Collée crème.
Crème Anglaise + gelatin + egg whites = Chiboust crème.
Crème Anglaise + gelatin + crème + liqueur = Bavarian crème.
Crème Anglaise + cream = Légère crème.
Crème Anglaise - eggs + starch = Blancmange.
Crème Anglaise - sugar + soy + dashi + mirin = Japanese savory custard.
Crème Anglaise - sugar + salt = Savory custard for quiche, moussaka & gratin.

CRÈME PÂTISSIÈRE ....

Warm or cold, thick, sweet, cream.

Sugar + eggs + milk + vanilla + starch.

Whisk together 4 egg yolks and ½ cup of fine sugar until pale and light. Stir in 2 tablespoons flour and 1 tablespoon cornflour, thoroughly, and set aside. Gently heat 4 cups of milk (or 2 cups each of milk and cream for a richer sauce), 1 teaspoon of vanilla seeds, essence or paste. Add the warm milk mixture to the egg, sugar and flour, and mix slowly, whisking continuously. Reheat on low to medium, stirring constantly until the sauce thickens. Do not allow sauce to catch on the bottom or to boil as it will curdle. Also known as French Pastry Cream. For filling profiteroles, éclairs, cakes, cream pies, Berliners, donuts, mille feuille, custard tarts and fruit tarts.

CRÊPE SUZETTE ORANGE SAUCE ....

Alcohol, hot, thin, sweet, sour, orange.

Orange + sugar + lemon + butter + brandy.

Method 1 used when crêpes are to be served immediately:

Heat, melt and simmer together, juice of 3-4 oranges and 1 lemon, zest of 1 orange and 1 lemon, 2 tablespoons caster or fine white sugar, 2 tablespoons unsalted butter and 2-3 tablespoons brandy (Grand Marnier and Cointreau can also be used). Sauté crêpes, folded into quarters, in the sauce to warm and flame with additional brandy.

Method 2 used when crepes are to be stored and then reheated in a covered pan or oven: Make a soft compound butter, by mixing the above ingredients together in a bowl and using an additional tablespoon of butter. Spread thinly on cool crêpes, fold into quarters and layer in oven proof serving dish or stovetop pan. Dot with any residual butter, cover and reheat gently before serving. If flaming, heat brandy in a small pan, ignite and pour over crêpes.

CUSTARD ....

See Crème Anglaise, Crème Pâtissière.

FRUIT ....

Other, hot or cold, thin, medium or thick, sweet, multi-colored.
Fruit + sugar + water.
Most fruits can be made into a sauce: most of the berries including, raspberry, strawberry, gooseberry and blackberry; apple, orange, peach, red or black currants, apricot, plum, quince, or pear.

FUDGE, HOT ....

½ cup sugar, 2 tablespoons unsalted butter, 6 tablespoons quality chopped chocolate, 200 milliliters thick cream, 2 tablespoons each of golden syrup and water and one teaspoon of vanilla.

GOOSEBERRY ....

Classic, secondary, compound, savory, lemony, creamy, white with pale green tinge.
Butter sauce (roux + water + egg yolks + cream + butter) + sieved pulp of gooseberries sautéed in white wine and powdered sugar.
For grilled or poached fruit, pastries and even white fish.

HARD SAUCE ....

Butter + sugar + vanilla.
Cream ½ cup soft butter with 1½ cups powdered or confectioners' sugar until light and fluffy then add 1 teaspoon vanilla extract, or 2 tablespoons rum or brandy.

LEMON ....

Egg + sugar + lemon + butter.

Heat, melt and simmer 1 beaten egg, 1 cup sugar, and the juice of 2 lemons and zest of 1. Stir until thickened then add 1 tablespoon of butter.

For gingerbread, pound cake, or hot pudding.

LEMON CURD ....

Fruit, emulsion, thick, warm or cold, sweet, sour, semi-translucent, pale to bright yellow.

In an electric mixer beat 6 egg yolks + 1 cup white sugar to a pale ribbon then add the zest and juice of 1 medium-large lemon. Heat and simmer some water in a saucepan big enough to allow your heatproof bowl to sit on top. Gently cook the curd sauce over the steam heat, scraping or whisking continuously until it thickens enough to coat the back of a spoon. Be careful not to curdle it. Take off the heat and add slowly ½ cup finely sliced butter, stirring until melted. When thin use as a sauce for pancakes, waffles, ice cream and desserts. When allowed to thicken use it cold for flans, tarts and cake fillings. If storing for later use it will form a skin as it cools so lay plastic wrap on top or store in a covered container.

MAPLE CREAM SAUCE AND HARD CRACK MAPLE CREAM ....

Heat, melt and bring to the boil 1 cup pure maple syrup, ½ cup heavy or thick cream, 2 tablespoons of butter and a pinch of cinnamon, then reduce heat and stir until it reduces a little and goes syrupy (about 5 minutes). When cream is first heated it thins out and then thickens again. More cream can be added for a lighter and slightly thicker sauce. Good on anything! The addition of 2 tablespoons of coconut oil after it is cooked will turn maple cream sauce hard when it chills or is used to top ice cream. Try thinly coating tropical fruit pieces like pineapple, banana or mango and refrigerate till the sauce sets to a brittle crack.

MARSHMALLOW SAUCE ....

Hot or cold, sweet, creamy, silky, white.

Heat, melt and simmer 2 cups packaged marshmallows (or make your own if you prefer) with ½ cup heavy cream and a splash of vanilla in a double boiler or bain marie. Stir until melted. This sauce thickens as it cools.

MOCHA SAUCE ....

Heat, melt and simmer chocolate (milk, dark or white), strong black coffee and butter, in a ratio of 4:2:1 (i.e. for 1 cup of chocolate, use ½ cup coffee and ¼ cup butter). Taste and add sugar, honey or maple syrup if you like it sweeter.

ORANGE ....

Heat, melt and simmer orange juice and sugar in a ratio of 2:1 (i.e. 1 cup juice to ½ cup sugar). Thicken to the desired consistency with an arrowroot slurry, (1 tablespoon arrowroot to 1 tablespoon water), beurre manié or a hydrocolloid of your choice. If you prefer, replace the thickener with demi-glace and reduce by half before finishing with butter for a rich gloss. Add chopped mint or orange flesh/zest for piquancy. Pairs well with turkey, duck, chicken and pork. Pans can also be deglazed with fresh orange juice, butter and additional flavor additives like cream, cherries or herbs.

ORANGE CUSTARD CREAM ....
Warm or cold, thin to medium, thicker when cool, creamy, sweet, tart, citrus, pale orange/yellow.
1 cup of sugar + 5 tablespoons flour + pinch of salt + 1 orange, zest and juice + 1 lemon, zest and juice + 3 egg yolks + dash of vanilla.
Heat, melt and simmer. Blend and stir well over low heat until thickened and smooth. Because citrus strengths vary, taste and balance the sweet and sour with the addition of more sugar or citrus then melt in 1 tablespoon butter. Allow to cool a little before folding in 1 cup of heavy or whipped cream.

PEANUT BRITTLE SAUCE ....
Heat, melt and bring to a boil ¾ cup sugar and ¼ cup each of both water and corn syrup. Do not stir; just leave it boiling until it colors a rich amber. Remove pan from the heat, stand well back and add $1/3$ cup of thick/heavy cream and 4 tablespoons of butter. (It will bubble dramatically when the moisture hits the hot sugar syrup.) Stir in 2 teaspoons of pure vanilla extract and a cup of chopped, skinned, roasted peanuts (bash in a mortar & pestle if you like or use dry-roasted honey peanuts instead). This sauce thickens and sets as it cools, but is great served at room temperature as a sauce and it can be reheated to thin.
For desserts, fruit, cakes and ice cream.

PRALINE SAUCE ....
Heat, melt and bring to a boil 2 cups of corn syrup, $1/3$ cup brown sugar and ½ cup water. Do not stir. Remove from the heat when it just begins to color. Add 1 teaspoon of pure vanilla extract and a cup of chopped pecans.

RHUBARB SAUCE ....

Heat, melt and simmer until soft ½ kg of chopped rhubarb, 1 cup of sugar and 2 cups water. Cool slightly, blend until smooth and sieve if you want a smoother sauce. Return to the pan and either finish with a knob of cold butter for a thin sauce or with an arrowroot slurry for a thick sauce. If a brighter color is required, a drop or two of natural red food coloring can be used.

For ice cream, fruit, ricotta or baked cheesecake, pound cake, sponge desserts.

SABAYON ....

Classic, emulsified, cold, thick, sweet, pale blonde.

Sugar + egg yolks + cream + acid (wine, sherry, lemon or vinegar).

Known in Italy as Zabaglione. Traditionally made by hand whisking for half an hour over a double boiler, sabayon works out just as well with electric beaters. Beat 4 egg yolks with an electric beater. Make a sugar syrup by heating 8 tablespoons sugar and 8 tablespoons water or white wine, boil for 3-5 minutes then pour in a slow stream into the egg yolks with the beaters on high. When the mix is pale and thick after a few minutes add 1 teaspoon of lemon zest, the juice of 1 lemon and 2 tablespoons of sherry, grand marnier or rum. It's not traditional but you can fold in 2 tablespoons of thick cream for a milkier-flavored sauce. Keep in the refrigerator until ready to serve. Good with fruit.

TOFFEE ....

Heat, melt and simmer ⅔ cup brown sugar, 200ml cream and 40g unsalted butter.

TURKISH DELIGHT SAUCE ....
Soft, fragrant, sweet, usually pale rose color.
Sugar + water + lemon + cornflour + cream of tartar + rosewater + coloring.
Before making this recipe, be warned: this sauce is not for the faint hearted or beginner cook. Lots of things can go wrong, like getting lumps, or even worse a rubbery ball, not to mention the potential to burn yourself. Turkish delight seems simple but is actually technically very difficult to perfect due to the precise control of the chemical reactions required.

1. Put 4 cups of sugar, 1½ cups water and the juice of a lemon in a saucepan and stir on high heat until it dissolves. As soon as it comes to a boil stop stirring, add a candy thermometer and cook until it reaches 230°F. (This achieves partial caramelization of the sugar by melting it in water and driving off the water with heat, creating an unsaturated polymer.)

2. While the sugar syrup is coming up to temperature, put 1 cup of cornflour and 3 cups of water in another saucepan, add 1 teaspoon of cream of tartar and on medium heat stir very gently until the lumpy mix turns to a smooth milky liquid. As it cooks further it will begin to thicken from the bottom of the pan upwards. As soon as your spoon picks up the thickening paste from the bottom, turn off the heat and keep gently stirring while this happens. Be very careful not let it over-thicken. (Heating melted cornstarch in water causes the molecular chains to unravel and form a mesh capable of capturing water molecules, a process called polymerizing.)

3. Once these two processes have been achieved the two substances must be joined together and then boiled until the

mesh of the cornflour polymer captures the remaining water in the sugar syrup. To achieve this the thickened, but not lumpy, cornflour must be added to the sugar syrup as soon as it reaches 230°F. The mix must be stirred and reheated until it boils and must be continuously stirred until it changes from its milky white to a clear gel. This part of the process may take half an hour and the result must be a sweet, silky and runny soft sauce. Take from heat and add 1-2 tablespoons rosewater and 1 drop of pink food color or grenadine.

Serve warm and soft. Pour left overs into an oiled silicon pan and cool uncovered to set before cutting and dusting with icing sugar and cornflour in a ratio of 1:1. Warm Turkish delight sauce gives an exotic Persian flavor to any dessert. Use as a flavor layer for sponge cake or in cupcakes, for saucing steamed puddings, with fruits and ice-creams, piped into donuts, for battered and frittered fruit, or even for dipping profiteroles.

YOGHURT HONEY ....

Cold, thin and pourable, sweet, sour.

Yoghurt + honey + lemon.

In a blender mix 2 cups natural yoghurt, 2 tablespoons each of lemon juice and honey. Pour into serving jug and sprinkle with nutmeg or cinnamon. For pancakes, fruit, cereals, curries. For a savory version add 1 cup of fresh mint and a pinch of salt to the blender and finish with a sprinkle of ground cumin instead of nutmeg or cinnamon.

ZABAGLIONE ....

See Sabayon

DIPPING SAUCES

"England has three sauces and three hundred and sixty religions, whereas France has three religions and three hundred and sixty sauces."
−TALLEYRAND

AIOLI ....
Mayonnaise + garlic.
Aioli is a flavored Mayonnaise, made by simply mixing crushed garlic into the process when making mayonnaise. For seafood, fish, potato, salads.

ASIAN ....
3 tablespoons rice vinegar or mirin
3 tablespoons light soy sauce
3 tablespoons chopped coriander
1 tablespoon toasted sesame oil
1 tablespoon chopped ginger
1 tablespoon chopped green or red chili pepper
1 tablespoon chopped garlic
1 tablespoon chopped spring onion
1 tablespoon honey or sugar
Mix all ingredients together.

AVOCADO ....

In a food processor or blender blitz the following:
For each whole soft ripe avocado, add 2 tablespoons mayonnaise, 2 tablespoons lime or lemon juice, ½ long green chili pepper (de-seeded, or 1 teaspoon of green Tabasco sauce or ¼ teaspoon cayenne pepper). Add water a little at a time if you want a thinner sauce. Top with thinly-sliced spring onion rings or chives.

BABA GANOUSH ....

Normally used as a dip, baba ganoush makes an excellent sauce when served thick or thin.
2 medium or large eggplant + olive oil for cooking the eggplant
2 tablespoons tahini sesame paste
2 garlic cloves, crushed
½ teaspoon cumin powder
1 lemon, juice only
salt and pepper
chopped coriander for garnish
The eggplant needs to be pre-cooked until soft with a smoky or caramel flavor imparted into the flesh. Slicing and frying in oil until soft and browned, baking in a hot oven, grilling, broiling or searing over a gas flame can do this. After this first cooking step, the eggplant can be peeled or left in its skin. To make the dip, blend all ingredients together in a food processor, blender or large mortar and pestle.

CHERMOULA ....

Also known as Charmoula, this wonderful Moroccan or Tunisian sauce can be used as a marinade or an accompanying or dipping sauce. It is a heady mixture of green herb, chili, oil, lemon pickle, citrus juice, salt, pepper, garlic and cumin. Ground coriander, chili, smoked paprika, pepper and or turmeric can also be added for variation depending on your preference.

½ cup extra-virgin olive oil

1 tablespoon each of lemon or lime juice, and finely chopped preserved lemon

1 teaspoon of powdered cumin

2 garlic cloves, crushed

1 cup of chopped fresh coriander

1 long red chili, finely chopped

salt & pepper

Excellent will all red meats, fish, chicken.

CHIMICHURRI ....

This wonderful Argentinian sauce can be thinned and used as a dipping sauce. Parsley + garlic + olive oil + oregano + red or white vinegar, varied by adding coriander, thyme or lemon. It also has a red version where chopped tomato and red bell pepper are added. This recipe is a thinner version of cold chimichurri used for steak.

½ cup extra-virgin olive oil

3-5 tablespoons of white or red wine vinegar

3-5 tablespoons parsley, finely chopped

2 garlic cloves, crushed

1 tablespoon oregano, finely chopped

salt & pepper

CHIPOTLE ....

½ cup of prepared mayonnaise or sour cream

1 tablespoon lemon juice

2 garlic cloves, crushed

1 chipotle pepper (smoked, dried, jalapeno chili), finely chopped, or a tablespoon of chipotle in Adobo sauce (canned chipotle chili paste).

Blend all together into a scrumptious sauce. Add extra mayonnaise or sour cream or use it as is on meats, with chili beans or roasts.

CHOCOLATE ....

100g best milk chocolate, finely chopped
100g best dark chocolate, finely chopped
300 ml of cream

Heat the cream gently, mix in the chopped chocolates, stirring until melted and smooth. Too much heat will curdle and separate the fats in the chocolate, so be patient.

Use with any desserts and especially as a dipping sauce for the deep-fried, piped Mexican donuts known as Churros, which are no more difficult than donuts or pancakes: simply make a smooth batter with 2 cups of plain flour, 1 level tablespoon of baking powder, a pinch of salt, ½ liter of boiling water and 2 tablespoons of olive oil. Using a ½" star tip in a piping bag, squeeze out 12 centimetre or 4" lengths of the paste directly over hot, but not smoking, oil. Cut them off with scissors to gently release them into the oil. They will cook through in a few seconds but turn the heat down if they colour too quickly. Lift the warm Churros into a mix of caster sugar mixed with cinnamon and serve with your chocolate sauce for dipping.

DASHI ....

Bring a piece of kombu (approximately 4x6" or equivalent) and 1½ cups water to a boil in a saucepan. Stir in 2 tablespoons of bonito flakes, remove from heat and let steep for 5 minutes. Sieve, return to saucepan, and add ½ cup soy sauce (we use mega chef or red boat brand), ½ cup mirin, ¼ cup peeled and finely-grated daikon radish and 1 tablespoon of freshly grated ginger; bring to a boil. Remove from heat, cool to room temperature and serve or use as a basis for other sauces.

EGG & CAPER
Chicken Velouté + cream + hard-boiled eggs + capers.
1½ tablespoons each of butter and flour, cook as a Roux
1½ cups chicken stock
½ cup heavy/thick cream
2 hard boiled eggs, peeled and chopped Brunoise
2 tablespoons capers, rinsed and chopped Brunoise

FISH SAUCE
Fish sauce is a commercially prepared Asian condiment sauce. There are many brands but few good ones. We choose to use brands that are naturally prepared without artificial additives or chemicals and with the finest taste. Good fish sauce should have no nasty smell or taste, and should preferably be the first press or extraction just like the best olive oils. Avoid the cheap supermarket brands and head to the best Asian grocers you can find. The brands we use and recommend are Megachef and Red Boat.
For sushi, sashimi, tempura, spring rolls.

GREEN GODDESS
Herbs + mayonnaise + vinegar + cream.
2 good tablespoons each of finely chopped parsley, tarragon or coriander, spring onion, chive, thin cream and white wine vinegar. Mix well with 1 cup of thin mayonnaise and season to taste.

FONDUE ....
Is melted cheese + wine a sauce? We think so; it certainly meets the criteria of the definition for a sauce, at least a dipping one. Fondue is the name of the Swiss dish, and cheese sauce is the medium for dipping bread, meats, and vegetables. A heavy pan is rubbed with garlic and grated cheese melted into slightly-heated white wine.

HUMMUS ....
Hummus is a Middle Eastern dip made from ground chickpeas, sesame tahini, spices and lemon juice. Blitz together cooked chickpeas, tahini, olive oil, lemon juice, salt and pepper and garlic. We add water slowly at the end and blend to make it lighter, thinner and smoother and use as a sauce for meats and vegetables. See our Hummus post at **TheCulinaryLibrary.com** for the full recipe.

MUHAMMAARA ....
2 red peppers, charred or roasted and skinned
1 cup walnuts
2 tablespoons each of lemon juice and olive oil
1 tablespoon each of red chili paste and pomegranate molasses
1 teaspoon cumin powder
salt & pepper

PEANUT ....
3-4 tablespoons crunchy peanut butter
1 large can coconut cream
2 garlic cloves, crushed
½ onion

2 tablespoons lemon or lime juice
1 tablespoon brown sugar
½ tablespoon curry powder
½ teaspoon red chili paste or flakes
Sauté onion and garlic, add the rest of the ingredients and simmer. Season with salt and pepper. Taste and adjust to your palate.

RED CAPSICUM

1 large red capsicum
1 garlic clove
½-¾ cup white wine vinegar
½ long red chili pepper
½ cup caster sugar
Chop and sauté the capsicum and when soft and slightly colored, add the garlic and chili and cook a little before adding the rest of the ingredients. Simmer for 5 minutes and then blitz in a food processor or blender. Use for dipping skewered meats like lamb, pork, beef or chicken, or pastries like samosas or pakoras.

SEAFOOD COCKTAIL

American: Tomato ketchup + horseradish
Australian/European: Tomato sauce + mayonnaise
Irish: Tomato sauce + mayonnaise + sour cream

SALTED CARAMEL

Stir 1 cup of sugar on a medium heat until it clumps and then melts totally, then whisk in 6 tablespoons of butter, one at a time. When melted, remove from heat and slowly add 1 cup of heavy/thick cream, whisking in with a good pinch of finishing salt.

SPICY SOUR CREAM ....

To each cup of sour cream add 2 tablespoons sweet chili sauce, 1 tablespoon lemon juice and ½ teaspoon each of cumin, cayenne pepper and/or smoked paprika. Taste and add salt and pepper if necessary. Another option is to add finely chopped chives or soft herbs of your choice. Great for dipping fried or roasted potatoes, pumpkin, asparagus, vegetables, pakoras and samosas, chicken, fajitas, taco, pastries and those wonderful, cheesy potato-filled fried noodle dumplings called pierogies.

SRIRACHA ....

This Asian chili dipping sauce is sold in bottles as a condiment but the homemade version is fresher and so easy to make.

2 long red chili, de-seeded and finely sliced

2 garlic cloves, crushed

6 tablespoons fish sauce

3 tablespoons each of light soy sauce and rice wine vinegar or mirin

3 tablespoons caster sugar

Simply blend together.

When Sriracha sauce + butter + vinegar are melted together in a ratio of 2:2:1 and simmered, the result is another dipping sauce traditionally used with fried chicken wings. In America this dish is known as Buffalo Chicken Wings.

TAMARIND ....

2 tablespoons tamarind pulp

1 teaspoon salt

¼ teaspoon dried red chili flakes

2 teaspoons sugar

½ cup water

Soak Tamarind pulp in hot water for about one hour. Drain and grind it in a mortar and pestle with the other ingredients. Add a little extra water if you like it thinner. Taste, season with pepper and salt and adjust sweetness.

TARAMOSALATA ....

If you love taramosalata then the option is to either buy your favorite commercial brand or make your own. Using a mortar & pestle or processor mix together:

4 slices day-old white bread, no crust, soaked in a little water and squeezed of excess

4 tablespoons Tarama (carp or cod fish roe)

2 tablespoons minced onion

¾ cup olive oil

5-6 tablespoons lemon juice

Grind or blitz the onion and roe, then the bread, then add the oil slowly until it thickens and goes creamy like a mayonnaise. Mix in the lemon and taste; add more lemon if you like it sharper and season if needed. Best as a sauce to dip all types of breads, from the crunchy-crusty loaves to flat Greek varieties.

ZA'ATAR ....

3 tablespoons Za'atar*

3 cloves garlic, minced

3 tablespoons coriander, finely chopped

3 tablespoons balsamic vinegar

6-8 tablespoons olive oil

salt and pepper

* If you want to make your own Za'atar blend see our recipe in *The Culinary Library*, Volume 1, *Alchemy of the Mortar & Pestle*.

ESSENCES, GELÉES, GLACES, JUS & SOILS

---◆◆◆---

"This is an age of intellectual sauces, of essence, of distillation ... conclusions without deductions."
–BENJAMIN HAYDEN, 1786-1846

ESSENCES ....

DEFINITION ....
Previously known in the 1800s as Ozmazomes, essences traditionally referred to the watery fluid released from meats as they cooked, which when reduced further but un-caramelized were used as meat essence sauces. When caramelized to a thick sticky residue, as in the meat roasting process, essences become 'fond'

and when fond is deglazed with stock and then reduced it becomes 'jus'.

When cooks think of essences today, they probably imagine those small bottles of liquid fruit, nut and alcohol essences found in the baking section of supermarkets, but for chefs and Molecular Cookery fans, if they don't wish to make their own essences they are able to buy commercially-prepared versions. Usually sold dehydrated as powders which when rehydrated make sauces or sauce additives, or as essence syrups used as flavor additives to food and sauces. Molecular Cookery essences including beetroot, tomato, soy, rice wine, blood orange, cranberry, passionfruit and raspberry. Prices average around AU$10-20 per 100 grams but you wont find these essence powders on your local shelf. Home cooks can buy essences online from businesses like ChefsArmoury.com and RedSpoonCompany.com and for a full range of wholesale-only supplies chefs can buy essences from companies like Metroz, an old Italian family-owned company based in Milan.

If you want to try making an essence sauce at home try the following recipes:

CITRUS ESSENCE ....
Simmer thin peelings of citrus fruit like orange, mandarin, blood orange, lime or lemon in water, juice, wine, port or madeira in a ratio of 1:1 and reduce. Taste, add sugar or salt and pepper depending on your use, then sieve.

HERB ESSENCE ....
Simmer fresh herbs in water, wine, stock, pear or apple cider in a ratio of 1:1, reduce, add a squeeze of lemon, strain, season and finish with a little butter.

MUSHROOM ESSENCE ....

Sauté 2 cups of your favorite sliced mushrooms (Swiss brown, morels, chantrelles, button, cèpes, field) in 2 tablespoons of butter/oil until they color then add 2 cups of water or stock and simmer until reduced by half or three quarters. Sieve and use.

ONION ESSENCE ....

Sauté 2 cups thinly sliced onions in 2 tablespoons of butter/oil until they color then add 2 cups stock and reduce to the concentration required. Sieve and use.

VEGETABLE ESSENCE ....

Use the same method above for any vegetable or combination of vegetables.

GELÉES ....

DEFINITION ....

Yes, we know. Gelée means a gel and jellies are not really sauces, but soft runny gels historically, both the sweet and savory (meat gelée) were once used as sauces. The setting agents were naturally occurring ones like gelatin, agar agar and pectin, but today we have a wider choice of natural and man-made jelling agents thanks to the molecular cookery movement. When liquids are set with a jelling agent they can be made soft or firm and served hot, warm or cold. Most firm gels will melt to a runny sauce when served on top of warm or hot foods. Gelées are simple or compound liquids that have been taken to a gel stage by the addition of gelatin or agar agar or one of the newer jelling agents like gellan. Many recipes use gelatin as it is commonly available as a powder or in sheets. See gellan, agar agar and hydrocolloids in the Thickeners chapter for alternative jelling agents you can experiment with and use.

The following definition of sweet gelée we provided in *The Culinary Library*, Volume 2, *Edible flowers & Leaves*, so if you have that volume you might like to skip to the recipes. Gelées are often made using flowers, leaves, herbs or fruit with sweeteners and jelling agents. Herb Jelly or Confit is flavored sugar syrup with a jelling agent added. An old French word that means 'to preserve', Confit comes from the Middle English word 'Confyt', derived originally from the Latin, 'Conficere' or 'Confectum', meaning 'prepare'. The process of Confit is used today mainly to refer to the process of cooking meat or vegetables at low temperatures in butter or oil, but the original cooking technique of Confit was invented in medieval France and meant preserving fruits and leaves by cooking and then storing them in sugar syrup. So we are now re-claiming the word to describe encouraging edible flowers and leaves to release their color and flavor essences, usually into boiling water, then straining, reducing, sweetening and setting with a jelling agent. Fresh leaves and petals can be added for texture and freshness to the confit when cooled but before set. As this will shorten its shelf life, confit with added petals, whole buds and leaves should be used as soon as possible. The intense color, flavors and texture of flower or leaf confit will take other foods to a new level of experience. Open flowers rather than buds give a more intense flavor and color and the freshest, youngest leaves with the brightest color should be selected.

The most commonly known rose confit gelée today is probably Turkish Delight, and the most commonly known single-leaf savory confit gelée is Mint Jelly, which a traditional accompaniment to Roast Lamb. Other commercially available confits or gelées from France include Violet, Jasmine flower, orange flower, red poppy, rose petal, nasturtium and rosemary. There is however no reason why the adventurous cook or chef cannot use any of the edible herbs and flowers to create confit gelée. The color and flavor extractions are intense and can be further altered by reducing the sugar and the addition of more leaves, different leaves, fresh strained juices or spices. Why not try Cinnamon Basil (lime green with suspended cinnamon dust), Rosemary (deep green), Rosemary and Orange (light green), Rosemary and Pomegranate (blue-purple), Lemon Verbena (pale honey yellow), Opal Basil (deep purple) or Rose Water or Orange Flower Water (clear and transparent)? For special occasions we suggest either adding some edible gold or silver leaf flakes or dust or adding more setting agent to set the confit to a consistency that will allow you to cut it into small cubes or sticks. Both of these variations add an exciting textural and visual element to your dishes. You can use gelatin, agar agar, gellan or any of the modern jelling agents.

Edible Leaves & Flowers confits can be either sweet or savory, salty or sour, and can be eaten on toast, brioche, croissant, with meat, fish, poultry or used to decorate cakes or to drizzle around desserts. Try a confit of Lavender (mauve), Rose (from colorless white petals, through palest pink to red), and Violet (pale to deep purple or blue). The possibilities are limitless. Why not try Clove dianthus (raspberry red), Hibiscus flower (pink), Frangipani (palest yellow) or Camellia sinensis, the plant we derive our tea from. Tea is, after all, only a dried green leaf. There are now a few specialist tea companies like the Mighty Leaf Tea company that supply Whole Leaf Teas with flavors like Organic Earl Grey, White Orchard, African Amber, Green Tea Tropical, Leaves of Provence and Chamomile Citrus. All can be confit. Adding fresh flowers or leaves to strained infusions makes for a more interesting confit. Try:

– Lapsang Souchong and Rosemary for a smoky-flavored green gel.

– Vanilla Tea confit with fresh seeds from a vanilla pod added.

– Leaves of Provence Tea Gelée with additional linden or tilleul flowers added.

– The burnt red color of African Amber Gelée with suspensions of gold leaf, firm set and cut into small cubes for use with white fish or chicken dishes.

The basic recipe ratio for edible flower or leaf gelée or gel is:

1 part water, 1 part flowers or leaves, 2 parts sugar and $1/8^{th}$ part acid (lemon juice or white wine vinegar). Pectin, gelatin, agar agar, gellan or any other jelling agent in the amount recommended by the manufacturer, depending on its properties for the amount of infused liquid and the set required. Try 1 ounce of pectin in the above ratio for a soft gelée if using 2 cups flowers. If the flower or leaves have an intense or overpowering flavor, reduce the flower to water ratio to 1:3 or experiment until the infusion is the color and flavor you desire. Varying the type and amount of setting agent will give you varying textures of gel set from soft to firm. Experiment a little to find what suits your intended use. For example, you might want a soft Rose Gelée to spoon over ice cream, toast, pancakes or waffles but a firmly set one like Turkish Delight to cube and arrange around a dessert or to accompany cheeses.

If you prefer gelée to be transparent and clean of plant matter, strain off the infused flowers and leaves. This will give a pure jelly with a longer shelf life. If you add fresh flowers and herbs in your gelée for texture, discard the infused matter and add some carefully selected, whole, clean, specimens that have perfect color and shape. Remember to wash and blanch fresh leaves and flowers in boiling water before adding to the jelly just before bottling or serving. Fresh matter in the gel will shorten its use-by date and it should be used as soon as possible before they deteriorate.

If you wish to intensify your gelée color further, dip the end of a wooden toothpick in a natural food-grade dye and swirl into the gel in its final heating stage, but be careful, the color needs to be pure, clear and delicate to be realistic. An alternative is to take a little citrus zest and/or a skin peeling of the plant where possible, wrap in a little infusing bag and use it in the steeping process with the leaves or flowers before cooking. It must be discarded before cooking to avoid bitterness.

You can also add food-grade powdered or flaked Silver or Gold. Imagine the palest pink rose gel with suspended Gold Leaf flakes, or the softest lime green basil gelée with Silver Leaf flakes. If you are experienced handling the fragile sheets of gold and silver leaf, you can try setting your flower or herb gelée in thin layers with perfect sheets of Gold or Silver in between or on top. Use a shallow, plastic-wrap lined dish to make it easier to turn out or remove the set gel. Dice into small or larger shapes/sheets depending on the effect required. Use in any way you can think of, to garnish hot or cold consommé or soups, in salads, with mains or desserts. You could even pour your flower gelée into the base of a cake tin to cover it, maybe add fresh petals or buds, set in the fridge, then pour in a cheese cake or dessert mix, or make a no-bake cake with a crumb base and after setting again, turn it out with the gel layer on top.

If you make a firm-set gelée by adding more pectin or jelling agent it can be cut with a knife into cubes, slim ribbons or made into shapes using mini cutters. Serve it nude or dusted in castor or powdered sugar. One of the better-known solid-set flower gelées is Turkish Delight, that sweet exotic rose flower flavored gel dusted in powdered confectioner's sugar. Try some of the different types of jelling agents to achieve the textures you prefer. The better quality firm-set gelées are the ones that are melt-in–the-mouth soft, and even though they are set enough to solidify, they melt to a sauce consistency with a little mouth heat. The sign of a skilled artisan.

BERRY FRUIT GELÉE ....

Heat, melt and simmer, sugar, water, macerated berries, muscat dessert wine or sauterne or sweet wine in a ratio of 1:1:2:2. Bloom 3 tablespoons of gelatin in 5 tablespoons of cold water for every 3 cups of liquid. Add fresh berries. Refrigerate until set and cut into cubes.

CACTUS GELÉE ....

3 cups cactus juice extracted by cooking de-spined, chopped, prickly pear fruit in water. You'll need about a kilogram of the magenta coloured fruit and just over 2 tablespoons or less liquid pectin, depending on how soft you want your gelée. Use 2 tablespoons lemon juice or a teaspoon of citric acid, and 3 cups sugar. Simmer fresh fruit with 2-3 cups water until tender and soft. Mash or blend and strain out the seeds, flesh and skins. If you don't have 3 cups of juice return the mashed cactus to the pan, add extra water, re-simmer and re-strain. Heat the 3 cups of juice and pectin to a slow boil, add the sugar very slowly, stirring and keeping up a slow, rolling boil. Boil for a few minutes, cool a few

minutes, add lemon juice or citric acid and bottle. Make a firmer gel for cutting shapes to replace a sauce, or set to a soft gel or pouring sauce for desserts or meat. Cactus gelée has a rich, fruity watermelon-strawberry-toffee-apple flavor and a beautiful deep red colour. For cheese, desserts, meats, poultry or on toast/bread.

CHAMPAGNE GELÉE ....

Bloom 3 teaspoons powdered gelatin in 1 cup champagne in a pan for 10 minutes. Heat gently and add 1 cup of sugar, stirring gently until dissolved. Tip into a bowl, add 2 more cups cold champagne and a small squeeze of lemon juice. Cool for 15 minutes, skim off any foam, and pour into a shallow pan lined with plastic wrap. Cool in fridge until set. Cut into squares or shapes to serve. When cool but before set try adding additions like gold or silver leaf, fine herb leaves, micro greens, edible flowers, finger lime or raspberry nodes. For sweet or savory foods.

CHOCOLATE GELÉE ....

½ liter of milk
120 grams dark chocolate (55-66% cocoa), finely cut
1.8 grams agar agar powder
Warm the milk and chocolate in a saucepan over low heat and stir until the chocolate is melted. Whisk in the agar agar until it dissolves then increase heat to the boil and simmer for a minute, stirring constantly. Pour into a mold, set at room temperature then refrigerate. Unmold, cube, ribbon or cut and serve.

CITRUS GELÉE ....

Heat, melt and simmer, sugar, water, orange juice, muscat dessert wine or sauterne or sweet wine in a ratio of 1:1:2:2. Bloom 3 tablespoons of gelatin in 5 tablespoons of cold water for every 3 cups of liquid. Add peeled, de-pithed, segmented and finely sliced pieces of fruit from citrus such as pink grapefruit, blood orange, tangerine, orange and/or lemon. Refrigerate until set and cut into cubes.

CUCUMBER GELÉE ....

5 gelatin sheets or 14 grams of powdered
2 long cucumbers cut lengthwise and de-seeded
8 grams of sugar and a pinch of good salt
Juice cucumber flesh in a juicer or blitz and strain the purée. Use a little of the juice to bloom the powdered gelatin then heat gently to liquefy. If using sheets, soak in water for 5 minutes, squeeze, then heat with the juice, whisking until dissolved with the sugar and salt. Line a shallow container with plastic wrap, pour in the gelée and set in the fridge until firm. Cut to required shapes. Alternatively pour a thin layer of liquid onto your plating plates, allow to set and then place your salads, meats etc. on top of the thin cucumber gelée layer.

JAPANESE SOY SAUCE GELÉE ....

Mix 6 tablespoons Japanese soy sauce, 6 tablespoons boiling water, 4 of white wine or mirin, 2 of sugar with ½ teaspoon of gelatin in a plastic container and stir until the gelatin dissolves. Refrigerate until it sets.

JUNIPER BERRY GELÉE OR GELÉE DE GENIÈVRE ....

Simmer 15 juniper berries in 2 cups of sweetened apple juice or cider with 3 tablespoons of sugar until soft. Blitz in a food processor or blender and strain. Return to the heat with a squeeze of lemon or orange juice and ½ teaspoon of gelatin or the equivalent of a setting agent of your choice. Cool to a soft gel. Serve with game and meat.

LAVENDER GELÉE ....

Simmer 3 cups water with ½ cup dried lavender flowers for 10 minutes, strain, return to heat and add juice of 1 lemon and 6 tablespoons liquid pectin. Stir, add in 2 cups sugar and then boil for 2 minutes for a soft gel or 4 minutes for a medium gel. Test for jelling thickness by placing a teaspoon of mix on a plate and into the freezer to cool for a minute or two. If it's too runny add another teaspoon of pectin and boil another minute before testing. Use for desserts, cakes, game, chicken and meats.

MINT GELÉE ....

Cut 4 green cooking apples (like Granny Smiths) leaving the skin on and seeds in. Bring to the boil with 2 cups of chopped mint leaves, 4 cups of water, a tablespoon of liquid pectin and the juice of 1 lemon (or replace lemon with ½ teaspoon of citric acid). Cook until the mint and apples are mushy and extract maximum flavor by squashing, then strain through a fine sieve, jelly bag or cloth, squeezing gently to allowing the mix to drip slowly. Measure your sieved liquid and return to the pan with sugar in a ratio of ½ kilogram of sugar to every liter of liquid. Reheat and boil until testing a teaspoonful by placing in the freezer indicates it has reached a point of setting to a loose gelée. Allow to cool slightly before stirring in additional finely-chopped mint leaves in a quantity that appeals to you.

PEAR GELÉE ....

3 cups pear purée

2 cups caster or superfine sugar

1 cup water

2 tablespoons lemon juice

2 tablespoons liquid pectin for a soft gelée, 3 for slightly thicker

Boil the sugar and water, add the purée and lemon juice and stir in the pectin then simmer until it reduces and begins to thicken, remembering it will jell as it cools.

PINEAPPLE GELÉE ....

Bloom 2 teaspoons gelatin in 8 tablespoons of pineapple juice. Heat gently with two additional cups of pineapple juice. Taste, adjust sweetness (sugar) or savory (salt) if needed. Set in a thin sheet before cutting into shapes or set in a mold.

PORT WINE GELÉE ....

Heat, melt and simmer 2 cups of your best port (ruby is good) with a squeeze of lemon or orange juice and 4 tablespoons of sugar. Bloom 2 tablespoons gelatin in 4 of water then add the softened gelatin to the port mix and simmer for a few minutes to reduce. Strain if needed and cool to a soft gel or set to a firm cutting gel depending on use. Use with desserts (soft) or meats and poultry (cubed or set in a thin sheet on the base of the serving plate). The port wine can be replaced by cranberry, pomegranate or cherry juice.

PRESERVED LEMON GELÉE ....

When whole cut lemons are packed into jars and preserved in lemon juice and salt for a few weeks, their sharp and bitter taste transforms into a pungent and sweet delight. If left longer, for a few months, the salty lemon juice turns into a soft gelée. There is a short cut way to imitate this amazing preserved lemon gelée if you don't want to wait. Bloom 3 tablespoons of gelatin in 5 tablespoons of water for 5-10 minutes or use the equivalent alternative jelling agent strength for a soft gel. Heat 3 cups of lemon juice, add 1 cup of finely minced or chopped preserved lemons, half a cup of sugar and 1 teaspoon of salt. When it comes to a boil add the bloomed gelatin and stir for a few minutes. Cool slightly and pour into sterilized jars to keep.

RED CAPSICUM GELÉE ....
3 red bell pepper capsicums + 1 teaspoon red chili flakes chopped in a food processor until very fine. Heat with 1 cup white wine vinegar, 1 tablespoon butter, a pinch of salt and 3 cups of sugar. Bring to a boil, stirring constantly and then add 3 tablespoons of pectin and it will thicken slightly. Cool before use.

SWEET WINE GELÉE ....
Heat, melt and simmer sugar, water, dessert wine and sweet wine in a ratio of 1:1:2:3. Bloom 3 tablespoons of gelatin in 5 tablespoons of cold water for every 3 cups of liquid. Add to the warm liquid until dissolved and cool in a thin layer in a dish until set. Cut into small cubes and use with desserts and cheese.

YUZU GELÉE ....
Bloom 1 teaspoon powdered gelatin in 4 tablespoons water. Heat gently with 1 cup of Dashi and 2 tablespoons of yuzu* juice. Adjust flavor with salt or sugar if needed.
* Yuzu is a Japanese citrus but a mix of lemon/lime juice is similar.

GLACES ....

"I want to do my share, you know that, Archie, but I can't make good glace de viande if I have to be watching murderers."
—Fritz the Chef, *Kill Now–Pay Later* (Rex Stout, 1961)

DEFINITION ....

Glace is a French cooking term meaning a glaze. Glace sauces can be either sweet or savory and are used as coating sauces. Sweet Glace sauces usually have a sweetener added that makes the sauce shine when reduced and concentrated. Savory Glace also glisten, usually from the breaking down of fine fat molecules and meat gelatins.

ASIAN ....

Quick Basic: Heat, melt and simmer 2 tablespoons each of palm or brown sugar, mirin and a good quality oil, then add 1 tablespoon each of chopped or crushed garlic, ginger root, red chili, lime zest and lime juice and 8 tablespoons of soy sauce. For glazing roast chicken, duck, lamb, pork, beef, spare ribs, chicken wings, and pumpkin

Teriyaki: Heat, melt and simmer ½ cup sugar, 2 cups of soy sauce with 1 cup each of water, mirin and rice wine. Then add 1 cup of orange juice + the zest of the oranges. Simmer for 45 minutes until it reaches the glace stage. Bottle and refrigerate.

See also our recipe for Lacquered Duck or Chicken at **TheCulinaryLibrary.com**

BALSAMIC ....

Heat, melt and simmer 4 cups of Balsamic vinegar, 1 cup sugar and 1 cup soy sauce. Reduce slowly to about a ¼ or until it thickens to the consistency you want. Taste. Add more sugar or a splash of lemon if required. Bottle. This keeps for months in the fridge.

BBQ ....

Heat, melt and simmer 2 tablespoons each of molasses or brown sugar, tomato ketchup, Dijon mustard and a good quality oil, 1 tablespoon each of chopped or crushed garlic, ginger root, red chili or chili sauce, orange zest and orange juice, 8 tablespoons of white vinegar. For glazing roast chicken, duck, lamb, pork, beef, spare ribs, chicken wings, and pumpkin.

CACTUS GLACE ....

Make the Cactus Gelée recipe without the pectin and boil longer to reduce the liquid to a deep red syrup. Add a little butter before using. Amazing deep red, rich fruity glaze with tastes of watermelon, strawberry and toffee apple. For all meats including, game, duck, and poultry.

DEMI-GLACE ....

Demi-glace is a rich reduction sauce made by combining and reducing the mother sauce Espagnole and veal stock. The classic version is Escoffier's recipe, but his version is too complex, time consuming and expensive for today's home cooks. The following recipe still takes a little time but is easily achievable. You need only make it once or twice a year and then freeze until needed.

1. Make a Basic Veal or Brown Stock: Place cut up veal and/or beef marrow bones (small ossobuco cuts are good) in an oven pan and

roast at 180°C or 450°F for an hour, turning occasionally and not burning. Remove from oven and pour over tomato paste slurried down with water. Cover with finely chopped onion, carrot and celery. Cover and return to the oven for 30 minutes. Transfer to the top of the stove, remove excess fat and deglaze the pan with a generous splash of red wine, making sure to scrape up all the pan juices. Move everything to a big pot, cover with water (for a final product of 4 liters add around 6-8 liters now), add salt, pepper and a bouquet garni and reduce on a gentle heat until the meat falls from the bone. Strain the solids from the stock.

2. Make an Espagnole sauce: Heat 4 tablespoons butter in a pot and add 4 tablespoons flour, stir the roux and color gently until it turns golden brown and has a nutty smell. Add 2 liters of your brown stock, stir until it thickens then simmer on low heat. In a separate pan, sauté until soft one cup each of finely chopped onion, carrot and celery in butter/oil. Add pepper, salt and 2 good tablespoons of tomato purée. Cook gently for a few minutes then add to the stock. Simmer gently until the Espagnole has reduced by half. Skim if necessary then strain.

3. Espagonole + Brown Stock = Glace: Return the Espagnole to the pot with another 2 liters of your brown stock and a new bouquet garni and reduce gently for 45-60 minutes until you have about half a liter of rich glace. Strain, taste and adjust seasoning. Freeze in ice cube trays until needed.

SEMI-DEMI-GLACE ....

Julia Child is credited with coining the word semi-demi-glace when she recommended slowly reducing 2 liters of beef or veal stock + 2 tablespoons red wine down to 1 cup of sauce. When it coats the back of a spoon it is said to be an acceptable compromise and substitute for demi-glace. We've tried this a few times with different stocks and each time have found the flavor lacks depth. Sautéing aromats like garlic, shallot, peppercorn and herbs first is recommended.

CAFÉ ....

Heat, melt and stir one cup of boiling milk, ½ cup strong black espresso coffee and 2 tablespoons of sugar. Off the heat, whisk in 2 egg yolks and stir over gentle heat until cooked and thickened.

CHOCOLATE ....

Heat 1 cup cream to boiling then pour over 8 ounces of chopped bittersweet chocolate. Beat or whisk until shiny. Add essence of Orange, Truffle or Mint if you like. Good for dipping madeleines, churros, fresh or dried fruit, cup cakes, bananas, marshmallows, or Turkish delight.

CITRUS ....

Heat, melt and simmer 2 tablespoons each of sugar and water, 1 cup of orange muscat dessert wine and 1 cup of sauterne or sweet wine. Add ½ cup peeled, de-pithed, segmented and finely sliced pieces of fruit from any citrus such as pink grapefruit, blood orange, tangerine, orange and/or lemon, and a teaspoon of citrus zest. When reduced by half, pass through a sieve, mouli or blender and then return to the heat and thicken slightly with arrowroot slurry or a hydrocolloid of your choice. When slightly cooled, flavor and color can be added in the form of chopped chives, micro-greens or mint, gold or silver leaf or crystallized edible flowers. For fish, chicken, duck, spicy foods, desserts and puddings.

GLACE DE VIANDE ....
Before the Nouvelle Cuisine movement embraced Demi-glace, Glace de Viande was popular. Make a Veal Stock recipe and reduce it up to 10 times its original volume. This super-concentrate was sometimes cut with a little butter before serving.

GLACE SAUCE FOR CAKES ....
Sieve 2 cups of pure icing/powdered sugar and add 2 tablespoons of cream or milk or fruit juice, 4 tablespoons of melted butter and a splash of your favorite flavor extract like vanilla, almond, lemon, orange, coconut, cherry, cappuccino, rose, tangerine, praline etc. Beat until smooth and creamy, adding a little more liquid if needed to keep it thin. Add some optional zest.
Use only on cooled cakes, e.g. for dipping cupcakes in or drizzling over larger cakes.

HAM ....
Heat, melt and simmer 2 tablespoons of brown sugar and 2 tablespoons of maple syrup or honey, ½ cup fruit juice (pineapple, orange, apricot, mango) or water, a pinch each of salt and mixed spice and 2 teaspoons of Dijon mustard.
Glaze sauce for baking ham, lamb or chicken.

MUSHROOMS ....
Sauté your favorite mushrooms in butter and oil with finely chopped onion or shallots until soft. Add demi-glace and reduce further. Add a small splash of sherry and lemon juice, taste and adjust seasoning.

PRUNES ....

Heat, melt and simmer 2 cups red wine, 1 cup water, 10-15 pitted Dagen prunes, 1 tablespoon white balsamic vinegar or white wine, 3 tablespoons honey or brown sugar and a pinch each of ginger and cinnamon. When reduced by half push gently through a sieve then reheat and thicken with a little beurre manié or arrowroot slurry. For pork, duck or lamb.

VANILLE ....

Heat, melt and bring to a boil then simmer 500 grams of caster sugar, 1 tablespoon glucose syrup and 5 teaspoons water until it turns a golden color. To stop the cooking process, immerse the pan bottom very, very gently in cold water. Add 2 teaspoons of vanilla paste and 100 ml cream. If you want to turn your glace sauce into hard crack for spinning lattices, baskets, springs or creating spiked hazelnuts then just increase the water to 100ml. Spin when slightly cooled.

JUS ....

DEFINITION ....

Jus is a sauce usually incorporating the juices from cooked foods like roasted meats, deglazed in the pan with stock or wine, flavored with herbs or vegetable mirepoix and reduced to intensify flavor. It is then strained and seasoned but not thickened. See also reduction sauces.

JUS GRAS ....

Jus gras is made from chicken, usually the cuts with the most skin and bones like the wings or thighs. Sauté 1 kilogram of chicken pieces with skin on in hot oil until browned, then drain excess oil and save. Add 2 chopped shallots, 2 chopped garlic cloves, a few peppercorn, a sprig of fresh thyme, 2 bay leaves and 1 liter of chicken stock to the pan with the chicken pieces. Simmer slowly uncovered for an hour or so, topping up the stock if needed. Let the sauce sieve itself slowly in a colander over a bowl pushing down occasionally on the chicken. Add the saved chicken fat and re-sieve the jus through clean muslin.

JUS LIÉ ....

Jus lié is made from veal stock and is essentially a demi-glace without the espagnole sauce and for this reason Julia Child called it a semi-demi-glace.

RED WINE JUS ....

2:1:1 red wine + beef stock + chicken stock, e.g. 250 ml dry red wine, 125 ml beef stock, 125 ml chicken stock, 2 cloves garlic and a sprig of rosemary. Simmer until reduced to a thin sauce consistency. Season & sieve. Serve warm or hot with an optional finishing butter whisked in to add gloss, or with chopped chives added.

ROASTING PAN JUS ....

After roasted meat or fowl has been removed from the baking pan, heat the pan juices including the fat and caramelize (if they have not already) on top of the stove. Add ½ cup stock, water or broth and deglaze the pan, scraping the bottom fond well. Strain, remove the fat that rises to the top and spoon the liquid over the plated dish. Because jus is intense, a tablespoon or two is usually enough per serve.

You can add other flavors to your jus if you prefer, either before the liquid reduces (e.g. garlic, rosemary, onion, mustard, chili, lemon grass, mushroom, soy, balsamic, butter, horseradish, wasabi, juniper berry etc.) or after the liquid has reduced (e.g. citrus zest or segments, pomegranate arils, baby capers or soft herbs like tarragon, parsley, chives, basil, chervil etc.)

WHITE WINE JUS

Sauté shallots or onions in oil and butter until soft and colored. Add crushed garlic and herbs, cook a further 2-3 minutes then add white wine and reduce by half. Add the same quantity of veal glaze and reduce to a sauce consistency. Season with salt and pepper and add a splash of balsamic vinegar for acidity. Sieve and use warm or hot.

SOILS

DEFINITION

Culinary 'soils' are associated with the molecular gastronomy movement and are foods that have been dehydrated by heat or chemicals then crushed to imitate the texture and appearance of soil or dirt. Japanese chef Yoshihiro Narisawa, Noma restaurant in Denmark, El Bulli, Joan Roca's restaurant in Spain and Heston Blumenthal in England have all invented and used their own 'soils'. Ingredients like beets, mushrooms, olives, oils and sauces have all been re-invented as soils and used as replacements for traditional sauces. They don't meet the definition of 'wet' as they are just the opposite, but they do fulfill the role of a sauce, accompanying other foods as partners.

Tips and Tricks when making Soils:

–Dry your fresh ingredients either in a food dehydrator or conventional oven at 65°C (150°F) for 12-24 hours depending on type and size until dry and brittle.

–As soon as soft, fine soils come into contact with liquid or heat they begin to melt. You want this to happen on the tongue, so don't serve around wet foods.

–Liquids with high fat content can be powdered by mixing with tapioca maltodextrin. Texture is achieved using a food processor or tami (drum sieve with flat paddle).

For online ordering of tapioca maltodextrin try Amazon.com, or:

Australia: melbournefooddepot.com

UK: creamsupplies.co.uk

USA: modernistpantry.com; lepicerie.com; bulkfoods.com

MUSHROOM SOIL ....

Place dried mushrooms in a blender or food processor and blitz.

NUTELLA SOIL ....

90 grams (3 ounces) Nutella chocolate-hazelnut paste

60 grams (2 ounces) tapioca maltodextrin

Whisk together manually or in a food processor then sieve.

OLIVE SOIL ....

Drain, de-stone, halve and dry 1 or 2 cups olives (black olives are good) until crunchy. Grind or crush in the food processor or mortar & pestle.

OLIVE OIL SOIL ....

This process works for all edible fats and oils. See Volume 1 of *The Culinary Library*, *Alchemy of the Mortar & Pestle*, for the chapter describing edible oils. Mix 5 tablespoons olive oil with 1½ tablespoons tapioca maltodextrin and a pinch of salt and stir until it powders. To make it fluffier just sieve. Keep in a sealed container. For breads, peeled tomatoes, cheese, chicken, fish, vegetables, eggs.

PEANUT SOIL ....

90 g (3 ounces) smooth peanut paste
60 g (2 ounces) tapioca maltodextrin
Whisk together manually or in a food processor then sieve.

SALTED CARAMEL SOIL ....

Make a basic caramel first using:
350 grams (12.3 ounces) sugar
365 grams (12.9 ounces) glucose
500 grams (1lb 1.6 ounces) heavy cream
100 grams (3.5 ounces) butter
Heat all ingredients together then cool in a greased tray or on a silicon mat. Blitz in a food processor with tapioca maltodextrin (65 grams for every 200 grams caramel). Before using add a pinch of finishing salt.

SAND ....

6 grams (0.2 ounces) kombu seaweed
80 grams (2.8 ounces) tapioca maltodextrin
25 grams (0.9 ounces) sweet biscuit like shortbread biscuit

30 grams (1 ounce) panko breadcrumbs, toasted with anchovy in a little oil

finishing salt to taste

Blend all ingredients together.

YOGHURT SOIL ....

1 cup vanilla yogurt

2 cups tapioca maltodextrin

Mix with a fork until thoroughly incorporated and a powder consistency is reached. You might need more or less tapioca powder depending on the fat content of the yoghurt. You can add a few tablespoons of orange blossom water or rose water to the yoghurt first for a flavor variation.

FOAMS & ESPUMAS

———•◆•———

*"A meringue is really nothing but a foam. And what is
a foam after all, but a big collection of bubbles?
And what's a bubble? It's basically a very flimsy little
latticework of proteins draped with water. We add
sugar to this structure, which strengthens it.
But things can, and do, go wrong."*
–ALTON BROWN

DEFINITION ....

Espuma is a Spanish word meaning a dense hot or warm foam or
froth. Introducing air or gas bubbles into a thin or thick liquid and
holding it there, often with the help of a stabilizer, produces
culinary foams and espumas. They can be made by hand-beating
liquids with a fork or whisk, using a stick blender, electric beaters
or food processor, or by forcing air or gas through them.

Don't be afraid of making foams, they're rather fun and not
scary at all and most of us began making them when we were kids
when we blew through our straw into milkshakes. Baristas make
foam every day with their coffee machines which blow steam
through milk to make froth. Meringue, soufflé, mousses, bread and
cakes are all just foams set by heat or cold and held firm by
stabilizers like cream of tartar, baking powder, fat, sugar and yeast.
In our view, foams definitely meet the criteria for inclusions in our
book on sauces. They have the same, although slightly more

flamboyant, culinary role as traditional sauces; they add flavor without significant substance, allowing cooks to introduce new flavors and startling new textures without changing the original dish.

The technique of making culinary foams is not new. Historically, it began in the 1700s when cooks began making sweet and savory foams by beating air into eggs, calling these soufflés. Today, culinary foams are associated with the work of Chef Ferran Adria from El Bulli restaurant in Spain. He first used a whipper syphon with nitrous oxide gas bulbs (non fizzy), instead of carbon dioxide (fizzy) to produce a range of both savory and sweet foams. The newer syphon food-foams include espresso, mushroom, beet, olive oil and coconut. If you want to try making these new whipper-syphon foams, which are the subject of this chapter, you're going to need to invest in a whipper-syphon.

There are several manufacturers on the market but we use and recommend the iSi brand. There are three main types of iSi to choose from: the Cream Profi, made for handling cream based sauces; the Gourmet Whip which is a good all-rounder for home cooks; and the Thermal Whip, which keeps hot or cold foams at temperature for hours, useful for restaurants. There are 2 main sizes, the ½ liter and the 1 liter models and for home cooks the ½ liter is going to meet most of your needs and will fit on your fridge shelf whereas the 1 liter may not.

Tips & Tricks when making foams:
- If you buy a ½ liter capacity whipper it charges with one cartridge or bulb of gas and a 1 liter capacity will charge with 2 cartridges. Generally the more gas used the more expensive it will be, but also the airier and less glossy your foam.

- A stabilizing agent like a thickener or jelling agent is needed in your liquids before you foam them. This stops them collapsing and holds their structure after plating. Some will be intrinsic to your ingredients but some you will have to add.

  For cold foams these options include starch, gelatin, eggs, agar agar, lecithin (good for juices and watery liquids used at 6% volume), fat, butter, cream, yoghurt, crème fraiche or milk (50-65°C is ideal). When not using dairy use gelatin at the rate of 2 leaves per ½ liter, it makes a shinier and better cold foam than agar agar in our experience.

  For hot foams the options include fat or starch, butter, cream, yoghurt, crème fraiche and milk, agar agar (because it stays jelled at higher temperatures than gelatin) and xantham gum (used at a concentration of 0.2-0.8%)

- Liquids to be foamed need more seasoning and stronger flavors than you would normally add because they are going to double in volume after foaming.

- Foam texture is determined by the amount of liquid in your mixture and the size and quantity of gas bubbles you induce. Hand whipping gives lighter foam and gas charges give denser foam similar to a mousse. Small bubbles give fine foam and large ones coarse foam; more liquid gives wetter foam, less liquid, dryer foam.

  Fine bubbles introduced by gas charger or strong whipping + a wet mixture = a dense foam e.g. whipped cream.

  Coarse bubbles + a wet mixture = coarse foam or froth.

  Course bubbles (whipping) + a dry mixture = light foams called 'airs'.

- Bubble structures, solidified using heat and/or dehydration = set foams like soufflé, mousses or bread.
- Foam structure in the iSi changes with shaking so shake lightly, try, then shake more.
- Lighter foams that are often baked or dehydrated to set their structure = meringues and choux puffs
- All particles must be strained from the liquid to be foamed. Anything that passes through the iSi strainer funnel will be fine, so invest in one of these. Any larger particles, once in the whipper, will clog the release mechanism. You will only know this after your whipper is charged but won't release the foam. Releasing the gas of a blocked whipper under pressure must be done carefully. There are two ways to do this safely:

  −By unscrewing the top a little at a time until you hear the pressure releasing, if you unscrew the top in one movement there *will* be a mess and there *will* be pain if the lid hits you on its way up.

  −By removing the threaded dispensing nozzle you can apply a firm pressure to the spring valve that will allow the pressure to release.

  Once you've cleaned the valve of blockages, with the brush that comes with the unit, and re-strained your mix, you can re-pressurize and start using.
- Use powdered pepper rather than ground pepper in your foams.
- Although foams are primarily used in the same role as traditional sauces, either as a garnish or accompaniment, they can also be further garnished themselves but you'll need to be inventive and find something lighter than the foam to avoid collapsing its structure. Try Flowers or Micro Greens

(see *Edible Flowers and Leaves, The Culinary Library*, Volume 2, for ideas), panko crumbs, dried black olive, finely chopped capers, bonito flakes, cracked black or pink pepper, powdered or crystalized food additives, jelly crystals, shaved chocolate or coconut.

The following recipes will serve 8 as garnishes or accompaniments and most can be made in a ½ liter whipper with one charge of gas.

AVOCADO FOAM ....
Bloom 5 grams of powdered gelatine in ¾ cup warm water for 5 minutes. Heat ¾ cup thick of double cream to a simmer and then add the gelatine water and stir until the gelatine is melted. Blitz the cream with a blender or food processor with 2 peeled, deseeded avocados, pepper and salt and a squeeze of lemon juice. Sieve, pour into an iSi whipper, charge and shake. Use while it is still warm or put the iSi in the fridge for a couple of hours and use cold. Serve with fish, chicken, vegetables like asparagus or beans, smoked salmon or with bruschetta or pasta.

BANANA FOAM ....
Blend together 1 ripe banana, ½ cup skim milk and ½ teaspoon sugar. Sprinkle with 3 grams of powdered gelatin and bloom for 5 minutes. Heat gently for a few minutes, stirring to dissolve the gelatin. Take off the heat and add ½ cup thick or heavy cream or crème fraiche. Sieve and pour into an iSi whipper. Charge and shake. Put in the fridge for a couple of hours and use cold. For desserts like banana split, trifle, stewed fruits, meringues, cakes, hot caramel or chocolate puddings.

BASIL FOAM ....

Mix 2 cups fresh basil leaves with 1 cup olive oil and purée in a blender. Season to taste with salt and pepper. Pour through an iSi funnel and sieve directly into a ½ liter iSi whip. Charge with one iSi cream charger and shake vigorously. Cool before use.

CHIPOTLE FOAM ....

½ cup of chipotle peppers in adobo sauce, diced
1 cup sour cream or soft cream cheese
½ cup thick cream
1 lime or lemon, juice only for foam, zest for garnish
Purée, sieve, and pour into a ½ liter iSi whipper. Charge once, shake, and chill in the fridge before use.

CHORIZO FOAM ....

1 cup chorizo, either minced or finely diced, Macédoine (¼" cubes)
500 milliliters cream or crème fraiche
100 milliliters milk
1 teaspoon agar agar
Sauté chorizo on medium heat until colored but not crisp, add in the cream, milk, agar agar and simmer, then purée and strain, pushing down a little with the back of a wooden spoon to extract flavor. Pour into iSi, charge, and shake.

COCONUT FOAM ....

Make a sugar syrup in a saucepan using 2 tablespoons sugar and 2 tablespoons water, boiling until the sugar dissolves. Remove from heat. Bloom 3.5 grams of gelatin powder on top of 400 grams of coconut cream and after a few minutes add to the sugar syrup and stir to dissolve the gelatin. Pour into the iSi whip and charge with N_2O. Shake vigorously. Refrigerate 2 hours before use.

GARLIC FOAM ....

Sauté 8 garlic cloves gently in a little olive oil, add 2 cups of milk and bring to a boil then simmer until the milk reduces by half. Add 300 milliliters of thick/double cream and 2 bay leaves or a bouquet garni and bring to the boil. Turn off the heat, season with salt and pepper, cover and infuse for 10 minutes. Sieve, pour into the iSi whip, charge, shake and refrigerate for 12 hours.

GOATS CHEESE OR FETA CHEESE FOAM ....

Blend 250 grams soft goat cheese or soft Persian or Danish feta, 125 grams sour cream, 2 tablespoons olive oil and some fresh herbs in the food processor or blender. Add 125 milliliters of thick or double cream, salt and pepper. Sieve, add to whipper, charge and shake. Refrigerate 1 hour before use.

HORSERADISH FOAM ....

½ cup milk
½ cup cream
½ cup cream cheese
½ cup commercially prepared horseradish
½ tablespoon cider vinegar
salt and pepper
Warm all ingredients to a gentle simmer, sieve into a 1 liter Thermo iSi, charge, shake, charge again, shake and serve hot with roasts and meat.

MUSSEL FOAM ....

1 kilogram (2 pounds) of fresh mussels
2 cups dry white wine
4 garlic cloves, crushed
2 shallots or spring onions, chopped
1 stick of celery, finely chopped
1 sprig of dill or French tarragon
Lecithin powder, 1 leaf per 250 ml or 1 gram powdered per 125 ml
salt and pepper
Bring all ingredients except shellfish and lecithin to a boil, then add the mussels and cook with the lid on until they open. Strain off the liquid, dissolve in the lecithin, pour into iSi, charge, and shake. Serve on the cooked mussels on a half shell. Garnish foam with a small sprig of dill.

OLIVE OIL FOAM ....

Heat 200 grams extra virgin olive oil with 16 grams glycerin flakes on a gentle heat until they reach 60°C, stirring until the flakes dissolve. Season well with salt then pour into the iSi whip. Charge and shake. Use warm. If you want to reuse at a later date, reheat the syphon in a double boiler until it reaches 32°C.

PARMESAN CHEESE FOAM ....

300 grams freshly grated parmesan cheese
200 milliliters milk
1/2 liter cream
1/2 teaspoon agar agar
Heat cheese, milk and cream until melted, add agar agar and bring to a boil then strain, cool, charge once and shake.

SAFRON FOAM ....

100 milliliters each white wine and vegetable stock
200 milliliters cream
50 milliliters Noilly Prat
1 teaspoon ground saffron
salt, pepper and sugar to taste
Bring the two wines and stock to a boil, season with salt, pepper, and sugar. Off the heat, stir in the cream and saffron powder. Sieve, pour into your iSi whipper, charge, and shake.

SPINACH, CHARD OR KALE FOAM ....

Sauté 1 tablespoon diced shallots and 1 garlic clove with 250 grams freshly chopped spinach, chard or kale then add 100 milliliters of chicken stock. Blend in the blender or food processor. Push through a fine sieve, add 150 milliliters heavy/thick cream, pepper & salt and pour into iSi whip. Charge. Shake. Chill 2-3 hours before cold use. If using warm serve immediately or re-warm in a bain marie to 70°C.

WASABI FOAM ....

For Wasabi Air: Mix the wasabi powder with a spoonful of water to create a paste. Using an immersion blender, mix the wasabi paste, the water and the rice vinegar in a high container wide enough to collect the air (about 25 cm). Add the lecithin powder and mix well. To produce best results, the mix needs to be cold. Place it in the fridge until one minute before you are ready to start plating and then produce the wasabi air. To produce the wasabi air, you will have to lift the blender to the upper part of the liquid surface to incorporate as much air as possible so that foam forms on the surface. Once you have enough foam on the surface, let it rest 1 minute so that the foam sets and the excess liquid is eliminated. Proceed to remove the foam with a slotted spoon and serve.

WATERMELON FOAM ....

½ liter fresh watermelon juice*

100 milliliters orange or lemon juice

2 sheets of gelatin or 2.5 grams of powdered gelatin

Soak sheet gelatin in cold water for 5-7 minutes, remove and squeeze and add to the juice. If using powdered gelatin bloom on your watermelon juice for 3-5 minutes. Heat the juice and gelatin until melted. Add to 1 liter canister, charge twice and shake.

* Any pulp-free and seed-free fruit, vegetable or citrus juice can be used in this recipe.

MODERN SAUCES

"Tomatoes and oregano make it Italian; wine and tarragon make it French; sour cream makes it Russian. Lemon and cinnamon make it Greek, soy sauce makes it Chinese, garlic makes it great."
—ALICE MAY BROCK

DEFINITION ....
Perhaps modern is too imprecise a word when applied to these Sauces but we use it in an attempt to distinguish the sauces in use today that are distinct from the old classic sauces developed in the

1800s. Traditional classic sauces derived flavor from a mirepoix of vegetables, usually carrot, celery and onion, sweated in fat and then simmered in stock. Modern sauces rely on herbs and aromats. Classic sauces used wine for their acid balance whereas modern sauces tend to use citrus, rice wine or vinegars. The use of rendered fats and butter has generally been replaced by the use of olive oil in modern sauces, which gives them a lighter mouth feel. This doesn't mean that modern sauces don't use wine, butter, roux and cream, simply less of them and not always all in the one sauce.

Some of the Asian, Mediterranean and Middle Eastern sauces are in this section not because they are recent inventions but because their spread and acceptance in Western cuisine is relatively new.

AVGOLEMONO ....

Chicken stock + lemon juice + egg.

3 eggs, separated

3 tablespoons lemon juice

2 cups warm broth or chicken stock

Beat the egg whites until foamy. Continue beating and add the yolks, lemon juice and then the warm broth or stock.

For stuffed cabbage and vine leaves, vegetables, meatballs and rice, soup, pasta, chicken, fish, pork, asparagus, roasts or eggs. Chopped herbs like dill, tarragon or chervil can be added.

CACTUS VINAIGRETTE ....

See also Cactus Glace. Make a cactus syrup and add to vinaigrette sauce. For salads, meats, fish, chicken or vegetables.

CASHEW ....

4 tablespoons vegetarian mushroom oyster sauce

2 cups roasted cashew nuts

2 cloves garlic, minced

3 cups mushroom, sliced

1 tablespoon each of light soy sauce and rice wine or mirin

1 piece each of long green and red chili, finely sliced

1 red capsicum, finely sliced

1 cup fried tofu, sliced into very thin squares

1 spring onion, finely sliced

chopped cilantro and green onion, for garnish

Fry chili peppers and garlic until soft, add vegetables and tofu and cook till tender. Stir in oyster and soy sauces and mirin or rice wine, then the nuts, and spring onion. Thin with a little water if needed, add fresh coriander and serve with chicken or beef strips that have been quickly stir-fried.

CHAMPAGNE ....

Blonde Roux (flour + butter, 1:1) + shallots + stock + champagne.

Sauté 2-3 chopped shallots or 1 mild onion in butter/oil until pale and translucent. Add 2 tablespoons each of butter and flour and make a roux, cooking until blonde. Add 300 milliliters of stock (fish or chicken depending on final use) and 300 milliliters of champagne. Simmer on a gentle heat and reduce by half and then add 300 milliliters of double/thick cream. Reduce to the desired thickness or until the sauce coats the back of a spoon. Season with finishing salt and white pepper. For fish, shellfish, crustaceans or chicken, veal.

CHIMICHURRI ....

Herbal, cold, thin and semi-solid, piquant, green.

Fresh herbs (parsley, coriander, thyme, oregano) + garlic + olive oil + acid (red wine vinegar, lime or lemon juice) + paprika.

Also known as Argentinian Sauce. Chop by hand or blend together in a food processor or blender 8 tablespoons chopped parsley, 3 tablespoons oregano and or coriander, 1 tablespoon thyme, 4 garlic cloves, 2 tablespoons paprika, 8 tablespoons olive oil, 6 tablespoons of red wine vinegar, 5 tablespoons warm water, and pinches of cayenne, pepper and salt. Serve cold.

For all grilled and BBQ meats, chicken, steak, lamb, sausages, vegetables, marinade, salad dressing.

COULIS ....

Fruit or vegetable, cold, thin or thick, sweet or savory, multi colored.

Fruit + sweetener if required, puréed and strained.

Cooked vegetables + butter or cream + seasoning, puréed and strained.

For desserts e.g. raspberry, strawberry, blackberry, mulberry, apricot, plum, prune, peach or mango coulis.

For meats, poultry, and fish and to garnish soups e.g. celeriac, pumpkin, sweet potato, pea or parsnip.

CUCUMBER RAITA ....

To 2 cups plain yoghurt add 1 teaspoon toasted cumin seeds, 1 crushed garlic clove, 2 tablespoons chopped coriander and mint and 1 large finely chopped and drained cucumber. Stir in a dash of fresh lemon juice and sprinkle with smoked paprika or cayenne.

GREEN PAPAYA SALAD SAUCE ....

Thai, cold, sweet, sour, salty, spicy.

Fish sauce + white vinegar + sugar + water + garlic + chili + lime juice.

Mix together 6 tablespoons each of fish sauce and white vinegar then add 4 tablespoons of sugar, 4 crushed garlic cloves, 3 thinly sliced red chilis, 2 tablespoons of lime juice. Stir in one cup of water. Pour all the sauce over a salad made from ½ green papaya and 2 carrots both shredded to julienne strips, 4 tablespoons each of fried red onion or Asian shallot and crushed roast peanuts. Finish with mint, basil and coriander.

GREMOLATA (MILAN) ....

Parsley + garlic + lemon.

Gremolata is a sauce made from finely mincing together parsley, garlic and lemon (zest and juice) in the proportions you prefer. Simply blitz, taste and adjust flavor and seasoning.

Serve with veal, fish or seafood.

GRIBICHE ....

Classic, motherless, cold, thick to semi-solid, herbal, salty, sharp, pale green.

Hard-boiled egg + oil + vinegar + cream + chopped capers and gherkins + parsley, tarragon and chervil.

Although we have listed Gribiche in the cold sauce chapter, we have included it here in more detail and with a recipe popular today.

2 medium eggs, hardboiled, yolks sieved, whites julienned

6 tablespoons mayonnaise

2 tablespoons cornichons, finely chopped

2 tablespoons baby capers, rinsed, drained (chop if using larger sizes)*
1 tablespoon white wine vinegar
2 tablespoons whipping cream
1 tablespoon each tarragon, chervil and parsley leaves, chopped
salt and black pepper
Traditionally for fish and seafood but good with vegetables and on bruschetta.

* In France, capers are classified by size:
< 7 mm = non-pareils
7–8 mm = surfines
8-9 mm = capucines
9-11 mm = capotes
11-13 mm = fines
> 14 mm = grusas
20 mm = caperberries (after caper buds flower they produce a fruit called a caperberry that when pickled are used in antipasti and mezzes)

HARISSA, MOROCCAN ....
Blend together 250 grams small hot red chili (stalks and seeds removed)
1 large red capsicum (stalks and seeds removed, roasted & peeled),
1 small preserved lemon, 2 garlic cloves, 1 small bunch coriander, 1 tablespoon ground cumin, a pinch of salt and a little water.
Serve with meat or vegetables or use as a marinade or dipping sauce.

HARISSA, GREEN ....

Blend together 2 jalapeño chilis, 2 spring onions, ½ cup Italian parsley, ½ cup coriander, juice of 1-2 lemons, 1 garlic clove, 1 tablespoon each of lightly toasted cumin and coriander seeds and ½ cup olive oil.

HOLLANDAISE (QUICK VERSION) ....

8 tablespoons unsalted butter, melted
3 egg yolks
1 tablespoon lemon juice
pinch of salt and a little white pepper
Blitz the egg yolks, lemon juice and salt in a blender on medium for about a minute or until light in colour. Then, blending on the low setting, slowly dribble in the hot melted butter and the sauce will thicken as it incorporates the butter. Taste, adjust salt, pepper and lemon balance and serve garnished with finely chopped chives or tarragon.

INDIAN MINT YOGHURT SAUCE ....

This is the thin sauce that most take-away Indian restaurants in Western countries serve, and is one of our favorite sauces. Mix 1 teaspoon of a good brand Kashmiri paste (Patak's works well), ¼ cup fine or caster sugar, 3 or more tablespoons of mint sauce (mint + sugar + vinegar) or mint jelly, ½ teaspoon chili powder and salt to taste. Bring to a slow boil until the sugar is dissolved. Blend in a blender or processor with 1 pint of milk and then add and blend 500 grams natural yoghurt. Adjust the salt. Serve at room temperature with pakoras, samosas, any spicy Indian foods or just about anything else you like.

MEXICAN MOLE COOK-IN SAUCE ....

Hot, semi-solid, sweet, spicy, red. Mole is probably Aztec in origin but has only recently been introduced to Western cookery as a cook-in sauce for pork, beef, chicken, lamb or sausages. Sauté hazelnuts and almonds (or peanuts) with garlic, onion, raisins, prunes, chili (reddish black, black or red), cinnamon and aniseed. Blitz to a paste adding a teaspoon of pure cocoa powder, taste, adjust flavors by adding more of any ingredient you prefer. Then add some grilled or fried tomatoes and thin with water. Sauté floured chicken pieces or steak in oil in a large pan, deglaze with a little stock or white wine, add the sauce, cover, and slow cook in the oven or on the stove top for a couple of hours, topping up the water if needed.

NACHO CHEESE ....

Melt 2 tablespoons of butter and stir in 2 tablespoons of flour until smooth, cook the roux for a minute or two then blend in 1 or 2 cups of milk depending on how thick or thin you want the cheese sauce. Whisk until smooth, add salt and pepper and a grating of nutmeg and/or hot smoked paprika and 1-1½ cups of grated tasty cheddar cheese.

ORANGE GINGER ....

1 orange, peeled and segmented
1 tablespoon fresh ginger, grated
3/4 cup each of orange juice and chicken stock
2 tablespoons coriander, chopped
1 tablespoon sugar
1 teaspoon sesame seeds
1 teaspoon sesame oil

finishing salt and pepper

Heat all ingredients and reduce by half, or alternatively heat and thicken with a little arrowroot slurry.

PARSLEY CREAM ....

In the early 1950s this would have meant a white Béchamel sauce with chopped parsley added, and in the '60s a Velouté with parsley, but the modern version of this sauce bears no resemblance to either. Firstly, it's a bright vibrant green. Use flat leaf Italian parsley (either raw or lightly blanched in boiling water and refreshed in cold water) and blitz it in the processor or blender with a little stock or coconut cream, olive oil, pine nuts, garlic, lemon, pepper and salt. Taste and balance.

For a slight twist we add a few drops of top quality fish sauce like Red Boat or Megachef at the very end which makes this sauce amazing. Use with everything from fish to chicken, steak and red meat, boiled or baked hams and corned meats, fried and deep fried foods, vegetables and pastas. You can also substitute or add chervil, basil, rocket, baby spinach, chives or tarragon and for a bitter twist we use frisée chicory (sometimes called frisée or frieze lettuce).

PESTO ....

Blitz together fresh herbs (basil, coriander, parsley, sorrel or baby spinach) + nuts (pine, cashew, walnut or brazil) + olive oil + garlic + parmesan cheese.

Of Italian origin, pesto is thought to have originated in Genoa in Liguria and the original is made from basil and pine nuts. Today most cooks are willing to embrace variation and use alternative herbs and nuts for their pesto. Best known as a sauce for pasta, it is also good on pizza, bruschetta, fish, gnocchi and vegetables.

RAREBIT ....

If you like cheese fondue but don't have a budget for Gruyere or Emmenthal cheese then why not make the English version with cheddar? It's not exactly modern and has a roux as a base, but it's a sauce that deserves to be made and eaten more often. It's so incredibly easy to make from fridge and pantry staples and with crusty bread makes a great winter lunch or Sunday dinner when you can't be bothered cooking but want something hot, filling and tasty. Simply make a roux with 2 tablespoons each of butter and flour in a saucepan, add 1 to 2 cups of shredded cheese, 1 teaspoon each of Dijon mustard and Worcestershire sauce, and a pinch of pepper and salt. Then add 1 cup or a little more of liquid. You can choose between milk, milk and cream or cream and ale/beer. Stir while melting and taste. Add a pinch of cayenne pepper or smoked paprika. Serve hot on toast or crusty bread and brown under the grill or broiler if you like. Good plain or with eggs, beans, avocado, smoked salmon, sausages, ham, bacon, chorizo or with a fresh green salad on the side.

ROMESCO ....

Blend together 1 large red capsicum (stalks and seeds removed, roasted & peeled), 1 clove garlic, 2 tablespoons each of Italian parsley, sherry vinegar, tomato purée and peeled almonds, 1 teaspoon smoked paprika, ½ teaspoon cayenne pepper, ½ cup olive oil, salt and pepper. For pasta, vegetables, fish, seafood, chicken, red meat or pizza.

SESAME SAUCE ....

Sesame sauce probably conjures images of tahini and hummus for most of us, and these certainly can be thinned and used as sauces, but the sesame sauces we want to introduce to you, also known as goma-dare, are of Japanese origin. Here are three recipes, beginning with the easiest. Use all three with salads, hot greens, asparagus or as a dipping or drizzling sauce for anything.

Recipe 1: Mix 4 tablespoons rice vinegar or sake with 2 teaspoons brown sugar and a teaspoon each of sesame oil and tahini.

Recipe 2: In a blender or food processor blitz 1 cup toasted sesame seeds with 1/3 cup each of Japanese soy sauce, sugar, vinegar and water, and 1 teaspoon each of miso paste, dashi powder, salt and sesame oil.

Recipe 3: Heat 1/3 cup each of water, mirin and bonito and boil a few minutes. Strain and add 1/3 cup each of Japanese soy sauce, vinegar and sugar, then stir in 1 teaspoon of red miso paste, 2 tablespoons of tahini and a pinch of salt. Bring to a boil then use warm or cold.

SOFRITO ....

Also known as Refogado. In Spain, Portugal, Brazil, Cuba, the Caribbean and Latin America there are many different variations of the recipe for Sofrito, but all agree onion, garlic and oil are the heros. The secret to making a good Sofrito is slow cooking on a low heat.

Green Sofrito: Finely chop 2 brown or white onions, 5-6 cloves of garlic, 2 green bell peppers, 1-2 long green chili peppers and sauté slowly for 10 minutes in a generous amount of olive oil. Then blitz in the blender or food processor with a bunch of coriander.

Red Sofrito: Finely chop 2 red onions, 5-6 cloves of garlic, 2 red bell peppers, 1-2 long red chili peppers and sauté slowly for 8 minutes in a generous amount of olive oil. Add 2 tablespoons tomato paste and cook a couple more minutes then blitz in the blender or food processor with a bunch of coriander.

STROGANOV ....
Sour cream + onion + mushroom.
This popular Russian sauce was first published in the 1860s. When Larousse included it in their book they replaced the sour cream with cream and added white wine and paprika.
Sauté one sliced onion and 2 cups of sliced mushrooms in 2 tablespoons of butter. When colored, add ½ cup of beef or chicken stock and a splash of white wine if you like. Simmer gently then add 1 cup of sour cream or cream. Stir until it reduces to the consistency you prefer. Sprinkle with a little smoked paprika to finish. Traditionally served with fine strips of sautéed beef, but chicken and other meats, including sausages, pair very well with stroganov sauce. Serve the meat and sauce with steamed rice, egg noodles or mashed potatoes.

TAHINI SAUCE ....
Sauté 4 cloves of minced garlic and 2 long red chilis (deseeded, finely chopped) in 3 tablespoons of olive oil. Add 1 cup tahini, ½ cup water or coconut milk, 1 tablespoon lemon juice, salt and pepper and simmer for a few minutes. Taste, adjust flavor if necessary. Stir in or garnish with finely chopped coriander and toasted pine nuts. An excellent sauce served with meats and vegetables.

TAHINI LEMON ....

Blitz 4 garlic cloves, ½ cup water, ½ cup lemon juice, and 1 cup of tahini in a blender. Taste and season then add a little extra water or lemon juice if you want your sauce thinner. Try with all battered, crumbed or fried foods including fish.

TAHINI TAMARI GINGER ....

1 cup tahini

½ cup water

2-3 tablespoons grated or finely chopped fresh ginger root

2 tablespoons good tamari

2 tablespoons lemon juice and a little finely grated zest

TARATOR ....

Tahini + lemon + herbs + garlic.

8 tablespoons tahini

4 tablespoons pine nuts, toasted

4 tablespoons finely chopped fresh herbs (like parsley, chervil, tarragon, mint, or coriander)

6 tablespoons lemon juice

2 garlic clove, crushed

a pinch each of ground cumin and cayenne pepper

salt and pepper

Excellent with cold salmon, hot fish like swordfish, shellfish, vegetables or poultry.

TARRAGON CREAM ....

2 tablespoons olive oil

2 tablespoons butter

2 garlic cloves, crushed

2 shallots or 1 small onion, finely chopped
3-4 tablespoons tarragon, chopped
1 scant teaspoon Dijon mustard
1 teaspoon lemon juice
1 cup cream
¼ cup dry white wine
salt and pepper
Sauté the garlic and shallots in butter and oil, deglaze the pan with the wine, add the mustard, lemon juice, cream, salt and pepper and lastly, just before serving, the tarragon. Use for fish, vegetables, pasta, or you can sauté chicken thighs in your oil and butter in the pan first, remove and then use that fat and the fond to make the tarragon cream as a pan reduction sauce.

TOMATILLO ....

Tomatillos, a staple in Mexican cuisine with a tart flavor, look like small green tomatoes but are actually a part of the gooseberry family. This is a delicious fresh, uncooked, cold sauce we love with meat, curries and especially fat luscious prawns in chipotle cream sauce.
5 or 6 fresh tomatillos, husks removed, boiled in salted water for 10 minutes and finely chopped (canned tomatillos also work well, drained and chopped)
1 green jalapeño or long green chili, finely chopped
½ onion, finely chopped
2 cloves garlic, peeled and crushed
1-1½ cups of water, depending on how thick you like your sauce
fresh coriander, finely chopped
All ingredients can be chopped in the food processor or by hand.

TOUM ....

Cold, emulsified, creamy, very garlicky.

Garlic + olive oil + egg white + lemon juice + water + salt.

Toum is a Lebanese garlic sauce easily made in a blender. Just add 8-10 cloves of peeled garlic, the juice of 1 lemon and 2 egg whites and whizz on high with the lid center out then reduce the speed to low, add a pinch of salt and drizzle in 1½-2 cups olive oil or one of the nut oils until emulsified and thick. To make it lighter and fluffier, just like when making hummus, add cold water a tablespoon at a time.

TZATZIKI ....

Place 1 cup each of Greek yoghurt and sour cream in a food processor with 2 peeled Lebanese cucumbers, 2 garlic cloves, 2 tablespoons lemon juice, salt, pepper and some fresh herb like dill, chive, tarragon or mint. Blitz until smooth. There is no need to salt or remove seeds from the cucumber, as the liquid is needed to achieve a sauce consistency. Thin with a little water or milk if required. Good with everything savory especially samosas, meats, vegetables, chicken, fish, lamb, tomatoes, avocado and eggs.

WALNUT ....

1 tablespoon each of butter and oil

1 cup walnuts, chopped

2 cloves garlic, minced

1 cup dry white wine

1 tablespoon each of chopped parsley, tarragon or chervil

Sauté the walnuts, add garlic until cooked then add wine and herbs and simmer for a couple of minutes. Season with pepper and salt. For pasta, fish or vegetables.

PASTA SAUCES

———◆———

"Fettucini alfredo is macaroni and cheese for adults."
—MITCH HEDBERG

DEFINITION ....
There are too many wonderful companion sauces for pasta to cover
them all so we have limited our recipes to ones we feel the average
home cook is likely to use. It is useful to know which sauce
traditionally pairs with the different shaped pastas so we have
included a summary. Any pasta shape can be eaten with any pasta
sauce, but some make better partners than others, although just
exactly what the best pairings are is by no means clear, even in
Italy. In general, any pasta can be traditionally served with the
mother sauce, tomato, and any of the tomato derivative sauces; see
them in the Classic Sauces chapter.

   Our tip is 'less is more' when it comes to the number of
ingredients in pasta sauces; aim for a concentration of a few flavors
rather than a confusion or mish-mash of multiple ingredients. If
you want to add complexity do it by offering garnishes and let your
family and friends choose their own. Sauce recipes below are for
approximately 500 grams or 1 pound of dried pasta or
approximately 4 serves. Freshly cooked pasta* is best used slightly
wet with a little of its hot cooking water, with some freshly grated
parmesan cheese forked through prior to the addition of a sauce.

* See the glossary section at **TheCulinaryLibrary.com** for the best way to cook pasta.

AGLIO E OLIO ....

Garlic + olive oil + red chili.

This is the quickest and simplest of all the pasta recipes and in our view one of the best.

2 tablespoons garlic, minced and sautéed

½ cup good olive oil

1 tablespoon finely diced red chili or 1 teaspoon dried chili flakes

Heat the oil and add the garlic and chili to sauté until light brown. Toss through hot cooked pasta with a little of the reserved cooking water.

ALFREDO ....

Cream + butter + parmesan + black pepper.

Make a Béchamel with 2 tablespoons flour, 2 tablespoons butter, 3 cups milk and salt and pepper, then add ½ cup cream and ½ cup parmesan cheese. Variations of the traditional recipe include the addition of sliced prosciutto and cooked baby peas.

AMERICANA (ALL'AMATRICIANA) ....

Tomato + bacon (or cured pork) + pecorino.

Variations of the traditional recipe include the addition of onion, garlic and red wine. Sauté 1 cup finely sliced or cubed bacon or pancetta in oil until colored. (Add 1 diced onion and a crushed garlic clove now, if using.) Deglaze pan with 1 cup red wine and 2 cups crushed tomato. Reduce a little and then stir in ½-¾ cup grated pecorino cheese. Season with salt and pepper.

For tube pastas, especially bucatini or penne.

ARRABBIATA ....

Tomato + hot chili + garlic.

Variations of the traditional recipe include the addition of sautéed onion, lemon and sugar. Sauté 1 finely chopped onion and 4-5 crushed garlic cloves in oil. Add 1 teaspoon dried red pepper flakes or 1 tablespoon finely diced fresh long red chili pepper. Stir in 1 tablespoon tomato paste. Add a splash of red wine and 2 cups crushed tomato, then 1 tablespoon each of sugar and lemon juice. Season with pepper and salt and garnish when serving with chopped basil or parsley and grated pecorino or parmesan cheese.

For tube pasta, especially penne.

BOLOGNESE ....

Tomato + soffritto + meat (veal, beef, pork) + pancetta or bacon + red wine + stock + herbs.

Also known as Bolognaise or Bologne sauce.

Make a soffritto by sautéing 2 onions, 2 carrots, 2 celery sticks, and 1 tablespoon each of butter, oil and sugar. When caramelized and soft, add 3 crushed garlic cloves and 3 good tablespoons of tomato paste and set aside. In a clean large pan, sauté 3-4 strips of chopped bacon with one kilogram or 2 lb mince meat in oil. Beef, veal, or pork, or a mixture of two or three of these can be used. Stir continuously, separating the meat as it browns to reduce clumps. Deglaze the pan with 2 cups of red wine, 2 cups of stock and 2 cups of crushed tomatoes. Add the soffritto, 2 bay leaves, salt and pepper and a wedge of citrus (orange, lime or lemon). Cook on a low simmer for 3-4 hours, stirring occasionally and adding more stock if needed until it thickens and darkens.

For ribbon pasta like tagliatelle, fettuccini and lasagna.

CACCIATORE ....
Tomato + onion + garlic + red or white wine.
Sauté 2 chunky-cut large onions in oil, add 4 crushed garlic cloves, 2 tablespoons of tomato purée and deglaze with 1 cup of wine and 2 cups of crushed tomato. Used as a cook-in sauce for chicken, and when bacon and mushrooms are added it is known as Huntsman's Sauce.
For ribbon and shaped pasta.

CARBONARA ....
Smoked bacon + egg + cream + black pepper.
Sauté 1 cup of chopped smoky bacon or pancetta in 1 tablespoon of oil until soft but not too colored. While this cooks, beat 2 egg yolks with 2 whole eggs, ½ cup cream, ½ cup grated parmesan cheese, salt and pepper. Cook pasta, drain and return to the pan with a little of the reserved cooking water. Add the bacon and stir through the egg, cream and cheese mixture, stirring gently over low-medium heat until it cooks enough to lose the raw-egg flavor. Too high a heat will curdle the eggs.
For spaghetti.

FORMAGGIO (CHEESE) SAUCE ....
Béchamel + cheese.
Make a standard 2 cup Béchamel, and to the warm sauce add 1 egg yolk, 1 cup of grated parmesan (or your favorite cheese), salt and pepper.
For tube, stuffed and sheet pastas, especially macaroni, lasagna, and tortellini or ravioli.

GARNISHES ....

Traditional garnishes for pasta sauces are chopped fresh herbs like parsley, basil or oregano, grated cheeses like parmesan or pecorino, black olives, virgin olive oil, anchovies, garlic, chopped chili, fresh ground black pepper, capers and lemon.

MARINARA ....

Tomato + garlic + parsley + onion + olives.

Sauté 1 chopped brown onion in olive oil until soft, add 3 crushed garlic cloves, 1 cup of white wine, 2 cups tomato pasta sauce or passata* and chopped parsley. Heat through marinara-mix seafood and shellfish of your choice just before serving.

* Tomato purée or paste is too strong for marinara sauce so use your favorite tomato-based pasta sauce, which is lighter and fresher. If you have no passata or fresh tomatoes, as a last resort substitute 2 cans of crushed tomatoes and 2 tablespoons tomato paste.

For spaghetti.

MUSHROOM ....

Mushroom + onion + tomato purée + white wine.

Sauté 1 chopped onion in 2 tablespoons oil then add 4 large mushrooms (halved and sliced) or 12 button mushrooms, sliced. When they have softened, add 5 tablespoons each of water and white wine and 2 tablespoons of tomato purée. Taste and season. A good splash of cream is optional. Garnish with fresh herbs and grated Parmesan cheese.

Serve with tagliatelle.

NAPOLETANA ....
Tomato sauce mother + basil.

PESTO ....
Basil + garlic + pine nuts + olive oil + pecorino cheese.
In a mortar & pestle, food processor or blender crush or chop ½ cup each of walnuts and pine nuts with 1 cup each parsley and basil. Add enough olive oil to give a loose sauce, then add a cup of grated parmesan or ricotta cheese. Taste and season.
For any pasta shape, especially ribbon and strand pasta.

POMODORO ....
Tomato + garlic + basil.

PUTTANESCA ....
Tomato + garlic + hot chili + anchovies + capers + olives.
For any pasta shape, especially ribbon and strand pasta.

QUATTRO FORMAGGI ....
Cheese + milk + white wine + pepper + nutmeg.
Heat 2 cups of milk and add ½ cup each of 4 different types of cheese. Fontina, mild gorgonzola or blue castello, parmesan, pecorino or romano are good. Sheep's milk, tasty or matured, is traditional but you can experiment with your favorites. Stir continuously until the cheeses have melted, then add white wine to thin to the desired consistency, a pinch of white pepper and a scrape of nutmeg.
For penne and other short pasta.

RAGÙ

Slow cooked meat (veal or beef) + bacon + tomato purée + mushroom + wine + mirepoix.

See **TheCulinaryLibrary.com** for our Ragù recipe.

ROMESCO

Tomato + red capsicum + garlic + olive oil + nuts (almonds, hazelnuts) + vinegar + herbs + red chili. See recipe on page 218.

TOMATO

See Tomato sauce and its derivatives in the Classic Sauces chapter.

TONNO OR TUNA

Tomato + tuna + garlic + oil + anchovy.

Sauté 1 clove of crushed garlic and one anchovy fillet in 2 tablespoons of oil, add 1 can of tomato (250 grams or 9 ounces) and simmer for 10 minutes, mashing the tomato as it cooks. Remove from the heat and fork in freshly cooked tuna or one can (120 grams or 4 ounces, of Italian tuna*). Taste and season with a little salt and black pepper. For spaghetti.

* Most Italian canned tuna is Yellowfin as the finer Bluefin is prohibitively expensive. Italian cans are color coded for type: red cans for the body fillet, yellow for the more tender, fattier belly meat which is lighter in color, and green for the leaner meat along the backbone which is darker in color.

SHAPE TYPES AND THEIR SAUCE PAIRINGS ....

SHAPED PASTAS ....
Campanelle, capunti, casarecce, cavatelli, cecioni, conchiglie, conchiglioni, corzetti, creste digalli, croxetti, farfalle, farfalloni, fiori, foglie di ulivo, fusilli, gemelli, gigli, gnocchetti, gramigna, lantern, lumache, lumaconi, mandala, orecchiette, pipe, quadrefiore, radiatori, ricciolini, ricciutelle, rotelle, rotini, sorprese, strozzapreti, torchio, torine, trenne and trofie.
Traditional sauce pairings: thick tomato sauces, pesto, sauces with herbs, meat sauces, chunky vegetable sauces and cheese sauces.

TUBE PASTAS ....
Cannelloni, canneroni, cannolicchi, cavatappi, ditalini, elicoidali, fagioloni, fideua, Florentine, fusilli bucati, garganelli, gomiti, macaroni, maccheroni, maccheroncelli, maccheroncini, manicotti, maltagliati, mezzani, paccheri, penne, penne lisce, rigatoni, tortiglioni, and ziti (smaller than rigatoni but larger than mezzani.)
Traditional sauce pairings: Use thick tomato sauces, meat sauces, chunky sauces, and thick cream sauces like béchamel.

RIBBON PASTA ....

Fettuccine, lasagne, linguine, pappardelle, pellizzoni, pici also known as pinci, reginette, tagliatelle, and trenette.

Traditional sauce pairings: meat sauces, thick tomato sauces and thick cream sauces for wider dried pasta or on narrow or fresh pastas, use light tomato sauces, butter-based sauces, light oil-based sauces, and light cream-based sauces.

SOUP PASTA ....

Acini di pepe, alfabeto, anelli, anellini, conchigliette, corallini, couscous, ditali, ditalini, farfalline, fideos, filini, fregula, funghini, grattini, grattoni, midolline, occhi di pernice, orzo, pastine, pearl pasta, putine, quadrettini, risi, risoni, seme di melone, stelle, stelline, stortini, tripolini and tubetti. Light sauces can be added to broths or soups with a light base e.g. Pesto is added to Pistou soup.

STRAND OR LONG STRAND PASTA ....

Bigoli, bucatini, bavette, capelli d'angelo (also known as angel hair; capellini strands curled into nests), capellini, chitarra, fedelini, spaghetti (alla chitarra, rigati, spaghettini, spagettoni) and vermicelli (vermicellini).

Traditional sauce pairings: light tomato sauces, butter-based sauces, purées that are thick such as basil or pepper purées, light oil-based sauces such as olive oils, and light cream-based sauces.

STUFFED PASTA ....

Agnolotti, cannelloni, cappelletti, casoncelli, fagottini, mezzelune, occhi di lupo, pansotti, ravioli, sacchettini, tortellini and tortelloni.

Traditional sauce pairings: light tomato sauces, light cream-based sauces and broth.

QUIRKY CHARACTERS

———•◆•———

"Confidence is going after Moby Dick in a rowboat and taking tartar sauce with you."
—ZIG ZIGLAR

BEER GRAVY ....
Served with 'bangers and mash' this quirky sauce is actually delicious. Simply sauté 3-4 finely sliced onions in oil/butter until soft and colored, then add a whole baby carrot, bay leaf, star anise or whole clove and a tablespoon each of butter and flour. Stir, allowing the flour to 'cook-out' for a couple of minutes, then add a cup of beer and the same of stock. Simmer slowly for 10-20 minutes, tasting as the flavor deepens and adding more beer if it becomes too thick. Remove the carrot and aromats before serving.

CARMELINE ....
There are many versions of this quirky old Middle Ages sauce from the 1300-1400s but few quantities of ingredients so you'll just have to experiment if it appeals to you. It's basically a bread sauce with spices and vinegar but was hugely popular in its day.
Carmeline 1: Crush or blitz peeled almonds or hazelnuts, currants, cinnamon, cloves, bread and vinegar.

Carmeline 2: Crush or blitz ginger, cassia, cloves, grains of paradise, mastic, thyme, long pepper, bread, vinegar, salt.
Carmeline 3: Crush or blitz fresh ginger root, cinnamon, cloves, mace, long pepper, bread, vinegar, salt.
Carmeline 4: Crush 2 slices white bread, ½ cup red wine, 1 tablespoon sugar, a pinch each of cinnamon, ginger, clove, saffron, salt.

CARROT JUICE SAUCE ....
From the Middle East, Iran and Afghanistan.
Carrot + butter + spices.
This delicious hot, sweet and spicy sauce is yet to be discovered by Western cooks.
2 cups fresh carrot juice or buy a good quality one from a health food store
4 tablespoons butter
pinch of cayenne pepper and sugar (or honey)
pinch of cinnamon and ginger
salt and pepper and chopped herbs
Simmer the carrot juice, whisk in the butter a little at a time then add a small pinch of some or all of the above spices, tasting and balancing the flavor as you go. Add freshly chopped herbs before serving and if you want a thicker sauce use beurre manié (flour and butter mixed in a ratio 1:1) or a splash of cream.
For meat, fish, chicken, vegetables.

CHAUD-FROID ....
Chaud-Froid is French for 'hot-cold' and is a classic jellied sauce invented to coat cold cooked chicken which was then decorated with bay leaves, parsley and cut vegetable shapes. It is no longer used today but can be made in several ways: gelatin can be added

to velouté, demi-glaze, mayonnaise, sour cream or Béchamel and it can also made by adding cream to warm aspic.

GARUM ....
From Ancient Rome comes this quirky sauce that the Romans ate daily. Take a quantity of fatty raw fish like sardines, sprats or mackerel, including entrails, and beat to a pulp. Leave the pulp to ferment in the sun for a few weeks with crushed aromatic herbs such as dill, coriander, fennel, celery, mint or oregano. Strain the liquid into jars and keep as long as possible.

GHEE SAUCE ....
This is a tangy, creamy, white sauce from antiquity. Ghee is stirred into cold water, salt is added and it is stirred until the ghee swells and slowly turns from a yellow cream into a thick, curdy, off-white mixture. A little extra cold water is added and the curds beaten and stirred until the sauce dilutes and turns smooth. Served with meat, especially game.

HARD WRANGLER ....
Other, cold or warm, thick or semi-solid.
Butter + sugar in a ratio of 1:1 + flavorings such as brandy, rum, whiskey, sherry, vanilla, orange, lemon, coffee, cinnamon and spice, or fruit purées.
For hot steamed puddings, plum pudding, fruitcake, desserts.

JEZEBEL ....
Recipe 1: Heat together pineapple or apricot preserves, horseradish, apple jelly, dry mustard and ground black pepper.

237

Recipe 2: Heat cranberries in water with brown sugar until soft and mushy. Sieve or blitz then reheat with Dijon mustard, horseradish, and orange juice in quantities that suit your palate. For pork, poultry, game, all white meat.

LEMON MYRTLE ....
Mix 1 cup of thick plain yoghurt, 1 tablespoon honey, 1 teaspoon powdered lemon myrtle with 2 teaspoons of hot water, salt and pepper. Serve hot or cold.

MONKEY GLAND SAUCE ....
Firstly we must state that The Culinary Library never supports inhumane animal treatment or slaughter and secondly that the sauce known in Africa as Monkey Gland Sauce has no animal products in it – more to the point, no monkey glands! Monkey Gland Sauce is made from fruit and spice and is served as an accompaniment to meat in South Africa.
To make this sauce, sauté the following ingredients in olive oil:
1 large onion, peeled and chopped
4 garlic cloves, chopped or crushed
1 tablespoon of fresh ginger, grated
½ cup of chutney, or sweet chili sauce
½ cup tomato purée
1 tablespoon soy sauce,
2 tablespoons each of mustard and Worcestershire sauce,
3 tablespoons ketchup or tomato sauce
½ cup muscat wine
⅓ cup chicken stock
2 tablespoons red wine
salt and pepper

Simmer for 10 minutes, stirring occasionally. Taste, adjust seasoning. Serve hot or cold. Great with any roasted or grilled beef or red meat.

ORCHID SAUCE (SAHLAB) ....

Most cooks probably don't know that vanilla is the pod of an orchid plant, so is it any wonder few cooks have heard of Sahlab Orchid Root powder? The ground root/tubers of a specific purple orchid, when ground to a powder, are called Sahlab, a reference to the Arabian liquid-custardy-slurry made by mixing Sahlab and milk. Sahlab powder is available from your Middle Eastern (Arabic, Turkish, Greek) grocer.

Heat to a simmer 1 cup of milk, 1 cup of cream, 2 tablespoons of sugar and 1 teaspoon rose or orange-blossom water. Mix 1½ tablespoons Sahlab Orchid Root powder with a little of the warm milk to make a slurry, then whisk it a little at a time into the milk until it thickens to your preferred consistency. Pour into cups or Moroccan glasses and dust with cinnamon and a grating of nutmeg. Use also over hot steamed puddings, steamed fruit, cakes, most desserts especially chocolate and caramel ones. Also known and sometimes labeled as Sahlep or Salep.

QUANDONG ....

Quandong is a wild desert fruit common in the Australian bush and used for centuries by indigenous Australians. The fruit are scarlet in colour, quite small at about 2cm across and have a large kernel that must be removed.

15 quandong fruit, kernel removed, chopped
¼ cup white vinegar

1 long red chili, deseeded, chopped finely
1-2 tablespoon brown sugar or palm sugar
salt and pepper
Simmer for 20-30 minutes, mashing the fruit. Dried fruit can be soaked in hot warm water for half an hour, and then drained. Quandong Sauce is sweet and spicy and can be paired with roast lamb or pork, thinned and used as a dipping sauce with spring rolls or meat, seafood or chicken skewers.

RED EYE GRAVY ....
Whether the origin of the name was President Jackson's red-eyed cook, or because the evaporating gravy is said to make a red 'eye' in the center of the pan, this is a traditional Southern United States accompaniment to Country Ham. It is often served with eggs or grits and biscuits. The distinguishing feature is that the pan is deglazed with black coffee.
Fry some thick slices of ham or kassler steaks, and soft fry an egg. Remove to serving plate and deglaze the pan with with about ½ cup of ready made black coffee, a dash of Worcestershire sauce, a teaspoonful of sugar and a pinch of black pepper. Thicken with a knob of beurre manié (about 2 teaspoons). Instant sauce!
We originally had this recipe in the pan sauces chapter, but on second thoughts and after a taste-test decided it really was a quirky character! Variations include the addition of a little mustard or tomato ketchup.

SCREAMING ROOSTER SAUCE ....
A street name for Kewpie (Japanese mayonnaise) mixed with Sriracha (Asian hot chili sauce) and sesame oil.

SPECIAL (BIG MAC) SAUCE ....

From Ancient Rome we jump two thousand years to modern America with an attempted copy of the sauce used on McDonald's Big Mac hamburger. How does the jingle go? 'Two all beef patties, special sauce, lettuce, cheese, pickles, onion, and on a sesame seed bun.' The brand names listed are only suggestions, try experimenting with your own preferred brands.

¼ cup whipped mayonnaise, Miracle Whip, Kraft

¼ cup normal egg mayonnaise

2 tablespoons French dressing, Wish-Bone Deluxe or any good quality brand

½ teaspoon sweet relish, Heinz (pickled cucumber + red bell pepper + cabbage + corn syrup + vinegar + thickeners)

2 teaspoons dill pickle relish, like Vlasic or Heinz (or you can substitute mustard pickles + chopped dill pickles)

1 teaspoon sugar

1 teaspoon minced onion

1 teaspoon white vinegar

1 teaspoon tomato sauce or ketchup

Mix or blitz all ingredients, microwave for 25 seconds, stir and cool before use.

SUBWAY OR SOUTHWEST SAUCE ....

This is not really a quirky character but given that we'd replicated the Big Mac special sauce in this chapter we thought you might like to try our replica of the sauce used at Subway outlets. We're big Mexican food fans, so although they call theirs Southwest sauce, we think it's really a Mexican chipotle chili mayonnaise. Mix the following ingredients together and see what you think:

1 cup of thick mayonnaise (or Miracle whip which works better)

1 teaspoon of chipotle chili in adobo sauce, buy it in the can at Mexican shops

1 teaspoon each of sugar and lime or lemon juice

1 teaspoon of finely chopped coriander

½ teaspoon of white vinegar

½ teaspoon each of paprika, thyme, cumin, garlic powder

a pinch of salt

Taste, sweeten more if you like or adjust flavor and leave in the fridge overnight to develop and soften.

WHITE BBQ SAUCE ....

Mayonnaise + mustard + horseradish + garlic.

From Alabama in 1925 comes this strange sauce, but it's easy to mix and worth trying.

1½ cups mayonnaise

¼ cup water

¼ cup white wine vinegar

1 tablespoon fresh coarse ground black pepper

1 tablespoon prepared mustard

1 teaspoon salt

1 teaspoon sugar

2 garlic cloves, crushed

2 teaspoons prepared horseradish

Mix all ingredients together. Reduce the amount of water if you like a thicker sauce. For chicken, meat or vegetables.

WORCESTERSHIRE ....

Worcestershire is quirky because of its unusual history and because it's one of the few fusion sauces to be embraced fully by

Western cooks. A Chief Justice of India brought home to England a curry powder recipe he shared with his niece, a Mrs. Grey, who in turn gave it to her friend Lady Sandys who took it to her chemists in Worcester, to replicate the powder. Messrs. Lea and Perrins made a powder, mixed it in solution and Worcestershire sauce was born. Lea and Perrins is now a part of the Heinz empire.

RECIPE 1: Boil gently for an hour 6 cups vinegar, 1 cup treacle, 1 cup plum jam, 3 crushed garlic cloves, 1 long red chili (deseeded and finely chopped) and a pinch each of ground allspice, nutmeg, ginger, cinnamon, salt, pepper, clove. Bottle and store as it improves with age. If you don't have treacle replace with ½ cup each of honey and maple syrup.

RECIPE 2: In a saucepan mix 2 cups of white vinegar, ½ cup molasses (golden syrup and/or maple syrup can be used as a substitute), ½ cup soy sauce, ¼ cup tamarind paste or concentrate, 5 cardamom pods (split), 4 finely chopped red chilis, 3 tablespoons each of salt and seeded mustard, 2 crushed garlic cloves, 1 tablespoon minced or finely sliced fresh ginger, 1 teaspoon each of black peppercorns and whole cloves, ½ teaspoon curry powder, 1 cinnamon stick, a chopped onion and an anchovy fillet. Bring to a boil and stir occasionally, then reduce to a simmer for 15 minutes. While the sauce is cooking, heat ½ cup sugar in a small non-stick pan on a medium heat, stirring until it turns to amber syrup. Add to the sauce and cook until it reduces a little. Taste, adjust, and balance the flavors to your preference. Can be thickened a little with arrowroot slurry if you prefer it a little thicker. Strain after it has cooled and bottle. You can give your Worcestershire an individual twist by adding plum sauce, homemade tomato sauce or sweet chili sauce.

WOW-WOW ....

Cold, thick, sour, spicy.

From England in the 1800s comes this sauce invented by an enthusiastic cook: Dr William Kitchiner, optician! The original recipe appeared in his book *The Cook's Oracle*, published in 1817.

Melt two tablespoons of butter in a pan, add 1 tablespoon of flour, stir and cook a little. Add ¾ cup beef broth or stock, 1 tablespoon each of vinegar, tomato ketchup and port wine or mushroom oyster sauce, and 1 teaspoon of mustard. Simmer, reduce and thicken, add chopped parsley and chopped pickled cucumber or pickled walnut.

XO ....

Dried seafood + fresh spices (red chili, onion, ginger, garlic) + sugar.

Invented in 1980 in Hong Kong.

In a mortar & pestle grind to a paste:

50 grams dried shrimp (pre-soaked for 2 hours)

4 dried shredded scallops (pre-soaked for 4 hours & steamed for 10 minutes)

200 grams long red deseeded chili

50 grams each of fresh ginger & garlic

2 teaspoons each of sugar & salt

Sauté the mix in 1 cup of oil for 30-45 minutes or until it is a deep red. Cool, bottle and store. XO has been gaining in popularity, especially on Western TV cookery shows, though we personally don't understand why. Find a more elaborate recipe for XO in the Asian Sauces chapter.

REDUCTION & PAN SAUCES

"A sauce adds something, really two things: a taste as well as the opportunity to think about how the thing was made. This is the same kind of pleasure we derive when we look at a painting: the eye is pleased, while the mind explores the esthetic windings of a technique and a willed structure."
–RAYMOND SOKOLOV

DEFINITION ....

Quite simply, a reduction sauce is a liquid infused with flavor additives that has been reduced by heat to at least a half its volume. A pan or pan reduction sauce is one made in the pan you have just cooked in (usually sautéing or roasting). Reductions are used as modern sauces and are one of the replacements for the classic roux-thickened sauces like Velouté, Espagnole and Demi-glace.

The following methods can be used when making reduction and pan sauces:

1. Take the pan you have pan fried or roasted your meat, fish, poultry, crustaceans or vegetables in and deglaze with a liquid like water, verjuice, wine, vermouth, liqueur, fruit juice, cream, milk, stock, champagne, vinegar, cider or any other liquid of your choice. Add additional flavor ingredients either before or after the liquid, and boil or simmer until reduced. Strain if required.

2. Undertake the above process but in a new, clean pan.

3. Retain liquids already used as a cook-in or base sauce, remove the meat or main dish components and reduce the sauce further.

BALSAMIC VINEGAR ....

Add 2 tablespoons finely chopped onion or shallots and 1 tablespoon butter to your pan after removing steak or chicken or vegetables. Sauté then add a splash of cognac, brandy or masala, 1 tablespoon honey, segments from ½ orange and 3 tablespoons balsamic vinegar. Reduce by simmering until slightly syrupy then season.

For meat, chicken, or duck. See **TheCulinaryLibrary.com** for our recipe for Lacquered Duck or Chicken where we add additional chopped walnuts and a splash of pomegranate juice to our balsamic pan sauce.

CALVADOS CREAM ....

Traditionally paired with pork, this is an addictive sauce. After sautéing or roasting pork and removing it from your pan, remove excess rendered pork fat and replace with a tablespoon of butter. Add 2-3 fresh apples that have been peeled, deseeded and cut into quarters or eighths. Sauté until coloured then deglaze the pan with a good splash of Calvados* apple brandy (about half a cup). Tilt the pan to flame if using gas, or light the spirit carefully. Then add 1 cup of apple juice or cider and 1-2 cups of cream. Season with salt and pepper then simmer gently until reduced and just starting to color and thicken. Remove from heat to stop the color developing and finish with fresh chopped or torn tarragon if you have it. Best served warm or hot.

* If you don't have Calvados use Cognac or any good brandy.

CHERRY PAN SAUCE ....

Next time you cook pork chops, fillet or tenderloin, try this wonderfully easy cherry sauce. Remove the cooked meat from your pan and rest before serving. Melt a knob of butter in the pan sediment and stir in an equal quantity of plain flour. Deglaze your pan with a cup or more of roughly chopped cherries that have been plumped up in a good splash of juice and a little port. Sweeten with a raspberry, redcurrant or quince conserve, sharpen with a little Dijon mustard or lemon juice and add gloss by finishing with a little extra butter melted in before serving. Season and serve with pork, duck or game.

CITRUS PAN SAUCE ....

After pan frying and removing chicken or fish from your pan, add a little butter and flour, deglaze with a little white wine then whisk in the juice of a lemon or lime, 1 cup of orange juice, a little zest from both and finely chopped fresh herbs of your choice (e.g. chive, tarragon, thyme, flat leaf parsley or coriander). An option is to add citrus segments.

MILK GRAVY ....

This is good to make after cooking bacon, sausages, and pan-fried or roasted meats.

¼ cup bacon, sausage or pan drippings

¼ cup plain flour

2 cups milk or cream

Add flour to your pan drippings and lightly brown while stirring. Add the milk or cream and heat gently, continuing to stir until it thickens. Season.

MINT PAN SAUCE ....

After removing meat, sauté:

1 chopped onion in 1 tablespoon butter

Deglaze with:

1 cup apple juice or cider

juice and zest of 1 lemon or 4 tablespoons vinegar

1-2 tablespoons honey or raw sugar (depending on how sweet you like it)

Season with salt and pepper and simmer. Before use add 4 tablespoons finely chopped fresh mint. Good for lamb chops.

MUSTARD APPLE CREAM ....

For pork, veal or chicken. Sauté apple slices in the pan fond until they color, adding a little extra butter if required. Deglaze the pan with apple cider then add Dijon mustard, cream, pepper and salt, and fresh tarragon or chervil if you have it.

POMEGRANATE REDUCTION ....

After cooking meats like pork, duck, chicken, beef or lamb in your pan, remove to rest and deglaze the pan with pomegranate juice or use pomegranate syrup and a little orange juice + berry jam or citrus marmalade + fresh chopped red chili + crushed garlic.

RED WINE REDUCTION ....

Red wine + stock + sautéed vegetables (onion, carrot, celery) + garlic + herbs (bay, parsley, chervil, tarragon) + seasoning.

VINCOTTO REDUCTION ....

Vincotto, also known as Vino Cotto, is a cellar-matured syrup made from the 'must' of freshly squeezed dark grape varieties. It has a sweet-sour-velvety flavor that in Italy is known as 'agrodolce' or sweet & sour. Vincotto reduction sauce pairs well with both savory and sweet foods. Simply add aromats and Vincotto to your pan fond and reduce gently by half or until it goes a little syrupy. Try:

Vincotto + rosemary + sautéed garlic. A reduction sauce for beef, lamb, rabbit, poultry, game and quail.

Vincotto + cherry flesh + cherry juice. A reduction sauce for duck, pork, venison and desserts.

Vincotto + cinnamon + any citrus flesh + zest + juice. A reduction sauce for icecreams, quince, figs, cheese, poached fruit and desserts.

WHITE WINE REDUCTION ....

White wine + stock + sautéed vegetables (onion, carrot, celery) + garlic + herbs (bay, parsley, chervil, tarragon) + seasoning.

WORLD'S BEST PEPPER SAUCE ....

This is our favorite pan sauce, from Anton Mossiman when he was at the Dorchester Hotel in London. For 4 serves, cook 1-2" thick slices of beef fillet, coated in roughly cracked black pepper, in a pan with ½ butter/oil on medium-high heat. When your fillet is medium-rare, splash some cognac or good brandy into your pan and if cooking on gas just tilt the pan to set the alcohol alight or use a match if using electric. Once the flame dies, remove and set the steak aside on a plate to rest under foil. Add a teaspoon each of pink and green peppercorns (but not their juice, which is too intense and vinegary) to the crusty black pepper left in the pan. Scrape the pan before adding 1½ cups of cream and a pinch of finishing salt. Simmer at a bubble until the sauce reduces and just starts to change color from white to beige/blonde*. This is the stage you must stop cooking, get the pan off the heat, tip in the juices that have seeped from the resting meat, place meat on a serving dish and spoon the sauce over it immediately.

* The sauce will go dark and bitter fairly quickly if the heat is too high at this stage so it's best to watch, stir and avoid this happening. Use immediately because it thickens and goes gluggy as it cools.

We serve our pepper steaks with fondant or mashed potato and steamed greens like spinach, broccolini or beans. Also great with a salad of edible flowers & leaves. See Volume 2 of *The Culinary Library*.

SALSAS

---◆◆◆◆---

*"If you're interested in a hot Mexican entering your life,
why not try a salsa."*
−THE CULINARY LIBRARY

DEFINITION ....
Salsa is the Spanish word for sauce, so it's not surprising that the
Spanish and Mexican cuisines have the most salsa recipes. Salsas
were originally made in the Mortar & Pestle, called a 'molcajete' in
mexico, but today can be made by finely hand chopping vegetable
or fruit into a uniform size then adding liquids like citrus or oil,
herbs, chili and spices for an extra flavor. They can also be made in
the food processor, but only using the pulse button sparingly to
retain some texture and crunch.

CACTUS ....
Cactus + tomato + onion + chili + garlic + lemon + queso blanco.
Prickly pear cactus is an ancient staple food of Mexico and Central
America, tasting similar to green beans. With the growing
popularity of Mexican cuisine it has now become a celebrity or cult
food. The whole plant is edible, the pads (called nopal), the flower
petals and the fruit (called pears or tuna).
1 bottle or can of cactus pieces* or 2 cups of fresh pads (de-spined,
steamed or grilled)

2 tomatoes
1 yellow onion
serrano or jalapeño pepper (depends on your taste)
2 tablespoons fresh coriander/cilantro, chopped
½-1 cup Mexican queso blanco cheese (or use ricotta)
2+ tablespoons lemon juice
¼ teaspoon salt
optional: 1 teaspoon garlic, crushed
Finely dice the 2 tomatoes, 1 onion, 1 de-seeded jalapeño (if no serrano) and add coriander/cilantro, garlic, salt and lemon. Crumble in the cheese. Taste and adjust flavors.
* Unless you live in Mexico or somewhere where you can buy fresh cactus you'll probably have to source your cactus in a jar or can. Rinse cactus pieces well under cold water and chop into very small cubes. Canned cactus often has a small serrano chili pepper in the jar, so finely chop a little of that or use jalapeño instead. (Mexican Serrano peppers are hotter than jalapeños!)

CITRUS ....
1 orange, zested, peeled, segmented, roughly chopped
1 lemon, zested, peeled, segmented, roughly chopped
1 blood orange or small ruby grapefruit, zested, peeled, segmented, roughly chopped
To the zests and chopped citrus add:
3 tablespoons extra-virgin olive oil
3 tablespoons fresh mint, finely chopped (leaves only, no stalk)
3 tablespoons fresh flat-leaf parsley, finely chopped
1 scallion or spring onion, finely sliced
2 tablespoons honey
1 tablespoons small capers, rinsed, drained

1 teaspoon crushed red pepper flakes
flaked salt and ground pepper
For fish and chicken.

GUACAMOLE ....
2 ripe avocado
1 red chili, deseeded
2 tablespoons coriander
1 lemon, juice only
1 tomato, skin removed and deseeded

MANGO ....
1 ripe but firm mango, cubed
2 round radish or 1 large avocado, cubed
1 small to medium red onion, cubed
1 spring onion, sliced fine
2-3 tablespoons each of coriander and mint leaves, chopped
½ long green chili, chopped
1 lime, juice and zest
sugar, salt and pepper to taste

MEXICAN BLACK BEAN & CORN ....
1 cup cooked black beans or use canned ones, rinsed
1 cup fresh corn kernels
2 long green or red chili
2 garlic cloves
2 tablespoons each of chopped tomato, coriander, red onion,
spring onion, sweet red peppers or capsicums and lime juice
Taste and season.

PEACH ....
3 or 4 fresh peaches, halved, stones removed
1 tablespoon brown sugar
2 tablespoons red onion, finely chopped
1 jalapeño or long chili, de-seeded and finely chopped
1 lime, juice and zest
2-3 tablespoons each of fresh coriander and mint
The peaches can be used raw or sprinkled with sugar and sautéed in a little butter or oil until brown but still firm. Chop all ingredients and refrigerate until use.

PINEAPPLE ....
Grill or sauté 4 fresh slices of pineapple, cored and skin removed. Dice finely and add 1 diced small red onion, 2 finely diced long red or green chili peppers, a bunch of coriander/cilantro, and some chopped mint leaves. Mix together and add the juice and zest of 1 lime or 1 lemon and finish with 1 tablespoon of honey, flaked salt and pepper.

TOMATILLO ....
10-12 tomatillo, husked, simmered 10 minutes until soft, then finely cubed (or use canned tomatillo)
1 red onion, finely chopped
1 garlic clove, minced or crushed
1 long green or red chili, de-seeded and diced Brunoise or Brunoise Fine
1 cup finely chopped coriander
1 lime or small lemon, juice and zest only
Mix together and dress with a tablespoon each of olive oil, sugar/honey, and ground cumin. Finish with a pinch of flaked salt

& ground pepper. For all BBQ or slow roasted joints of meat, especially when served in Mexican tortilla wraps with salad.

TOMATO ....

3 large tomatoes, chopped
1 large Lebanese cucumber, peeled and chopped
2-3 round red raddish, chopped
1 red onion, finely chopped
½ long green or red chili, de-seeded and diced Brunoise or Brunoise Fine
1 cup finely chopped coriander
1 lime or small lemon, juice and zest
Mix together and dress with a tablespoon each of olive oil and sugar. Finish with a pinch of flaked salt and ground pepper.

ROASTED TOMATO ....

6-8 ripe tomatoes, cut in halves, seasoned with salt, pepper and sugar and roasted in olive oil in the oven. If you place them on baking paper in your roasting pan and twist the corners to bring the sides up a little it saves cleaning up and catches the caramelized juices for more flavor. Cook about 45 minutes in a medium-hot oven.

Meanwhile, sauté in a pan with some oil 1 onion (red or white, finely chopped), 1 long green or red chili pepper (finely chopped) and 2 crushed garlic cloves. Hand chop or blitz gently in a food processor the roasted tomato with the sautéed onion/chili/garlic. Turn into a serving bowl and stir in a little lime or lemon juice and ½ cup freshly chopped herbs like coriander, basil or parsley. Season with a pinch of finishing salt and ground pepper.

SALSA VERDE ....

Verde is the Spanish word for green, as in salsa, or green sauce.

The French version of Salsa Verde uses vinaigrette or mayonnaise flavored with chopped tarragon, parsley, sage* and lemon juice.

For the Mexican version of salsa verde see the Tomatillo salsa recipe.

For the Italian version use parsley, vinegar, capers, garlic, onion, anchovies, olive oil and mustard.

For the Argentinian version see Chimichurri.

For the German version use hard-boiled eggs, oil, vinegar, salt, sour cream, borage, sorrel, garden cress, chervil, chives, parsley and salad burnet.

* Many seasonal herbs can be used in the French version of salsa verde including dill, lovage, lemon balm, rocket, shallots, spring onions or spinach.

WATERMELON ....

3 cups seedless watermelon, diced Macédoine or Parmentier

1 red onion diced Brunoise or Brunoise Fine

1 long green or red chili, de-seeded and diced Brunoise or Brunoise Fine

1 cup finely chopped coriander

1 lime or small lemon, juice and zest

finishing salt

SAUCE THICKENERS

———◆◆◆———

"The assistance of the stock, the roux, brings to the brown sauce only a flavor note of little importance, beyond its thickening principle, and it has the disadvantage of requiring, in order that the sauce be perfect, an almost absolute elimination of its components. Only the starchy principle remains in a sauce properly skimmed. Indeed, if this element is absolutely necessary to give mellowness and velvetiness to the sauce, it is much simpler to give it pure, which permits one to bring it to the point in as little time as possible, and to avoid a too prolonged sojourne on the fire. It is therefore infinitely probable that before long, starch, fecula, or arrowroot obtained in a state of absolute purity will replace flour in the roux."
—ESCOFFIER

DEFINITION ....

Food thickeners are edible substances that we add to watery mixtures to increase their viscosity and body without substantially changing their flavor. Sauces can be thickened by a variety of methods, some of which have changed over time, like replacing meat bone gelatins with vegetable, plant and seaweed extracts, and others that have stayed the same, like applying heat. The majority of sauce thickeners are either starches or proteins, and many of

257

these thicken initially and then lose this ability with long cooking or heat that is too high. We therefore recommend you use your thickeners at the end of the sauce-making process. In this chapter we cover as many as possible, including the new range of hydrocolloids made available through molecular cookery and the older, classic thickeners like roux, grains and flours. It's up to you to choose the ones you feel best suit your cooking or to try others you've never used before.

AGAR AGAR ....
See also Hydrocolloids. Also known as kanten, Japanese gelatin or simply agar. Agar agar is a reduced derivative of seaweed, stronger than gelatin and commonly used as a vegan alternative. It has a high melting point, sets quickly and well and is useful for savory, vegetable and non-acid sauces. Because acid effects its performance, citrus, strawberry and passion fruit sauces need more agar agar to thicken than non acidic foods. For this reason it is not used for kiwi, mango, pineapple, papaya (paw paw) or fig sauces because their natural plant enzymes counteract and lessen its thickening ability. Available at Asian grocers and health food stores as a block, powder or in strands.

ARROWROOT ....
Arrowroot is made by a simple, natural process, gives a high gloss, is good for thickening acids but makes milk-based sauces slimy. This starch thickener has several advantages over cornstarch:
– a neutral flavor which is suited to delicately flavored sauces
– thickens at a lower temperature
– tolerant of acidic ingredients
– doesn't thin with long cooking times

While sauces thickened with cornstarch turn into a spongy mess if they're frozen, those made with arrowroot can be frozen and thawed with impunity. The downside is that arrowroot is pricier than cornstarch, and it's not a good thickener for dairy-based sauces since it turns them slimy.

For acidic foods, arrowroot is a better choice than cornstarch, which loses thickening potency in acidic mixtures. At acidic pH levels below 4.5, like guar gum, it has sharply reduced aqueous solubility and reduced thickening capability.

If the food is to be frozen, tapioca or arrowroot is preferable to cornstarch, which becomes spongy when frozen.

AU SANG ....

Au sang means 'with blood'. Historically, animal blood was used to thicken game sauces, but today it is seldom used and most modern cooks and chefs have relegated it forever to the 'quirky customers' section as a barbaric throwback. Blood is however still used in many traditional cultures as a legitimate thickening component of sauces.

BEURRE MANIÉ ....

Also known as Manié Butter. Butter, softened to room temperature, is kneaded (usually with a spoon) with flour in a ratio of 4:3, until it is a smooth paste. It is best added in pea-sized balls and stirred in at the middle or end of the sauce, or whenever it is at its hottest.

BLOOD ....

See Au Sang. Blood was historically used as a thickener for sauces, such as the cook-in sauce for coq-au-vin, but it is rarely used today.

BUTTER ....

Plain or flavored softened butter, added at the end of cooking, off the heat, gives a richer flavor and a slightly thicker, shinier, glossier sauce. Sauces must not however be boiled after a finishing butter is added or they will split and go oily.

BUBBLES ....

Sauces thickened with bubbles can be seen in the chapter on Foams or Espumas. A foam occurs when gas is introduced into and dispersed through a medium, usually a liquid of some kind. Bubbles can be added by air (aerating), air and water vapor (steam), carbon dioxide or nitrous oxide. The slow way is to aerate either by hand or machine whisking, a faster way is using steam under pressure, as in coffee machine attachments that foam milk, and the super quick way is using carbon or nitrous oxides under pressure with a foaming device like the ones used for whipping cream. The iSi ½ liter stainless steel foam gun handles both hot and cold sauces and costs around $170.

Foams are unstable, and just like emulsified sauces they are strengthened using stabilizers like plant purées, starch, pectin, gums, heat, proteins like egg yolk or with foam stabilizing products like Versawhip. Examples of traditional home-whisked foams, if somewhat heavier than modern foams, are sabayon, meringue, whipped cream, mousse and sponge cake. Using a foam canister with air, CO_2 or N_2O, you can make all sorts of light modern foams including lecithin based airs, sugar glass, fluid gel and methylcellulose. Almost any liquid will foam using this gaseous technique and innovations have included salt-water air, yuzu foam, parmesan, Tabasco, truffle, horseradish and even prune juice foam.

Airs and Foams as replacements for sauces were made popular by the rise of the Molecular Cookery movement and, like all modern discoveries, they have their champions and detractors. We like to think there are places for all inventions and innovations in cookery, no matter how narrow their appeal, as long as they do not involve cruelty to animals, but because all new culinary ideas must withstand the test of time, only time will tell if they are a fad or not. In any case, the journey of food is supposed to be fun and inclusive, not elitist and over-serious. We all accept the protein based foam in our café latte or mousse, the egg foam in our soufflé, meringue and sabayon, the fat foams in our whipped cream, so why not the modern, unpronounceable, seemingly-unachievable ones? Just because we can't reduce their texture to something more solidly tangible doesn't mean they have no place. Good foams are to food as perfume is to skin: elusive, ephemeral and with a different effect on each consumer.

CARRAGEENAN ....
See also Hydrocolloids. The Irish villagers of Carragheen discovered a red seaweed and algae extract, carrageenan. Also known as Irish Moss, it was initially used to make health syrups and a staple food similar to a saucy blancmange. It is not only a thickener but also a jelling agent, emulsifier, stabilizer, colloid and gum. There are three types: Iota is used most for thickening commercial convenience sauces as it will set them to a soft, silky stage or a light gel, whereas Kappa and Lambda are stronger and used for setting firmer gels. The downside to carrageenan is its implication as a producer of allergies and abdominal discomfort, and degraded carrageenan is reported as a known carcinogen causing inflammatory arthritis, bowel disease and tumors. You

probably already eat carrageenan because it is widely used in thickening flavored milks as well as in soy and almond milk, yoghurt, low-fat dairy and meat products, apple cider, ice cream, thickened cream, condensed and evaporated milk, chocolate and thickened convenience sauces. (Many sauces in canned pet food are also thickened with carrageenan.) The world of molecular cookery may love its properties but the World Health Organization has recommended it be withdrawn from inclusion in commercial infant foods and formulas.

CARBOHYDRATES ....
See Agar Agar and Carrageenan.

CHEESE ....
Many cooks would be familiar with adding cheddar or parmesan cheese to béchamel or velouté and their derivatives to thicken them. Macaroni and cheese sauce is an example of a cheese-thickened béchamel, but sauces can also be thickened with other cheese types including mozzarella, blue cheese and cream cheese.

CLEARJEL ....
This is a manufactured hydrocolloid, a commercial, registered brand name for a modified cornstarch product used as a thickener, jelling agent and stabilizer. It is dearer than cornstarch but works better in some applications because it is one of the few starches that will thicken acidic ingredients like fruit, so it's useful in thickening fruit sauces. You'll need to order it online, as the powder and pearls are not widely retailed. There is also an 'instant' version that thickens without heat.

COLLAGEN ....
A jelling protein extracted from meat tendons, skin, bones, muscle and feet or hooves. Gelatin is denatured collagen.

CORAL ....
Coral is the roe or eggs of shellfish like scallop, sea urchin, crab, lobster and prawns. It is a coral color when cooked and is classically used to garnish or thicken sauces. Crab or lobster liver, known as Tomalley, is also used as a thickener for sauces.

CORNFLOUR OR CORNSTARCH ....
Cornstarch was discovered in 1842 by grinding the tissue that surrounds the embryo of the corn kernel. Cornstarch was first used as a laundry starch, but by the 1920s it was being used in kitchens as a food thickener. Today it is highly processed and treated with chemical bleaches and toxic extracting agents. As a thickener, it:
– Is suited to milk and cream sauces
– Must be mixed with cold liquid to a slurry before use
– Does not like thickening acids like fruit, citrus, wine, vinegars
– Doesn't like prolonged cooking
– Breaks down when frozen and re-thawed
One tablespoon thickens one cup of liquid.

CREAM ....
Thick or heavy cream can be used to thicken sauces. It is usually added towards the end of sauce preparation. The initial effect when added will be to thin your sauce. Don't worry, it's just excess water which must be gently boiled off before it begins to thicken. Sauces thickened with cream tend to be glossy and rich in flavor. For a fresher, less rich flavor, crème fraiche or sour cream can be used.

EGG YOLK ....

Egg yolk + a little liquid, usually stock or milk, is mixed to a paste and added, off the heat, at the end of the sauce. If added to hot sauces without flour it can curdle.

EGG YOLK AND CREAM (OR BUTTER) LIASON ....

The ratio of cream or butter to egg yolk is usually 3:1 when butter or cream is whisked into egg yolks over heat to thicken. Examples include butter whisked into egg yolks for hollandaise, egg yolks mixed with cream for Velouté and Supreme sauces. Cream and egg yolk liaisons are usually added just before serving and must not boil or they will curdle.

FÉCULE ....

Also known as Slurry, Jayzee or Whitewash, fécule is a starch + a liquid. Fecula is the name of the starch. Most home cooks would be familiar with making a fécule, like cornflour and water, even if they didn't know its traditional name. A fecula starch such as arrowroot, cornflour, plain flour or potato flour has water or liquid added, is mixed to a paste and then added at the middle or end of the sauce cooking process. The thickening power of a starch fécule is reduced by sugar and acid. If either a sugar (granulated, in fruits, jams or chocolate) or an acid (vinegar, wine, lemon) is present in the sauce, more starch will be needed to thicken it.

FLOUR ....

Plain flour can be used to thicken gravies and sauces but must be cooked to avoid that uncooked-flour flavor. Adding flour to hot sauces is a sure way to get clumping and lumps, so mixing it with fat to make a paste or roux either before or after the liquid is added is more common.

FURCELLARAN ....

This is a hydrocolloid, a seaweed extract similar to carrageenan, that comes as either a liquid concentrate or dried flakes. It jells liquids above 40°C. It also stabilizes and thickens and is used with sweet and milky sauces mainly because it gives a soft, shiny, smooth result. Only a tiny amount is used, from 0.5-1% concentration.

GELATIN ....

Also known as Gelatine. The thickening, jelling and clarifying agent is collagen, usually derived from rendering animal skin, ligament, tendon, cartilage and bones. It is cheap, widely available and its strength varies by type, by brand, and by batch. Most of the animal parts used to make gelatin come from the carcasses of cattle and pigs left over from the live animal slaughter industry and the leather processing industry. Vegans and vegetarians use a gelatin substitute to thicken their sauces, one made from vegetable or fruit carbohydrates, such as agar agar or pectin.

Gelatin works by absorbing liquid, up to 10 times its own weight, each granule becoming enlarged and saturated; this is known as 'blooming' and it is always done in cold liquid, by sprinkling the powder or submerging the sheets in enough liquid so that each particle is able to touch the water. Agitating the powder during bloom creates undesirable lumps. Once dissolved or softened, gelatin is then usually heated at a low temperature of 130°F or less (because it will not set if boiled). It sets to a gel when chilled and re-liquefies if re-heated.

Gelatin is sold as a colorless (or slightly yellow), tasteless, odorless solid, as flakes, powder or sheets (also known as leaves). Because leaf or sheet gelatin dissolves slower than powdered gelatin, it requires soaking for 5 to 7 minutes in cold water, is drained or squeezed before adding to warm liquids to dissolve, is used by count, not weight, jells clearer than powdered gelatin and is sold in different strength grades known as 'bloom strengths'. Different applications require either a higher bloom for a firmer set or a lower bloom for a softer set.

Bloom strengths of sheet or leaf gelatin (from softest to firmest):
Bronze Leaf
Silver Leaf (most widely used in confectionary)
Gold Leaf
Knox Powder
Chrome Platinum
Titanium (pig skin derived)

Conversion ratios:
Powder to Silver Leaf..approximately 1:1.2
Powder to Gold Leaf ....approximately 1:1.1
1 sheet gelatin = approx. 1 teaspoon powder = approx. 1 ounce
3 sheets gelatin = approx. 1 tablespoon powder = approx. 3 ounces
1 sheet of gelatin generally sets ½ cup liquid. 3, 4 or 5 sheets or leaves, depending on bloom strength, will be required to set 2 cups of liquid.

Neutralizers: 'Bromelin' is a protein-splitting enzyme that prevents gelatin from setting. It is found in raw paw paw, guava, pineapple, fig, ginger root and kiwifruit. These fruit sauces should all be cooked before thickening with gelatin.

Gelatin is also made from fish, and an ancient form of fish gelatin called 'Isinglass' is still available and made from the 'sounds' or 'air bladders' of fish. It is the purest commercial form of gelatin, with a firm texture and whitish color. Isinglass is manufactured in Russia from sturgeon, in the US from many fish varieties including cod, hake, sea-trout & sturgeon, in China from algae or seaweed and in Japan from gelidium algae. Agar agar is also known as Bengal Isinglass. Grades of Isinglass are *lyre*, *leaf*, and *book*.

GELLAN ....

See also Hydrocolloid. Gellan is a gum derived from a bacterium called *pseudomonas elodea*. It is used with sauces for thickening, jelling, stabilizing and emulsifying. Sugar inhibits gellan's action and calcium aids it, so if used for sweet sauces it should be mixed with liquids and hydrated in a blender for a couple of minutes before the sugar is added. There are two types: low-acyl which is soft and pliable and high-acyl which is hard and brittle.

GLACES ....

Both meat and fish glaces can be used as sauce thickeners.

GUAR GUM ....

See also Hydrocolloid. Guar gum, also known as Guaran, is a gum derived from the endosperm of the guar seed. It is used for thickening yoghurt sauces, improving cream and ice cream texture, and in dressings and sauces to hold emulsions together. It is similar to but much stronger than cornstarch, and hydrates in both hot and cold water.

GUM ARABIC ....
See also Hydrocolloids. Gum Arabic is a gum, extracted from the sap of two species of acacia trees, traditionally produced in the Arabic world. Sold as powder, syrup, pellets and pieces. Gum Arabic binds and truly emulsifies ingredients that would not normally blend together (oil + water), thereby preventing separation and splitting. It also prevents sugars from precipitating out of solution, useful in molecular gastronomy as well as the soft drink industry.

GUM TRACAGANTH ....
See also Hydrocolloids. Gum Tracaganth is a gum made from legumes produced and used primarily in the Middle East. Used for thickening and stabilizing with similar properties to Gum Arabic and Xanthan.

HEAT ....
Heat thickens sauces by reduction (evaporating water particles), by expansion (increasing the molecule size in some foods like starch) or by both at the same time.

HYDROCOLLOIDS ....
Any substance, like a protein (gelatin) or complex sugars (all the rest), that form a gel upon contact with water are called hydrocolloids. They can be used as thickeners, emulsifiers or gel setters, and when properly dispersed they stabilize (foams) and prevent crystallization (sweet sauces). Most are derived from seaweed, seeds, sap, bacteria or fruit peels and they include agar agar (seaweed), cornflour (vegetable seed), carrageenan (red seaweed and algae), furcellaran, gelatin (animal bone and skin),

gellan (bacteria), gum Arabic (acacia tree sap), locust bean gum (carob seed gum), lecithin (soy bean), pectin (fruit peel), sodium alginate (brown algae) and xanthan (bacteria). There are also man-made hydrocolloids like MD (maltodextrin), MC (methylcellulose) & HPMC (hydroxypropyl-methylcellulose). Hydrocolloids can be classified by the flow texture they produce, but with only small quantities being required, measurement is crucial. For best results, blend your liquid on high before adding hydrocolloid.

ISOMALT

Made from sugar beets, isomalt sugar crystals have been available since the '80s. They are less sweet and contain only half the calories of normal sugar. Used as a thickener, sweetener and texturizer because they don't crystallize as easily as sugar and don't clump with humidity.

KATAKURI

Katakuri is a Japanese lily sometimes called dog-tooth violet. The bulbs are ground to make a thickening starch called katakuri-ko, which is traditionally used in Japanese cooking for thickening sauces and soups and for using in tempura batter and dusting foods before frying to give a crisp surface. Many of the katakuri starches commercially on sale in the West are actually made from potato starch because the finer, authentic katakuri is expensive.

KONJAC

See also Hydrocolloid. Also known as Konnyaku. Konjac is derived from the corm (stem) of the Konjac plant and is used mainly for setting gels and sauces to give a slightly fatty texture.

KUZU ....

Kuzu is a starch made from the tuber of the Japanese kudzu vine. Sold in either powdered or chunk form it is natural and unprocessed and when mixed to a slurry and added to hot liquid sauces it turns transluscent. Although similar in thickening properties to arrowroot and cornflour, it is superior in taste and jelling strength and has a smooth texture or mouth feel without the starchy flavor. When used as a sauce thickener it produces bright, glossy, translucent sauces and when used as a dusting starch before frying vegetables, fish or chicken it makes a crisp light coating. It is a foil for acid so is ideal for tart fruit sauces.

For thickening sauces: 1½ tablespoons of powdered Kuzu per cup of liquid.

LECITHIN ....

Also known as Soy Lecithin. It also occurs naturally in egg yolks but commercial quantities are derived from soy beans. Being both water and fat soluble, it is used as an emulsifier and anti-oxidant. It stops chocolate sauces from splitting and emulsifies and stabilizes foams and airs. A little added to liquids (e.g. milkshakes and mousses) before frothing will create spoonable, stable foam bubbles.

LOCUS BEAN ....

See also Hydrocolloids. Also known as Carob Bean Gum, Carob Gum or LBG. The Locust Bean is a gum derived from the seed or bean of the carob tree, the same tree that gives us the chocolate-substitute carob. It is a powerful thickening, jelling and stabilizing agent that is used with cold sauces because it hydrates at >90°F.

Similar to xanthan gum and kappa carrageenan. Use with fruit sauces, glaces and gels.

LOTUS ROOT FLOUR ....

Also known as Lotus Root Powder, this product is actually the dried powdered stem of the lotus plant. Used in Chinese medicine as a lung-cleansing tonic. When dissolved in liquid it is an excellent sauce thickener. Use 1 teaspoon per cup.

MALTODEXTRIN ....

See also Hydrocolloids. Maltodextrin is a man-made and artificially produced hydrocolloid derived from rice, corn, potato, wheat or barley starch. This white, powdered carbohydrate is used widely in commercial sauce production and is one of the cheapest thickeners available. Uses include milk and custard sauces, cheese sauces, cream sauces, and salad dressings including mayonnaise.

METHYL-CELLULOSE ....

See also Hydrocolloids. Another man-made artificial thickener and emulsifier that will bind but not separate sauces. Use for thick gels.

NUTS ....

Crushed or powdered nuts thicken with their oils and also because they are dry and absorb liquids. Picado, Romesco and Walnut sauces are all thickened with nuts.

ORCHID ROOT FLOUR ....

Also known as Sahlab or Salep, this flour is made from the tubers of the orchid genus *orchis*, species *mascula* and *militaris*. Paracelsus, a famous scholar and medic in the mid 1500s, invented toxicology and claimed that orchid flour restored male virility and passion. This aromatic floral powder is a Middle Eastern sauce thickener.

PECTIN ....

Derived from fruit, especially apples, grapes, blackberry, grapefruit, lemon, plum, melons and quince, pectin is a jelling agent, thickener and stabilizer. For fruits low in pectin (like rhubarb, apricot, cherry, kiwi, fig, pineapple, strawberry, peach and nectarine) powdered pectin can be purchased and added as a jelling agent. If making fruit sauces, pectin needs both sugar and an acid such as lemon juice to set. Adding 20 grams of pectin per 1 liter of liquid usually gives a good sauce consistency.

POTATO FLOUR OR POTATO STARCH ....

Made from cooked, dried, powdered potatoes, potato starch is mass-produced and the extraction process accelerated with chemicals. It is used as a gluten-free thickener for people who are gluten intolerant or just reducing their gluten intake. Used for both savory and sweet sauces. Can also be used to coat meats before frying to thicken a cook-in sauce like Ossobuco, Chicken Chasseur etc. Unlike cornstarch, potato starch does not need to be boiled to thicken a sauce; this makes it ideal for a slow cook-in sauce in the oven.

PURÉES ....

Both fruit and vegetable purées can be used as thickeners. Tomato purée is the most common vegetable purée sauce thickener, but puréed herbs and fruit also contribute to sauce thickening through their fiber and pectin. Pesto, for example, is not thickened by heat, egg protein or starch, but by vegetable purée, nuts and oil emulsion.

REDUCTIONS

A liquid or sauce thickened by reducing it in volume, by the application of intense heat, is called a reduction sauce. This method is preferred by modern chefs because the sauce making requires little attention, does not split, re-heats and refrigerates well and achieves intense flavors, deep colors and lighter textures when compared with the classic sauces.

RICE FLOUR

Before flour, ground roasted rice was the main sauce thickener. Rice flour, still used today but made from finely ground rice, is a gluten-free thickening starch that inhibits liquids separating. For this reason it is useful if you are thinking of freezing your sauces. There are two types: non-glutinous, also called sweet rice flour, which is used for sweet sauces; and glutinous, used for savory sauces. It gives sauces a shiny, transparent look that is similar to arrowroot rather than the cloudy one that you get from corn and wheat starches.

ROUX

Butter + flour. Traditional ratio 1:1.

Other fats are occasionally used instead of butter to make a roux. For example, the fatty pan juices of roast or pan-fried beef, pork, chicken, sausages or duck. The butter and flour are usually cooked together at the beginning of the sauce.

Roux, like the mother sauces, is classified by color, which depends on the amount of cooking it has had before other ingredients and liquids are added.

–White Roux: cooked only long enough to cook the flour but remains white. Flavor: milky.

–Blonde Roux: cooked long enough to cook the flour until golden but still pale. Flavor: biscuity.

–Brown Roux: allowed to color to a light brown, until it gives off a stronger aroma. Flavor: nutty.

Roux sauces appear to not only have fallen from favor with modern chefs, but are often reviled by them as being 'too gluey' or 'too old-fashioned'. Many of today's professional chefs self-righteously claim they have never made a roux-based sauce and never want to, preferring extreme reductions, coulis, glace-bases, foams, broths and modern thickeners like gellan, xanthan gum or agar agar. To a classically trained chef it is unthinkable to reject the classics outright. Béchamel, at the least, demands a roux, and judging the strengths and weaknesses of roux-based sauces can only be done by comparison and with a knowledge of how to make them.

SAGO STARCH ....
Also known as Sagu or Sago Flour. Sago starch is extracted from the pithy, spongy center of several members of the palm family and comes in the form of white, pink or brown pearls or powder. It is an all purpose thickener, generally made into a slurry before being added to hot liquids.

SEEDS & SPICES ....
Dried seeds and spices like turmeric, cumin, coriander, cinnamon, allspice, clove, nutmeg, dried chili, paprika, ginger, mustard and fenugreek all soak up liquid and swell in size when heated. Ground up plant tissue in the form of seeds and spices are the bases for most Indian curry sauces and the milk and cream extracted from the coconut is very popular as a sauce thickener in Thai cookery. In the whole of the Asia-Pacific region, as well as the Arabic world, seeds and spices are involved as thickeners in most sauce preparations. In Mexico, a marvelously complex and delicious sauce, called Mole, is made and thickened with pumpkin seeds and dried chili.

SORGHUM STARCH OR FLOUR ....
Also known as Milo or Durra flour. Sorghum is ancient, one of the oldest known grains cultivated and eaten by man. Although it is widely used in Africa and India, where it is the main ingredient in the amazing Roti (jowar) bread, it is only just experiencing popularity in the Western world. The whole grain kernel is ground to make the flour and can be used as an excellent gluten-free substitute for other starches.

STARCHES ....
There are literally hundreds of different food starches that can be used to thicken sauces, and we have covered a few (see arrowroot, ClearJel, cornflour, lotus root, orchid, potato, rice flour, sago, soy, sweet potato, tapioca and water chestnut). Starches don't usually add flavor, rather they change the texture of liquids, but they must be cooked to avoid a pasty-starchy flavor in sauces.

SWEET POTATO STARCH OR FLOUR ....
Sweet potato flour is slightly off-white in color and slightly sweet in flavor. It is produced from white sweet potatoes and used when gluten-free sauces are needed.

TAPIOCA OR CASSAVA FLOUR ....
See also Hydrocolloids. Also known as cassava powder or tapioca powder. Derived from the cassava or tapioca root. When used as a sauce thickener, tapioca starch gives a glossy sheen, thickens at room temperature and is stable when frozen. Good with acids like fruit and citrus sauces.

TARA GUM ....
Also known as Peruvian carob, this is a white or cream-colored, odorless powder produced from the seed or endosperm of the tara shrub from Peru. Its viscosity or thickening properties are less than guar gum and greater than locust bean gum, and it tolerates heat better than xanthan gum. It is good with acids (fruits etc.) and stable in hot sauces.

VERSAWHIP ....
Also known as soy protein isolate, Versawhip is a trade name of a modified soy protein, derived from soybeans. It can be used as a replacement for gelatin or egg whites (it doesn't over-whip) for making hot or cold foams. It's good with acid and high temperatures and can simply be whisked into any juice or liquid to make a stable foam. A large-bubble air (see chapter on Foams & Espumas for information on airs) can be produced by whisking together Versawhip, xanthan gum and egg white.

WATER CHESTNUT FLOUR ....
Also known as water chestnut powder. Used in Asia as a substitute
for cornflour. As well as thickening sauces, it is used for coating
fried foods for its nutty flavor and crispness. It usually comes in
boxes of coarse white or grayish chalky flakes, so you'll need to
powder it in the mortar & pestle before mixing well to a slurry or
adding to crumbs or batters for coating. It gives sauces a shiny
sheen.

XANTHAN GUM ....
See also Hydrocolloids. Xanthan gum was first discovered over 50
years ago and is still seen as an amazing revelation. Derived from
bacteria in cabbage and fermenting glucose, xanthan gum can
produce very large increases in the viscosity or thickness of a liquid
by adding only a very tiny amount (about 0.5-1%). Widely available
and very cheap, it stabilizes salad dressing sauces and prevents
them splitting apart, thickens sauces, and when added to foams
makes them lighter, creamier and more stable.

YOGHURT ....
Thick yoghurt breaks down and thins when heated so it is used
only as a thickener for cold sauces.

MISCELLANY

———◆————

"A good upbringing means not that you won't spill sauce on the tablecloth, but that you won't notice when someone else does."
—ANTON CHEKHOV

TIPS & TRICKS WITH SAUCE MAKING ....

ENHANCING FLAVOR ....
If you have a good sauce recipe then reduction is the obvious way to enhance flavor, but we have found there are a few simple additions you can also make if you don't want to change the recipe but feel it needs an additional boost to its flavor.

—Add a few drops of acid just before serving. Choose between lemon, vinegar, verjuice, vincotto or sherry.

—When your sauce recipe requires caramelizing or sweating onions or shallots, add a star anise and remove before proceeding to the following step.

—A knob of cold butter stirred in before serving will add richness and shine or gloss to your sauce.

—If thickening a savory sauce with buerre manié, a little soy sauce added will deepen the color and acidity and give an umami boost. Especially good for meat dish sauces.

THICKENING WITH STARCH ....

−When flour is browned its thickening ability changes and decreases, so a brown roux will give you a thinner sauce than a blonde roux.

−Never use bread flour in your sauces because they will give a stringy quality to the texture.

−Because cornflour contains no gluten it gives a clear unclouded sauce but it also means it gets a lot thicker as it cools, so replace it with Arrowroot if you're going to serve your sauce cold.

−If you are going to freeze your meal and it is in a sauce, use arrowroot instead of cornflour as the thickener because this will not breakdown when frozen or reheated as both corn and normal flours do.

−If your cream or white sauce is too thin use beurre manié to thicken, but if your cream or white sauce is too thick add milk or pouring cream, beaten in a little at a time.

−Most starch thickeners reach maximum gelatinization (where all the starch granules have absorbed enough water to touch each other) at 93°C or 200°F, so long cooking is not required and will actually make many sauces thinner.

−The sauce thickeners beurre manié and the egg yolk + cream liaisons are excellent soup thickeners as well as sauce thickeners.

−Too much heat under flour-based sauces will prevent the starch molecules expanding and thickening.

EMULSIFYING TIPS ....

−Oil and water don't want to mix, so in an emulsified sauce you need to force them to. Do it right and they'll stay together, do it wrong and they'll separate. It's best to put all the water based liquids into your bowl first, then add a little of the oil or fat that is to be dispersed, along with any stabilizer in the recipe (mustard, egg yolk, acids like lemon juice or vinegar, milk proteins) and emulsify by beating or whisking. Then add the rest of the oil or fat slowly at first, a teaspoonful at a time. You need to get the emulsion going well, until it has some bulk and is stable and viscous, then you can safely start adding it more quickly and the emulsion is unlikely to split.

–Most water-based liquids can only disperse (break-up) a maximum of three times their own volume, e.g. 1 part vinegar to 3 parts or less of oil. If you exceed this ratio your emulsion will go stiff, clumpy and lumpy. Adding more liquid relaxes and rescues it again.

–High temperature is too violent for most sauces because it makes the molecules collide and coalesce (break-up), which splits your emulsions, so unless stated otherwise it's always best to simmer sauces.

–Egg proteins harden above 60°C or 140°F which means your sauce will curdle, so even if you stay below this temperature when making your egg-based sauces they can still curdle later if they come into contact with other food that is too hot. So it is best to let your steaks 'rest' after cooking before spooning over your perfect hollandaise.

–Butter solidifies at room temperature as oil does in the fridge, so emulsions will clump when cooled and will then split if stirred or re-heated. Commercial emulsion sauces are made with fats that stay liquid with refrigeration.

–If the fat is added too quickly it overwhelms the emulsifier and the sauce will split. That's why it's best to add it slowly until it thickens.

–Emulsified sauces may also split when kept warm for too long as their ratio of liquid to fat decreases with evaporation.

RESCUING SPLIT SAUCES ....
When a sauce 'splits' it means the fats, which were previously emulsified with the other solids, have begun to separate. It's usually due to too much fat or too much heat. The texture will go grainy and the sauce will thin dramatically. There are warning signs to look for, like oil droplets forming around the edge of your bowl or pan. If you see this, stop adding fat and add water or liquid instead, or the result will be a lumpy, watery mess. For many 'splits', applying force like a blender will re-emulsify them, but there are exceptions to this like the curdled egg type sauces. There are various ways to rescue a split sauce:
–Remove from the heat, especially egg sauces, and strain immediately as soon as they begin to curdle or go lumpy. With egg sauces where the egg has begun to cook into curds it's easier to start again unless you're low on eggs.
–Rebuild by beginning with some new water-based liquid in a bowl and adding the sauce a little at a time while whisking. It should tighten immediately and you can pick-up where you left off and finish your sauce.
–Begin again with a new emulsifier like an egg yolk, milk or cream and add your strained split sauce a little at a time.
Adding a stabilizer, like mustard or tomato paste, or a starch, like flour or arrowroot, helps prevent splits.

Mastery of the Sauces leaves you with the immortal, slightly modified words of Julia Childs:

"Sauces are the splendour and glory of cooking, yet there is nothing secret or mysterious about making them and no one is ever born a great cook, but one learns by doing."

BON APPÉTIT — THE CULINARY LIBRARY

INDEX

288

INDEX

19240003R00187

Made in the USA
Middletown, DE
04 December 2018